Digital Bridges
Developing Countries in the Knowledge Economy

John Senyo C. Afele

IDEA GROUP PUBLISHING

Hershey • London • Melbourne • Singapore • Beijing

Acquisition Editor:	Mehdi Khosrowpour
Managing Editor:	Jan Travers
Development Editor:	Michele Rossi
Copy Editor:	Maria Boyer
Typesetter:	Amanda Appicello
Cover Design:	IBT Global
Printed at:	IBT Global

Published in the United States of America by
    Idea Group Publishing (an imprint of Idea Group Inc.)
    701 E. Chocolate Avenue, Suite 200
    Hershey PA 17033
    Tel: 717-533-8845
    Fax: 717-533-8661
    E-mail: cust@idea-group.com
    Web site: http://www.idea-group.com

and in the United Kingdom by
    Idea Group Publishing (an imprint of Idea Group Inc.)
    3 Henrietta Street
    Covent Garden
    London WC2E 8LU
    Tel: 44 20 7240 0856
    Fax: 44 20 7379 3313
    Web site: http://www.eurospan.co.uk

Library of Congress Cataloging-in-Publication Data

Afele, John Senyo C., 1958-
  Digital bridges : developing countries in the knowledge economy / John Senyo C. Afele.
    p. cm.
  Includes bibliographical references and index.
    ISBN 1-59140-039-2 (cloth) — ISBN 1-59140-067-8 (ebook)
    1. Knowledge management—Economic aspects—Developing countries. 2. Information technology—Economic aspects—Developing countries. 3. Telecommunication—Economic aspects—Developing countries. 4. Digital divide—Developing countries. I. Title.
  HD30.2 .A35 2003
    658.4'038'091724—dc21   2002012901

British Cataloguing in Publication Data
A Cataloguing in Publication record for this book is available from the British Library.

NEW from Idea Group Publishing

- **Digital Bridges: Developing Countries in the Knowledge Economy**, John Senyo Afele/ ISBN:1-59140-039-2; eISBN 1-59140-067-8, © 2003
- **Integrative Document & Content Management: Strategies for Exploiting Enterprise Knowledge**, Len Asprey and Michael Middleton/ ISBN: 1-59140-055-4; eISBN 1-59140-068-6, © 2003
- **Critical Reflections on Information Systems: A Systemic Approach**, Jeimy Cano/ ISBN: 1-59140-040-6; eISBN 1-59140-069-4, © 2003
- **Web-Enabled Systems Integration: Practices and Challenges**, Ajantha Dahanayake and Waltraud Gerhardt ISBN: 1-59140-041-4; eISBN 1-59140-070-8, © 2003
- **Public Information Technology: Policy and Management Issues**, G. David Garson/ ISBN: 1-59140-060-0; eISBN 1-59140-071-6, © 2003
- **Knowledge and Information Technology Management: Human and Social Perspectives**, Angappa Gunasekaran, Omar Khalil and Syed Mahbubur Rahman/ ISBN: 1-59140-032-5; eISBN 1-59140-072-4, © 2003
- **Knowledge and Business Process Management**, Vlatka Hlupic/ISBN: 1-59140-036-8; eISBN 1-59140-074-0, © 2003
- **IT-Based Management: Challenges and Solutions**, Luiz Antonio Joia/ISBN: 1-59140-033-3; eISBN 1-59140-075-9, © 2003
- **Geographic Information Systems and Health Applications**, Omar Khan/ ISBN: 1-59140-042-2; eISBN 1-59140-076-7, © 2003
- **The Economic and Social Impacts of E-Commerce**, Sam Lubbe/ ISBN: 1-59140-043-0; eISBN 1-59140-077-5, © 2003
- **Computational Intelligence in Control,** Masoud Mohammadian, Ruhul Amin Sarker and Xin Yao/ISBN: 1-59140-037-6; eISBN 1-59140-079-1, © 2003
- **Decision-Making Support Systems: Achievements and Challenges for the New Decade**, M.C. Manuel Mora and Guisseppi Forgionne/ISBN: 1-59140-045-7; eISBN 1-59140-080-5, © 2003
- **Architectural Issues of Web-Enabled Electronic Business**, Nansi Shi and V.K. Murthy/ ISBN: 1-59140-049-X; eISBN 1-59140-081-3, © 2003
- **Adaptive Evolutionary Information Systems**, Nandish V. Patel/ISBN: 1-59140-034-1; eISBN 1-59140-082-1, © 2003
- **Managing Data Mining Technologies in Organizations: Techniques and Applications**,   Parag Pendharkar/ ISBN: 1-59140-057-0; eISBN 1-59140-083-X, © 2003
- **Intelligent Agent Software Engineering**, Valentina Plekhanova/ ISBN: 1-59140-046-5; eISBN 1-59140-084-8, © 2003
- **Advances in Software Maintenance Management: Technologies and Solutions**, Macario Polo, Mario Piattini and Francisco Ruiz/ ISBN: 1-59140-047-3; eISBN 1-59140-085-6, © 2003
- **Multidimensional Databases: Problems and Solutions**, Maurizio Rafanelli/ISBN: 1-59140-053-8; eISBN 1-59140-086-4, © 2003
- **Information Technology Enabled Global Customer Service**, Tapio Reponen/ISBN: 1-59140-048-1; eISBN 1-59140-087-2, © 2003
- **Creating Business Value with Information Technology: Challenges and Solutions**, Namchul Shin/ISBN: 1-59140-038-4; eISBN 1-59140-088-0, © 2003
- **Advances in Mobile Commerce Technologies**, Ee-Peng Lim and Keng Siau/ ISBN: 1-59140-052-X; eISBN 1-59140-089-9, © 2003
- **Mobile Commerce: Technology, Theory and Applications**, Brian Mennecke and Troy Strader/ ISBN: 1-59140-044-9; eISBN 1-59140-090-2, © 2003
- **Managing Multimedia-Enabled Technologies in Organizations**, S.R. Subramanya/ISBN: 1-59140-054-6; eISBN 1-59140-091-0, © 2003
- **Web-Powered Databases**, David Taniar and Johanna Wenny Rahayu/ISBN: 1-59140-035-X; eISBN 1-59140-092-9, © 2003
- **E-Commerce and Cultural Values**, Theerasak Thanasankit/ISBN: 1-59140-056-2; eISBN 1-59140-093-7, © 2003
- **Information Modeling for Internet Applications**, Patrick van Bommel/ISBN: 1-59140-050-3; eISBN 1-59140-094-5, © 2003
- **Data Mining: Opportunities and Challenges,** John Wang/ISBN: 1-59140-051-1; eISBN 1-59140-095-3, © 2003
- **Annals of Cases on Information Technology** – vol 5, Mehdi Khosrowpour/ ISBN: 1-59140-061-9; eISBN 1-59140-096-1, © 2003
- **Advanced Topics in Database Research** – vol 2, Keng Siau/ISBN: 1-59140-063-5; eISBN 1-59140-098-8, © 2003
- **Advanced Topics in End User Computing** – vol 2, Mo Adam Mahmood/ISBN: 1-59140-065-1; eISBN 1-59140-100-3, © 2003
- **Advanced Topics in Global Information Management** – vol 2, Felix Tan/ ISBN: 1-59140-064-3; eISBN 1-59140-101-1, © 2003
- **Advanced Topics in Information Resources Management** – vol 2, Mehdi Khosrowpour/ ISBN: 1-59140-062-7; eISBN 1-59140-099-6, © 2003

To my parents

Digital Bridges
Developing Countries in the Knowledge Economy

Table of Contents

Preface .... **vii**
   Prelude .... *vii*
   Acknowledgments .... *xi*
   Reference .... *xiv*

Chapter I. Introduction **1**
   References *16*

Chapter II. Standards of Knowledge Communities **19**
   References *30*

Chapter III. Nurturing Knowledge Communities **32**
   The Corn Industry and Nurturing Knowledge Communities *33*
   Facilitators of Knowledge Networks *40*
   Identifying Talents *47*
   References *52*

Chapter IV. Splicing Modern Knowledge and Ancestral Wisdom **56**
   General Development Knowledge Needs of Rural Communities *61*
   Global Benefits of Indigenous Knowledge *66*
   Some Features of Indigenous Knowledge *71*
   Yam and Oil Palm in Holism of Indigenous Knowledge *75*
   References *79*

Chapter V. Digital Bridges and Digital Opportunities for Developing Nations **85**
   The Digital Divide *85*
   The State-of-the-Art Technology *86*
   Defining National Knowledge Needs and New Competitive Advantages *94*

Brain Gain, Human Resources, and Institutional Capacity
   Building *99*
Education and Talent Grooming *113*
Food or IT?: Convergent Communications and Rural
   Agriculture *126*
E-Business Culture *130*
Women and Development Communication *136*
Health Security and Connectivity *138*
Leadership and Governance in the Information Age *144*
References *149*

Chapter VI. Globalization and Frameworks for Digital Opportunities **160**
   Global Development Institutions *161*
   Globalization and Activism *167*
   Understanding Local Issues at the Global Level *170*
   References *177*

Chapter VII. Capitalizing the Knowledge Economy of Developing Nations **181**
   Private Sector and Foundations as Funding Sources *184*
   Local Funding Sources *186*
   References *189*

Chapter VIII. Preservation of Cultural Identity and Preventing Piracy of Indigenous Intellectual Properties **190**
   Internet Language and Information Liaisons *191*
   Preventing Piracy of Indigenous Intellectual Properties *194*
   References *196*

Chapter IX. Postlude **198**

About the Author **205**

Index **207**

Preface

"WISDOM, like an inheritance, is a good thing and benefits its possessor ... Wisdom is a shelter as money is a shelter, but the advantage of knowledge is this: That wisdom preserves the life of its possessor ... Wisdom makes one wise person more powerful than ten rulers in a city ... Whatever wisdom may be, it is far off and most profound—who can discover it? So [we turn our] mind to understand, to investigate and search out wisdom and the scheme of things ... Adding one thing to discover the scheme of things. ... Who is like the wise person? Who knows the explanation of things? Wisdom brightens a person's face and changes its hard appearance." (Ecclesiastes 7:11– 8:1)

PRELUDE

For the fact that so many initiatives exist at the highest levels of global diplomacy that seek to employ the tools of the most powerful technological innovations in ensuring prosperity and security of the weakest communities of human civilizations, and for the fact that that there are fledgling outcomes in the impact communities, some may pose the question: 'When will you be satisfied?' The answer could be deduced from the visions, intelligence, and eloquence associated with similar circumstances prior. King Jr. for example would have drawn attention to the global 'pledge to honour the sacred obligation of equity for all' and reminded the audience that the communities of the developing world 'live on a lonely island of poverty in the midst of vast oceans of material prosperity;' in view of 'the fierce urgency of now,' he would have advocated for immediate, concrete, and sustainable measures because 'this is no time to take the tranquilizing drug of gradualism' dismissing the oft-repeated problems of 'insufficient funds,' as the bank of development was not bankrupt or for the fact that there are sufficient funds in the great vaults of global opportunity (King Jr., 1963).

In the light of existing initiatives, who can say with certainty the proportion of Africa's 700 million people, in 54 countries and low *per capita* income and productivity, that would become users of information from global sources to generate enhanced knowledge solutions in their livelihoods attainment in the next decade or so?

Building a knowledge community necessitates that talents and ideas are identified; creativity is nourished, capitalized, and translated into tangible services and products for the primary impact zone; and lessons learned are shared among global partners in development. Current schemes emphasize access to information, but there should be a systematic manner in which individuals, institutions, and communities integrate knowledge generation, utilization, and dissemination and ensure that the lessons learned are fed back into the system in a perpetual growth mode. The existing initiatives appear to be discrete and lack scientific standards to measure the impact of programs and to project the stages of growth within the local impact areas. The idea of knowledge networks in development philosophy may have resulted in an increase in the concentration of power and resources within the traditional development agencies instead of seeding the option of knowledge utilization in the impact communities through effective support of locally grown networks. Networks that are not the result of the direct activities of the traditional development agency, or of those related to people and groups of influence, face a glass ceiling even if they were ingenious. But the transparency afforded by the digital tools of the information society implies that each group that is responsible for aspects of constructing digital bridges can be evaluated by future generations as to their thoughts and deeds when their imagination would have mitigated human tragedies and contributed to global prosperity and security. The digital imprints therefore become the oversight, which conscientious institutions and networks would revere and ensure that they reach the innermost parts of their imaginations in the conceptualization, capitalization, implementation, and supervision in orchestrating the digital bridges into modern knowledge-starved communities under their mandates. The need for ingenuity and sincerity in nurturing the transition of such communities into knowledge-based communities is a burden on both local and external actors.

The analytical tools that are employed in this book derive from mechanisms that enable access to information, the assessment and characterization of information, the splicing of information from external domains with the local knowledg,e in line with the strategic positions of the community, infrastructure, and capitalization of the ideas emanating to generate prototypes of enhanced knowledge outcomes for the local impact areas. Generating knowledge solutions is therefore considered as a factor of tools (technologies, resources, and a nourishing environment), themes (ideas and content), and teams (networks and partnerships). The tools aspect, though inadequate and often of poor standards, has been the principal focus of some groups, especially in the private sector; the content aspect and that of thematic networks lag behind or are not clearly defined. The International Telecommunication Union's 'Telecom Africa 2001' exhibition in Johannesburg was clear evidence of the abundance of technological solutions relevant to these communities, but the value added to tools due to themes and teams are less advanced or robust, hence the networks resulting are hollow; even if doctors at an advanced research centre in an advanced community can be connected to patients in a rural area of a developing nation, how are the drug prescriptions going to be honoured? For this and other cases, the aspects of seeding the notion of seeking information and knowledge and their applications through innovative schemes in the local area may be hard to find in the impact regions. This is a result of both gradualism and genuine challenges such as the existing intellectual gaps and lack of access to resources.

Social development schemes are usually not subjected to the rigorous examinations of the performance of investment capital in the major financial exchanges, which effectively determine the expectations of dividends on investments; the businesses that meet or exceed the expectations are rewarded with increased availability of capital and the overall business worth. Yet the promises and expectations of global prosperity and security, and the activities of the groups so mandated, demand even greater scrutiny. Connectivity and knowledge flows for development in the communities of interest here are also expected to create wealth among the stakeholders, which now includes the impact communities; hence, such schemes could be evaluated with the same free-market notions and features that these communities are obliged to operationalize. Of course, this does not imply that the operators and capitalists of these schemes would demonstrate the greed that some private-sector actors display, for example the cases involving failed businesses such as Enron and WorldCom (others have paid fines without accepting wrong-doing), and so on. The 'markets' are not rigid; they respond to policy and even 'stimulus packages' during crises, such as economic recessions and the post-September 11 attacks against the United States. Therefore this socio-economic philosophy of connectivity and knowledge flows for global prosperity and security should be operationalized with human aspects of capital and investment.

Indeed, the human, technological, and financial resources that are at the disposition of the major institutions, which are active in the development community, are greater than what it took some ingenious investors in the private sector to generate dividends to the possessors of ideas and capitalists: KFC (Kentucky Fried Chicken) began at a petrol station and grew to the trans-national corporation that it is today. But as free-market features of the West begin to be expressed in African urban centres, petrol or gas stations in that region are looking cleaner, sometimes similar to cases in the West, where people dine though remain squalid, with consequences in health, for example the spread of typhoid and cholera. Therefore, what knowledge is flowing through the system, or is it due to gradualism–first petroleum, then human? The ideas behind the various schemes and their stages of growth have often been discussed with the public in order to broaden participation, but invariably, the ideas from outside the 'institution' receive little consideration, or when used have little return to the contributors in the form of capitalizing the translation of ideas into products for their benefit; the more endowed 'stakeholders' may therefore 'consult' the less-resourced groups but without remuneration to the latter? Therefore, it would be inhumane to expect market-rate returns on investments in such schemes when the actors and environments are not equitably equipped.

A major challenge in contemplating knowledge communities in the developing world is how to relearn, and this is an issue that is relevant to all the stakeholders that may be involved. Some of the architects of the fledgling connectivity and knowledge systems of the developing world conceptualize the transformation of the traditional international development agencies into a global development community through knowledge and investment partnerships; their challenge may be that cells within the institution would perceive this as a process to self-destruction by the institution writing itself out of existence, therefore people and groups hold fast onto the kingdoms they have created in order to protect their relevance. Thus teams as artificial matrices arise and are of little relevance to the impact communities; the counter notion of an organic nature of networks in which groups evolve by each realizing its role and contribution to the pool, and which may not have originated from the traditional actors, is a threat to some interests and positions. Currently, small, self-evolving, and grounded organizations that arise from local needs and potentials are not supported to a significant extent by the groups that are mandated to do so; instead the new networks must originate and be supervised from within the establishment. This position is not supported by the theories and practices of free-market that are sounded to the impact communities by the external bodies of capital and resources; free-market systems realise that small- and medium-size enterprises, often self-business, are the engines of economic growth.

Communities in the developing world are making some efforts toward their knowledge economies: the policy environments are improving for investments in information and telecommunications, market forces are intensifying, tools are being deployed, and children, adults, institutions, businesses, and communities are increasingly curious about the Information Age tools and functions; much of the success is due to the interventions of the emerging atmosphere of development partnerships. But more is required.

Issues remain in several aspects, notably generation of content that is pertinent to realization of opportunities in the primary impact communities, severe gaps in ingenuity, human resources, reliable infrastructure, investment capital, and prototypes of the ideal partnerships, services, and products that meet people's needs.

ACKNOWLEDGMENTS

My friends and colleagues facilitated my transition into the environment of knowledge networks and convergent communications for development. For example Kofi Anani informed me about the Global Knowledge for Development (GKD) Listerv, which was part of the activities leading up to the Global Knowledge summit held in Toronto, Canada, in 1997 (dubbed GK'97), and Aket Adzimahe helped me to purchase and install my first computer and I am deeply indebted to them for these invaluable gifts, and to the GKD community and Janice Brodman for the depth of substance and friendships that ensued.

I was fortunate that I found an article written by John de la Moth and Paul Dufour in 1995 on globalization and science and technology policy at a time that I could effectively make use of the lessons acquired in shaping my interests. This lesson, combined with my formal education and career activities in the industrialized nations of Belgium, Canada, and Japan, and as a child of an African village, Woadze in the Volta Region of Ghana, increased my understandings about knowledge creation and utilization in the industrialized communities as contrasted with the situation in my indigenous home of origin and similar communities. As a testament to the efficacy of virtual knowledge networks, my participation in a virtual think tank on identifying critical technologies for developing nations, organized by the Volunteers in Technical Assistance (VITA, Washington, DC) and moderated by Caroline Wagner of Rand Corporation, translated into meeting Caroline, Paul, Maurice de Maurivez, and others during a science and technology policy forum in Ottawa just after the conclusion of that electronic forum. All these activities enriched my themes and teams in the subject area; I am grateful for these opportunities and indebted to Caroline, Paul, and Maurice.

I needed to be reminded less about the situation in Africa regarding innovations in science and technology and the means of livelihoods. When I observe that rural African's hunt for mushrooms from the wild-like diamond gems, or grate vegetables on rocks, it is because I have lived them; when I state that rural African women sometimes give birth on farm roads, it is because I know of such cases in my Ghanaian village. A significant part of my values derive from this village of 800 people, and influenced my search for understanding and actions about poverty, atavism, knowledge deficits, and the opportunities that the new communications present. I am therefore appreciative of the informal institutions and people who socialized me in the indigenous knowledge system.

I found the GKD Listerv very nourishing: I learned about what opportunities may exist for communities such as mine to prosper through knowledge networks; I tested my ideas in the GKD community and gleaned information from several contributors at various sessions around the globe. With this background preparation, I met people and institutions of great repute that in turn introduced me to others, and I have been able to participate in several conferences around the world, which focussed on knowledge solutions for knowledge-deprived communities; and my network chain grew. For all this, I am pleasantly indebted to a number of people and institutions, therefore, let me just say 'thank you' to all.

The University of Guelph, where I had earned my doctorate earlier and had returned to in some research capacity, gave me the opportunity to harness my activities and networks as the International Program for Africa, and I am grateful to the architects of that opportunity—Professors Rob MacLaughlin, Clarence Swanton, and Alistair Summerlee. Following my participation in the second Global Knowledge conference in 2000, this time held in the South (Kuala Lumpur, Malaysia), I applied on behalf of my program to join the Global Knowledge Partnership (GKP), and was admitted and further enriched by those in the knowledge for development business. I am particularly thankful for the roles the GKP membership committee, Joan Hubbard, Nalan Yuksel, Deena Philage, Brenda Juntenen, Rinalia Abdul Rahim, Kwan, and others have played in giving me the opportunity to represent my perspectives and to interact with others. Through my activities in the Global Knowledge Partnership, I was able to identify the groups that could impact my program's deliverables, and have benefited in that direction. I am grateful to Roger Dumelie and Tony Zeitoun, both of the Canadian International Development Agency (CIDA, Ottawa), for the chance to study some aspects of the governance of knowledge societies; to Gerolf Weigel and Walter Fust and their teams at the Swiss Agency for Development and Cooperation (SDC, Bern) for supporting my overview and analysis of some of the major connectivity and knowledge for development schemes that impact the Africa region; and to the Acacia initiative of the International Development Research Centre (IDRC, Ottawa), particularly to Gaston Zongo, for enabling my input into the RuralCom'99 deliberations in Cotonou, Benin.

Angelika Loeper of *Arbeitsgemeinschaft fuer Tropische und Subtropische Agrarforschung* (ATSAF e.V.), or the Council for Tropical and Subtropical Agricultural Research, facilitated my participation in the second conference of the European Federation for Information Technology in Agriculture (EFITA/99) held in Bonn, Germany; Angelika also introduced me to Anton Mangstl of the Food and Agriculture Organization of the U.N., which culminated in my participation in the First Conference on Agricultural Information Management convened in Rome in 2000. I am very grateful for these opportunities and wish to thank Angelika and Anton for the intellectual nourishments I have received as a result. I also benefited tremendously from the activities of Takeshi Utsumi and Steve McCarthy of the Global University System; Utsumi allowed me to contribute to the design of a possible African component and gave me a depth of information and wisdom on the subject, while Steve created my first homepage on the Internet and gave me a window to the world. Thank you Steve and Tak. Professor (Emeritus) Parker Rossman also contributed to my understanding of virtual education and what it would mean to the communities about which I have been concerned; I have enjoyed the fruits of his long period in educational matters, for which I am grateful.

I am thankful to other global institutions, which gave me the opportunity to make contributions and to learn from others on their panels devoted to the subject area. For example, the World Bank Institute sponsored my participation in the GK II forum; the International Telecommunication Union sponsored my presentation during the Bamako 2000 conference in Mali; the International Food Policy Research Institute sponsored my participation in a roundtable they convened in Washington, DC to discuss the subject. I also benefited tremendously from SDC sponsorship to participate in a workshop on nurturing knowledge communities organized by Helvetas in Bern, where I heard Stephen Denning's statement that these days, you either share knowledge or you perish, and where I learned from others; Esther Oettli and Marc Steinlin also taught me a great deal about the use of Geographic Information Systems in community resource management and development options. I am grateful for these opportunities. I am equally appreciative of the help that I received from the Indigenous Knowledge program of the Africa Region of the World Bank, particularly to Nic Gorjestani and Reiner Woytek.

My African colleagues in the Diaspora have also helped me to develop my themes and teams in the subject area: Fred Oladeinde and Anthony Okonmah, through the activities of the Washington, DC-based Foundation for Democracy in Africa, permitted me to present my perspectives and to meet both African and African-American leaders in the field of investments in Africa; I met Mel Foote of the Constituency for Africa, another Washington, D.C.-based organization as a result; Mel subsequently gave me the opportunity to speak at the 1999 science and technology forum of the Ronald H. Brown African Affairs Series during the U.S. Congressional Black Caucus Legislative Forum. Osei Darkwa and Kojo Arthur of the Chicago-based Ghana Computer Literacy and Distance Education Project (GhaCLAD) also gave me the early chance to participate in their program. I wish to thank Fred, Tony, Mel, Osei, and Kojo for these opportunities. I thank Okey Onyejekwe, Egondu Onyejekwe, and Solomon Tunde Aiyeru of the Center for African Studies at Ohio State University for inviting me to their session on the Internet and national cultures, and to Doris Dartey as well.

I also learned a lot through the Diaspora Focus Group of the U. N. Economic Commission for Africa's Africa Development Forum, and wish to thank Nancy Hafkin, Kate Wild, Raymond Akwule of George Mason University, and others for allowing me to do so. A number of other groups and individuals in Africa, including Jan Mutai of the African Telecommunications Union and Clement Dzidonu have encouraged me, for which I am appreciative; others who have inspired me include Malele Dodia and her emerging African Renaissance Committee, Eliud Wakwabubi of the Participatory Methodologies Forum of Kenya (PAMFORK), Meron Genene, Mansour Diouf, Toni Cela, among others, whose own search for knowledge and networking has given my work some relevance. Several institutional leaders in Ghana allowed me to interact with their programs to generate hypothetical solutions, and I am grateful to all of them.

My brainstorming sessions with my friend Kofi Anani were invaluable, and I am truly grateful to Kofi. Toni Cela was the first North American student in my network, who went to Africa to further explore some of the themes I espoused, and I look forward to further explorations by Toni and others.

I wish to thank Joanna Bendayan for revising my manuscript and making succinct comments while we brainstormed about these issues. I also wish to thank Kidist for her friendship that is dear to me; and I am thankful to David and MaryAnn for hosting me several times during my visits to Washington, DC for networking. And to my mother, my siblings, and the rest of my family, thank you for your investments in me, and your love, kindness, and patience toward me; this feeling is mutual. (And to my father who passed away one month before my final manuscript was due, you are a part of me, still.)

It is my fervent hope that all the help I have received in developing the themes I now espouse can be translated into practical outcomes in my village of origin and similar communities, which are the principal impact areas of this book, and add to the pool of knowledge about telecommunications and the prosperity and security of the developing world.

John Senyo C. Afele
Ottawa, Canada
May 29, 2002

REFERENCE

King, Jr., M. L. (1963). *I have a Dream*. Speech delivered on the steps at the Lincoln Memorial in Washington, DC, on August 28, 1963. [Online]. University of Minnesota, College of Education & Human Development, Office of Information Technology and Center for Applied Research and Educational Improvement. <http://web66.coled.umn.edu/new/MLK/MLK.html> [2001, March 25].

Chapter I

Introduction

Issues about global security have become preeminent in the hallowed corridors of global diplomacy, especially following the September 11, 2001, terrorist attacks on the mainland of the United States of America. The events of September 11, 2001, stand alone in their nature and causes, but they have also aroused a renewed sense of urgency in the implementation of policy decisions and deployment of technological responses to issues and regions of insecurities around the world. World leaders, writers, experts, and groups have pointed to the need for a comprehensive understanding of the anger that some societies harbour against other segments of the global community and leadership, and for the implementation of policies and programs to eliminate poverty, injustice, and discontent around the world. The expected outcome of the global coalition to defeat terror was echoed by the Prime Minister of the United Kingdom, Tony Blair, in his *Churchillian* speech to his governing Labour Party:

> *"It is that out of the shadow of this evil, should emerge lasting good: destruction of the machinery of terrorism wherever it is found; hope amongst all nations of a new beginning where we seek to resolve differences in a calm and ordered way; greater understanding between nations and between faiths; and above all justice and prosperity for the poor and dispossessed, so that people everywhere can see the chance of a better future through the hard work and creative power of the free citizen." (Blair, 2001:1)*

As the global economy faced the threat of a recession in the wake of the events of September 11, 2001, the world's poor and the majority faced the prospects of further being marginalized or the possibility that their insecurities could become integral to global security strategies. The World Bank's preliminary estimates of the impact of the terrorist attacks and the ensuing measures to control global terror indicated that the economies of the developing world could contract further by 0.5-0.75 percentage points in 2002, condemn as many as 10 million more people to live in poverty, and hamper the fight against childhood diseases and malnutrition (World Bank, 2001). The reinvigorated search for global security on the other hand has also brought a sense of urgency into measures that were being considered among world leaders to address poverty as an insecurity feature; for example the leaders of the G8 Nations at their 2001 Genoa summit initiated the 'Plan for Africa' and committed to several initiatives to *make globalization work*; to establish a new global health fund to combat HIV/AIDS, malaria, and tuberculosis; and to *continue progress* on debt relief for the poorest countries (G8, 2001).

The challenge may not be the stated intentions of leaders to address the issues of poverty, but the ability of the multitude of individuals and institutions through which the marching orders must resound for the translation of policy decisions into tangible initiatives, and to carry the process to completion and effect changes in the lives of the majority may the critical determinants of actions due to policy positions. Many of these issues had long been identified, but the action plans have often been bogged down in the processes that have often emasculated major initiatives and decisions to combat global insecurities and to spread economic opportunities and other desired benefits around the world. The British Secretary for International Development, Clare Short, and the U.S. Secretary of State, Colin Powell, noted during the U.N. Special Session on HIV/AIDS in 2001 that the global response to the HIV/AIDS crisis, for example, could have been stronger and earlier, blaming the machinations inherent in the environment of global diplomacy for the slow response. Short remarked that: "We waste too much time and energy in U.N. conferences and special sessions. We use up enormous energy in arguing at great length over texts that provide few, if any, follow-up mechanisms or assurances that governments and U.N. agencies will carry forward the declarations" (Linzer, 2001: A18). The convoluted processes in the implementation of global policies in these matters have created a suspicion of lack of interest in the issues that affect the world's majority and increased the power of civil society as the ultimate adjudicator in the issue of global justice—they can organize marches, boycott products, reduce the bottom-line of private capital, and defeat political candidates at the polls. The challenge for globalization is the ability to foster dialogue among groups of broad representation so that the majority can channel their energies synergistically to make technology, human intelligence, and investment capital empower deprived communities without diminishing prosperity in the traditional industrialized communities, which perhaps underlies the ideas of knowledge partnerships for development that are being sounded in the development corridors as the new form of relationship among nations.

While there is a need for communities to interact, the mechanisms and bases for such relationships are not equitably possessed by the various domains that would constitute the global community of harmony, hence the notion of partnerships to spread innovation and prosperity around the world. This is a task that requires the participation of the global community and not a few.

The end of the Cold War has left one superpower nation—the United States of America—with a myriad of tasks around the world, even as the world begins to chart a new order of partnerships. Therefore, the victor would be magnanimous; but that should not be difficult for the people of America when they recall their own struggles for freedom—The American Revolution or the American War of Independence (1775-1783). Kennedy (2001) referred to the leadership challenges that the U.S. as the sole superpower nation now needs to address: issues in all aspects of globalization - peace and security, rule of law, and prosperity through the management of trade, capital, and investment. The twenty-first century was supposed to be America's; the Warsaw Pact had collapsed; the Russian successor to the Soviet Union was still grappling with basic needs; the Japanese 'challenge' was disappearing; American economic style was the standard around the world; and American technology such as the Internet, and American-led Western culture as conveyed through music, movies, and news programs, were being embraced around the world. In spite of the competence of the U.S. in these and other vital sectors of interest to the global community, no single nation is capable of satisfying the various needs of the emerging global community, which is more likely to remain diverse than behave as a family of clones—regarding needs, thoughts, and deeds. The U.S., or any other nation for that matter, as the sole superpower is likely to offend one group or the other, at least inadvertently, in attempting to choose where it placed its power in a world full of social, political, and economic upheavals, ranging from cross-border military conflicts that have regional and global implications to famine. Others have posed the question, whether the U.S. alone could resolve the Israeli-Palestinian conflict; appease the nations of the Middle East; ease the tensions of the Korean peninsula, Taiwan Strait, and the Kashmir; contain rogue regimes; police the Balkans; build a space shield to ward off rogue missiles; win the war against the drug trade; and at the same time ward off recession and remain the motor of the global economy? (The Star, 2001). Many potential 'hot spots' in the world are contained with temporary compromises that are convenient for the parties in the short term. These simmering conflicts could be ignited with any apparent shifts in policy and actions perceived by any of the parties to be biased in favour of the 'other,' thereby increasing the possibility of further disturbance to global prosperity, stability, and lives. As Kennedy noted, "the relentless drumbeat of [U.S.] free-market doctrines has been seen as a threat to many religious and class groups, especially in traditional societies; its powerful corporations are viewed by American critics as having an undue and powerful influence, say, in blocking international agreements on climate control, in forcing changes upon restricted markets, in overawing weak Third World governments" (Kennedy, 2001: 8B). This unenviable leadership position of the U.S. makes every policy decision so sensitive that its weak participation or absence from any global framework paints its leadership and citizens as arrogant and isolationist, say, when some of its lawmakers and citizens view the U.N. and its activities with suspicion.

The ability of other nations, coalitions, and global bodies to champion some of the global issues of human and environmental security would determine the extent to which global peace becomes a reality. In the ensuing new global community following the end of the Cold War, and through the magnanimity of the victor in helping to forge a globally secured world, several communities could be empowered to become 'superpowers' in areas of their global comparative advantages related to partnerships for development. Canada for example, which has a lot in common with the world's only superpower nation and the rest of the advanced and industrialized communities, as well as being a champion in global equities toward the developing and transition communities, could perceive itself as a superpower in that regard; perhaps the leadership role that Canada is playing in the mobilization of global resources to capitalize the proposed New Partnership for African Development (NEPAD, 2001) would become a systematic dialogue in Canadian businesses and knowledge institutions for the mutual benefit of Canada and its bilateral and multilateral development partners. The impact of the failure of such programs on the citizens and businesses of the donor nation has often not been sounded loudly enough to make a sufficient number of businesses and institutions of the developed nations contribute to the global development dialogue and implementation in substantial ways. Obviously, the parallel seeding of such development options in the impact communities themselves is more urgent. That the new initiatives would generate widespread and lasting positive outcomes, because NEPAD for example emanated from African leaders themselves, may be unfounded as alluded to herein and elsewhere.

The realization of global security and peace may be unrealistic, given the different experiences and values of the different elements that inhabit a common space, but efforts toward such a goal are worthwhile, and have been the foundation of global institutions.

This book considers global security from the perspectives of poverty alleviation and enhancement of livelihood opportunities through knowledge sharing as global peace and security would derive from global equity and prosperity. Prosperity, however, stems from knowledge and the translation of knowledge into wealth and wisdom in perpetual growth modes. Thus knowledge conquers all challenges. Knowledge is accrued from information, and information-on-demand in multimedia formats is now instantaneous.

Prosperity in the twenty-first century hinges on peace and security, good governance and democracy, environmental responsibility, and sustainable human communities. These values are facilitated by advances in nanotechnologies in the biological and physical sciences that engender improved nutrition and health through application of biotechnologies in the design of crops and drugs, in new health technologies such as gene therapy, and in precision farming aided by space technology on earth, among others. But the principal driver of the new economic development models has been the unprecedented revolution in information and communication technologies (ICT) or information technologies (IT), which afford, among others: the processing of information; the utilization of information in knowledge creation through enhancing learning, creativity, and problem solving; sharing of information regarding lessons learned; and innovation in the local environment. These technologies combined to create a period of economic prosperity for Western economies beyond any other period. For almost the entire duration of President Clinton's two terms in the White House, the U.S. economy experienced economic growth far stronger than could have been predicted accurately by any growth model. The chair of the U.S. Federal Reserve Board, Greenspan, described the features of the impact of these technologies in the U.S. economy: the economic expansion achieved a record length, labour markets were tighter than any experienced in a generation, while inflation was basically subdued; this business cycle differed from the other cycles that the U.S. economy had experienced since World War II. Such an unprecedented economic expansion was made possible by the high productivity of the networked economy during which output per hour in the nonfinancial corporate sector increased at an average annual rate of 3.5 percent, nearly double the average pace over the preceding quarter-century (Greenspan, 2000).

Intensification of globalization has brought the realization that sharing the knowledge that underlies technological advances and prosperity in the industrialized world with other communities that have been traditionally excluded from such knowledge, while protecting their own unique features, is an important value in building global prosperity and security. The advances in IT have created opportunities for global prosperity and security through a distributed leadership on global issues, and they provide the potential to spread innovations in production and management as global public goods, backed by global investment capital. Access to such knowledge and capital can empower local groups to build secured livelihoods so that they can make positive contributions to the wealth of global knowledge and foster global peace and security.

These settings require critical analyses of the preparations that the non-industrialized nations, particularly the developing countries, and their development partners are making toward the transition of their impact communities into an effective Information Age. Indeed, the current development philosophies of the global development community are increasingly based on sharing information and knowledge globally through IT, but more specifically how information-starved communities could become a part of the networked world for local prosperity.

Increasing the knowledge quotient in economic models is pertinent to both the industrialized and the developing worlds; developing countries are searching for new knowledge, technological and managerial iniquities have meant inefficient and inadequate productivity and poor service capacities of formal and informal institutions. These knowledge needs of developing countries have become a part of the global knowledge needs as the industrialized economies are no longer insulated against the insecurities of the developing world; economic meltdowns, human health, animal diseases, or environmental insecurities in a local community, country, or region quickly become the concern of distant communities as well.

Several groups are therefore devising frameworks and networks in which both the industrialized and developing nations can learn from each other and share experiences through convergent communications toward evolving a sustainable global economy with human, and environmental security. Others point to the *digital divide* or the poor telecommunications infrastructure and the technological laggard state of the poorer communities of the non-industrialized world, which are herein referred to as developing nations (assuming that other communities that are not industrialized but are transitional or emerging economies remain on track toward the security levels of the industrialized nations) to declare that the advances in convergent communications are inoperable in these regions. However, had George Orwell relied on the state of technology in 1949, without the imagination of technological evolution due to scientific investigations innovation, he would not have published one of the most prophetic books in modern times – *1984* (Orwell, 1976). In Orwell's *1984*, Big Brother uses *newspeak* and *telescreens* to manipulate citizens into convenient modes of thinking. The telescreens constantly monitor each citizen that is allowed to be educated, watching for any action, word, or possible thought that could be unorthodox. The sole purpose of *newspeak* is in abolishing all unorthodox thought; for example, 'bad' is replaced by 'ungood.' "These two Orwell inventions were foretelling: we see the equivalent of *newspeak* every day in present day society when we are 'politically correct,' and *telescreens* are present in nearly every commercial institution, and sometimes in our own homes" (Anonymous, 1997).

Those who underestimate the relevance of the Information Age to the developing world point to the challenges but are unable to conceptualize the required interventions to overcome them. Often, the tele-concentration of the industrialized economies is contrasted to the level in developing nations, without contemplating ingenious features of *digital bridges*. The 'digital bridge,' unlike the 'digital divide,' counters challenges with opportunities; there are no mountains too high or rivers too wide for modern communications to bridge. Reality television shows, such as the 'Survivor' series (CBS, 2001) and 'Temptation Island' by CBS and Fox Television, respectively, have demonstrated that IT can penetrate remote areas in multimedia formats.

Attacking poverty on a sustained basis, with the aim of eventually eliminating this feature from the target or program impact community, requires an honest understanding of the root causes. It would take deep imaginations to reinvent knowledge systems in developing countries that seem to have long ago lost their own strengths. The ingenuity of indigenous knowledge systems from which the majority of the world's population—mostly rural communities and the urban-poor of non-industrialized economies, and some rural and native communities of the industrialized world—draw their knowledge for economic, technological, social, and political existence alone is not capable of supporting the current needs and aspirations of communities, institutions, businesses, administrative, and other sectors of the local economy. These local knowledge systems, in spite of modern education and industrialization attempts, are not capable of generating new knowledge solutions to challenges that did not confront them before, old challenges that were never really conquered or which have returned with a vengeance. However there are valuable remnants within the decaying indigenous or local knowledge domains that could be identified, refined, and spliced with modern knowledge to create the capacities needed in both formal and informal sectors to help their people meet their needs. Yet it is essential to ensure that globalization does not become a one directional flow of goods and information from North to South. Clear definitions of the insecurity levels of a community are the initial steps in making the right diagnoses that could lead to development of appropriate frameworks and effective intervention models. The First Nations or Native Peoples in advanced economies such as the United States, Canada, Australia, New Zealand, and Scandinavia, who are in the minority in their countries, are recognized as indigenous communities. However, the word 'indigenous,' as used in this book, is broadened to represent the local practices and beliefs of communities that may not be in the minority in their countries but whose practices are distinct from those of the generalized industrialized and advanced societies; for example, the knowledge system of the ethnic groups in Africa, Asia, or Latin America. Furthermore, modern knowledge has influenced the state of indigenous knowledge in the light of colonization, cultural interchanges, and education. Hence, indigenous knowledge may contain 'local' practices that are variants of the norm within an ethnic group;

for example, rural communities and the urban poor across Africa may use twigs as dental sticks (chewing sticks), but the species and other practices may vary between communities and ethnic groups. Indigenous knowledge and local knowledge are interchangeable throughout the manuscript for these reasons.

This book therefore describes the painful state of poverty and the underlying knowledge and network deficits among communities of the developing world. These descriptions, however real, are not intended to be disparaging to such communities, as the book originated from among them and is aimed to help address those insecurities. For, in the dark of the night or in a dimly lighted environment of an African village, where a grandmother with failing eyesight may be washing the wounds of the children of the household, the children would be warned early in life that it is the person whose limb bears the sore who could develop a gangrene if left untreated; this was to mitigate the tendency that a child who may be carrying a wound on one leg could turn the healthy leg to the nurse. The bluntness of the human insecurity states described herein is necessary for a synthesis of the appropriate hypothetical response models or for simulation of best-fit scenarios.

Similarly, other elements within the development community and industry are scrutinized for their models and actions. In the same way that the manuscript expresses dejection at the failure of Southern experts and institutions to meet their peoples' needs, it takes equal notice of where external development institutions might have exhibited lapses, and discusses where such weaknesses could be shored up and guided to coincide with the expected adjustments in the primary impact communities.

In the case of Southern experts, their failure to integrate their ancestral wisdom into nation building in the post-colonial era reaches a point of rebuke. The literary works of many indigenous writers of the generation that ushered Africa into independence in the 1960s depicted local communities in which much of the calendar year and the local cultural activities revolved around food crops; for example, in Achebe's African villages, yams were abundant, and farm productivity (the size of the fields and harvest barns) was related to the social status of the family (Achebe 1958, 1964). Much has since changed in many developing nations: failed development schemes, corruption, rapid population growth and increased pressure on the land, and perhaps a more erratic climate, among others, have conspired to intensify poverty or introduce it into areas that it did not exist before. The economic fallouts include factories as wastelands, high national debts, retrenchments, depreciation in real incomes, increased human morbidity, and an increase in the prevalence of communicable diseases; the damage to the environment and encroachment on previously uncultivated fields are also exposing new and strange diseases that are spreading faster than local capacities can contain. Many scholars have identified these problems and causes over the decades, giving rise to several development frameworks in the last five decades or more, but many of the interventions have failed to create the sustained improvements in human security sought. Easterly for example, in his book, *The Elusive Quest for Growth: Economists' Adventures and Misadventures in the Tropics* claimed that the various development programs and the one trillion dollars in aid to developing nations, in which the International Monetary Fund (IMF) and the World Bank participated, have all failed to attain the desired results because of miscalculations by economists, lenders, and the impact communities, and that these are some of the causes of global protests against internationalism (Easterly, 2001).

Hence, there is little optimism that the new opportunities unveiled by modern concepts and tools of globalization could create equity among the various communities of the perceived global village. However, considering the advances in modern telecommunications and the abundance of programs that have been initiated to provide such tools and opportunities to developing nations, this book discusses some of the issues to which these tools could be applied for resolving the development gap, and the environments that would unleash the potentials of knowledge and telecommunications-led sustainable development. This is not a manual for technical engagements, as the telecommunications industry has already developed tools that have minimized the human and topographical hindrances to communications; these tools are advancing in sophistication yet user-friendliness, there are few human physical conditions that can prevent the individual from engaging the tools, they are becoming cheaper and ubiquitous in all corners of the world, and assembly lines are now engaged in the production of the telecommunication hardware.

What is important now is how to deploy these assembled instruments and to what purpose such deployment.

Connectivity initiatives of governments, the private sector, foundations, and the development community abound in the developing world: the tools are being deployed, the policy environments are improving for investments in IT, and children and adults are increasingly curious about the Information Age tools and functions. Several ingenious IT applications and knowledge flow schemes also exist, covering several grounds in themes and stakeholders. However, challenges remain: much of the Internet traffic from communities of the developing world in these connectivity schemes are directed to communities external to the local economy, for example students looking for schools, and children seeking pen-pals. The applications of the tools in networking and increasing the knowledge quotient of institutions, businesses, and communities are less advanced. Some of the initiatives focus on building the knowledge component in 'connectivity and knowledge for development,' but the knowledge that is flowing through the current networks are heavily in a North-to-South direction, and there is very little formal South-to-South, or South-to-

North flow. Intranets (or local area knowledge networks) may even be less active, and the North-to-South flow terminates in the capital cities, but the poor nations are not able to develop the internal networks to diffuse the Northern knowledge transmitted.

Furthermore, these initiatives and schemes are approached as if they constituted a separate sector in the local economy of the developing nation. The proportion of researchers, university teachers, students, businesses, and civil servants who are generally aware of any of the multitude of global development knowledge networks that are aimed to facilitate their institutional roles and livelihoods is insignificant, and there is very little evidence that the activities of these elements and communities of the developing world have been enhanced by these networks as may be evident in the translation of the information into local realities. For example, some university professors who purchase services from their university Internet service providers (ISPs) do not have active phone lines in their offices even if they have their own personal computers (PCs), hence their interaction with existing knowledge networks, such as the Global Development Network, may be limited. Also, very few schoolteachers or pupils from these communities may be aware of the World Links for Development (WorLD), a pre-university school connectivity initiative. Moreover, the localization of these initiatives may not have been addressed to sufficient depths, for example, whether the African Virtual University would mean using IT to teach and learn in all of a local university's classrooms, if it should be a separate entity in one corner of the campus, or if the virtual university would operate 24-hour, 365-day 'sessions' or should 'open' and 'close' within daylight alone.

While there is a significant access to IT and connectivity in some urban centres of developing nations, the quality of access is poor and remains a major hindrance– lack of reliable energy sources, frequent technical glitches such as truncation of electronic messages, narrow bandwidths, and slow Internet access. The initiatives may also not have been programmed to adjust rapidly to fast-changing market trends in the local economies, probably because the programs of bilateral and multilateral agencies in the regions are housed in their headquarters or in regional programs, from where they interact with local actors of their choice. The in-country bureaux invariably do not have their own budget sources, but depend on headquarters for annual allocations; and the global and regional programs are invariably in the principal cities of the developing world.

Global development involves global and local actors; the current connectivity and knowledge network initiatives satisfy the global dimensions. Many global initiatives in knowledge sharing since the 1990s reflect partnerships among different stakeholders; however, there is a preponderance of partnerships within groups of similar features than a major shift toward active participation of local actors and diverse stakeholder types. The multilateral and bilateral development agencies and their organizational units interact with each other, hence the various initiatives involve the same core participating development organizations; a handful of private-sector organizations and civil society groups participate in the initiatives but are often international in scope, therefore of foreign origin so far as local communities and regions are concerned, as local non-governmental organizations (NGOs) lack critical knowledge and capacity to effectively represent their own constituencies on global platforms, and most of the major initiatives rely on the same donors. These features are healthy for cross-fertilization of ideas and coordination of donor programs, but it is important to prepare the local environment to match the incoming large pipe of knowledge and resources to effect local networks. Moreover, the existing initiatives have reserved roles for the formal sector or public sector of the developing nations regardless of the expressed interests of these institutions in the initiatives although it is doubtful that these institutions are able to make effective use of these privileges. This practice while facilitating institutional capacity building initiatives could also stifle creativity leading to intellectual atrophy, and may perpetuate dependency among the impact groups. This lack of local capacity could be demonstrated with the impact of the Development Gateway in Africa, where after nearly two years of existence globally, only one African nation (Namibia) had an active Gateway as of December 2001, which was about 1.85 percent crude penetration of the continent. The contents of the Namibian gateway at that time was also minimal and questionable as to goals, sophistication, and development impact. This suggests the need to broaden activities and partnerships, and institutionalization of processes to identify talents and champions of knowledge for development, and strategies to translate ideas and concepts into tangible outputs, because many of the 700 million people in 54 countries of Africa, say, are yet to be reached by the current programs.

The themes of the book are intended for the interests of the development communities of the South, as a reminder of the values in their indigenous knowledge systems and the benefits that may be obtained through knowledge networks for purposes that include digitization of their oral cultures. For the development communities located in the North, they may be able to glean some of the issues related to local knowledge needs, IT and knowledge sharing in building prosperous and secure communities through their bilateral, multilateral, non-governmental and private-sector activities, as seen from an indigenous perspective. The general reader, students of international development studies, businesses, technologists, and other groups whose activities impact, or are impacted by, global efforts toward poverty alleviation, prosperity, and security--may also be able to discern areas in which their knowledge resources, investment capital, or personal momentum may be beneficial to the process.

While activities of multi-stakeholder initiatives toward connectivity in developing countries have resulted in some communications capacity of these nations, further bridging of the digital divide may be contingent upon the impact that the introduction of IT causes in these communities. The period of a weakening ability of the dot.com machinery to attract investment capital in the industrialized economies could be an ideal period to ponder the value of connectivity initiatives for developing nations as well. The opportunity costs of any failed investments in this communications trend could be expensive to the local communities and could cause a further marginalizing of the poor; consider the opportunity costs, if a developing economy opted for communications at the expense of other vital sectors of human security, such as health, education, food, shelter, and water. Therefore, connectivity initiatives in development need to be translated into knowledge for increased food production, improved health, talent development and education, skills acquisitions of the youth, gender empowerment, and integration of local economies into the global marketplace, and so forth. It is important to begin developing models to push the Information Society in the developing world to critical tests that are designed from the perspectives of economic gain and social responsibility. These tests could determine if current connectivity frameworks and their deliverables would make major dents in poverty alleviation and cause improvements in human security in these communities.

Therefore, the manuscript considers the hypothetical models of networks and communications contents that would actualize *leapfrogging* in the impact communities in the form of human and environmental securities. The outcomes of establishing information and telecommunications infrastructure in developing countries should necessarily translate into quantifiable and significant gains in human security in the primary impact zones, as well as herald intangible benefits to all program partners as lessons learned, and as input into new growth models. Examples are drawn about emerging and industrialized economies to illustrate digital opportunities in the transformation of communities that are traditionally considered as most in need of knowledge resources and outputs, but perceived as regions of uneconomic investments.

The book advocates investments in the innovative experimentations of local talents and institutions, as part of nurturing knowledge cells, knowledge clusters, or knowledge communities at the local level by development partners. The traditional aid and relief agencies could still engage in rushing food to starving communities and other practices during emergencies, but a serious rethinking of development should employ what experts have long called for—investing in people for their own development through knowledge partnerships.

Knowledge partnerships between the industrialized and non-industrialized economies would not 'take away jobs' from the industrialized nations. The notion of partnerships in global development is not for a relocation of factories, but the spreading of innovation through investment to realize the competitive and comparative advantages of each community or sub-region so that the inhabitants and their activities would be of positive value to the global economy. Spreading innovation is not the same as the interaction between Northern capital and Southern communities in which manufacturing outfits were relocated to some economies with the resulting 'disappearance' of such jobs in the affected industrialized nations. That interaction was founded on the principles that developing nations or regions could manage with undervalued human resources, lower rewards to talent and skills, poorer workplace ergonomics, poorer health of the natural environment, and other lowered conditions of industrialization compared to the industrialized societies. That system may have presumed that global productivity had reached its carrying capacity, although only a few consume the goods and services that are generated globally in the formal economy, leaving the majority to the state of penury and unsophisticated technological practices of the Dark Ages. The 'poverty line' for the world's majority has been somehow determined to be one dollar per day, while in other communities, it is more than several thousand folds—more than 10,000 times higher; on the other hand, the costs of basic goods and services, such as health care products and energy, are determined in the global market.

However, this is not a call for, or the endorsement of, copious consumerism, and it is certainly not a support of product-push consumerism in which the television informs consumers in the industrialized economies about new drugs and encourages viewers: 'ask your doctor'; over-consumption may be unethical, but under-consumption can lead to atavism. The production, processing, storage, distribution channels, financing, and management systems in such communities could benefit from modern knowledge and capital to support a higher level of productivity and sustainable consumption. The causes of many divisions and tensions in human communities lie in the imagined or real gain of financial or material assets of some elements of the community to be at the expense of others. This real or imagined bias stems partially from the inability of global productivity to provide for all while the poorer regions of the world are becoming more aware about the quality of life in communities of the industrialized nations. The proliferations of information technologies and applications in media have brought Western media into the neighbourhoods of the poor, who may only view how others live and begin to yearn for similar livelihoods, although they may not have the knowledge and resources to reach such levels of prosperity under existing regimes. Local opinion leaders may create their own slants about the causes of local insecurity and engage the same advances in communications to disseminate their biases, and in the process divert the frustrations energy of the large population of active youth to other groups as the cause of local insecurities.

It is the lack of access to modern intelligence for technology, production, and management that is at the root of extreme poverty. However, assuming that a community in a poor region can access knowledge to solve problems and enhance productivity and outputs in agriculture and health care, the productive labour force would increase, beginning at the local level, and perhaps with that there could be increases in global productivity and prosperity. The knowledge, technologies, skills, and financial resources to establish such communities exist; it requires the integration of such features and demonstrations that poverty, which devours the afflicted, can be conquered with knowledge in a sustainable productive environment.

These scenarios should not be a threat to any community or economy of the industrialized world or elsewhere.

If the current industrial economies would falter and lose their economic status, it would not be due to the spreading of innovation and opportunities to the poorest regions so that they could create a decent state for their inhabitants. Long before the current schemes in globalization, Prince Albert, Victoria's consort, was endeared to the idea of the global community that was realized as the Great Exhibition of 1851, which attracted six million visitors and 17,000 exhibitors from almost every region. The exhibition envisaged a great collection of works in art and industry, based on competition and encouragement, to provide a true determination of the state of global advances and development and to configure a new beginning for all; its success was supposed to have set the format for globalization, based on economic and trade partnerships (Speel, 1996), but the early death of Albert closed the doors of the royal courts to the champions of this model, and the notion of internationalism that was built on the supremacy of one or a few over the rest triumphed. A century and a half after the Great Exhibition, the world is trying to define a new form of relationship among nations, based on trade and knowledge partnerships.

Like the nanotechnologies that have led Western economies into the new growth era, global capital could replicate itself several fold in the non-industrialized world when such investments impact productivity, management, and distribution systems where there is need, like the polymerase chain reaction (PCR) protocol in molecular biology allows the researcher to build up sufficient quantities of biological blueprints from minute levels under appropriate physical and enzymatic conditions. As investors are becoming more ethical in the choice of businesses in which to invest, some private-sector businesses inform the global investor that they are making all efforts to feed the world's hungry—making plants grow in previously barren lands, or increasing the vitamin content of crops so that starving children in Africa and elsewhere could be nourished. Their television advertisements speak about these noble goals and contain a disproportionately large amount of photo frames depicting such insecure communities as beneficiaries of global technological advances. Such presentations may be misleading, as the crops that have benefited significantly from nanotechnologies are neither the tropical root and tuber crops that are the staple food crops of many communities in the developing world nor the tropical diseases such as malaria; these are not of preferred research focus in Western laboratories. Instead, the subliminal account of technology application by some global capital borrowers is an acknowledgment of the power of nanotechnologies in global prosperity, including applications to the needs of the world's majority. Indeed, global technology and capital can make crops grow on denuded soils, make the desert bloom, and crops to be harvested from where they had not grown in living memory. However, such research and applications would not be determined by technology-push factors alone; the interaction of capital and technology in development should produce relevant, sustainable, and scientific results in the management of health, economy, society and ecosystems, among others, but not the often-experienced wild cycles of hope and despair.

Global capital and technology could interact to support the fledgling democracies and their institutions in the South. Many of these nations have borne enough of strange economic models that imposed adjustments that the proponents themselves had never experienced in real life. Just as the industrialized economies could use 'economic stimulus packages' to inject liquidity into their economies, the South could also benefit from infusion of development knowledge and capital into their fragile economies. However, such stimulus packages in the South could avoid labels that trumpeted the economic weakness of the recipient nation; the designation should provide the possibilities for psychological as well as economic uplift and not despair. Individuals and businesses in the North that may be indebted to the financial regimes are not paraded with their levels of indebtedness displayed on them, but developing nations that are being helped to come out of the debt trap they find themselves in are referred to broadly by their debt status and poverty levels, for example the heavily indebted poor country initiative (HIPC).

Since military intelligence and communications needs influenced the new trends in civilian use of telecommunications, programs that intend to use information and communication technologies to facilitate information and knowledge sharing for development could engage in reconnaissance activities of the defence environment: In the year 2025, the future soldier would have the capabilities of today's battle tank, complete with a body suit with a controlled microclimate and integrated communications that would enable the future soldier to sense an oncoming attack, blend with the environment, and react to the source of the attack (Veltman, 2001). In the same vein, wiring agricultural extension officers, public health nurses, teachers, and others in rural communities so that the field worker functions as an integrated database and solutions provider to the farmer, a pregnant and nursing woman, pupils, and the community should not be viewed as Utopian and grandiose, but real and urgent.

This book therefore explores some of the pertinent issues in nurturing knowledge societies in developing and transition economies, and the manner in which the information and knowledge societies of these communities could be orchestrated to achieve desirable outcomes. It discusses a knowledge economy from the perspectives of sustainable development that is founded on intellectualizing local knowledge and ideas through the splicing of information from modern and indigenous knowledge domains, the validation and capitalization of ideas, and translation of ideas into products. It also discusses how the process of modernization and diffusion of such knowledge blends could be facilitated by IT-led systems, and the partnership arrangements that would foster building knowledge bridges between modern and indigenous systems. Arguments are provided for customized IT systems that are realistic, given the infrastructure, social, and inherent intellectual capital of the impact communities. It surmises that a sustainable impact of IT in these communities would be in the transformation of indigenous or local practices into continuously evolving and learning systems.

Efforts are made to provide universal resource locators as further readings, notes, or citations, so that regardless of where a reader might be in the world, he or she could explore the subject area further, provided there is connectivity of some sort; this is also to demonstrate the Web as a learning environment. There is the real possibility that some Web links might become inactive over time, especially in the wake of dot.com failures; however, efforts are made to select links or Web pages that are hosted on the servers of institutions of repute, where possible.

If the concept of globalization is to remove the inequities in fundamental aspects of human and business organizations, then the digital age is the ideal opportunity to found such a world. The visionary community in the digital world is not prejudiced by the state of technological sophistication in the so-called old economy, hence the notion of leapfrogging of developing nations; but imagination is the prerequisite for actualizing leapfrogging.

REFERENCES

Achebe, C. (1958). *Things Fall Apart*. London: Heineman Educational Publishers.

Achebe, C. (1964). *Arrow of God*. London: Heineman Educational Publishers.

Anonymous. (1997, May). [Review of *1984* by G. Orwell] [Online]. <http://www.angelfire.com/id/audreyspage/1984.html> [2001, January 17].

Blair, A. (2001, Oct. 2). Speech by Tony Blair, Prime Minister (UK) at the Labour Party Conference, Brighton, 2001. [Online]. Labour Party, United Kingdom <http://www.labour.org.uk> [2001, Oct. 3].

CBS. (2001). Survivor. [Online]. *CBS News*. <http://www.cbs.com/primetime/ fall_preview/survivor_africa.shtml> [2001, July 8]: "It's a whole new terrain, but the formula's the same: 16 strangers, two tribes, one Survivor, a million bucks, and an executive producer. The executive producer, Mark Burnett, of the CBS show Survivor was to return with the latest installment of his record-breaking phenomenon that pits the best against the best and often brings out the worst, with each trying to outwit, outplay and outlast the others in the quest to be declared the Ultimate Survivor. Survivor Africa is not a camping safari.'' See also: Temptation Island. [Online]. *Fox Television.* <http://www.fox.com/temptation/information.htm> [2001, July 8].

Easterly, W. (2001). *The Elusive Quest for Growth: Economists' Adventures and Misadventures in the Tropics.* Boston, MA: MIT Press.

G8. (2001, July). Genoa Summit of the G8: Few Outcomes and Many Hopes. [Online]. <http://www.genoa-g8.it/eng/summit/in_diretta/in_diretta_7.html> [2001, Aug. 31].

Greenspan, A. (2000, Mar. 6). The revolution in information technology. [Online]. The Federal Reserve Board, U.S. <http://www.federalreserve.gov/boarddocs/ speeches/2000/20000306.htm> [2001, July 16].

Kennedy, P. (2001, Sep. 16). The colossus with an Achilles' heel. *The Daily Yamiui*, Tokyo, p. 8B.

Linzer, D. (2001, June 26). Africa pleads for AIDS help. *The Globe and Mail, Toronto*, p. A1 and p. 18.

NEPAD. (2001). *New Partnership for African Development* (NEPAD). [Online]. NEPAD Secretariat, South Africa. <http:// www.africanrecovery.org> [2001, Nov. 20].

Orwell, G. (1976). *1984.* Mass Market Paperback. (Originally published in 1984). See also: The George Orwell Archive at the University College of London, which has "the most comprehensive body of research material relating to the author George Orwell (Eric Blair) (1903-1950) anywhere." [Online]. University College of London. <http://www.ucl.ac.uk/UCL_Info/ Divisions/Library/special_coll/orwell.htm> [2000, Dec. 15].

Speel, B. (1996). The Great Exhibition of 1851. Homepage. [Online]. <http:// www.speel.demon.co.uk/other/grtexhib.htm> [2001, Aug. 16].

Star, The. (2001, Sep. 17) Going Rome's way? *The Star*, Malaysia [Online]. <http://thestar.com.my/lifestyle/story.asp?file=/2001/9/17/features/ usfall&newspage=Search> [2001, Sep. 22].

U.N. (2001, June 27). Declaration of commitment on HIV/AIDS: Global crisis -
    Global action. [Online]. U.N. Special Session on HIV/AIDS, New York,
    NY, June 25-27, 2001. The United Nations. <http://www.un.org/ga/aids/
    conference.html> [2001, July 13].

Veltman, C. (2001, Sep. 21). Nanotech future for soldiers. *The British Broad-
    casting Corporation,* [Online]. <http://news.bbc.co.uk/hi/english/sci/tech/
    newsid_1554000/1554130.stm> [2001, Sep. 24].

World Bank. (2001, Oct. 1). Poverty to rise in wake of terrorist attacks in U.S.:
    Millions more people condemned to poverty in 2002. *Development News.*
    [Online]. The World Bank. <http://www.worldbank.org/developmentnews/
    stories/html/100101a.htm> [2001, Oct. 1].

Chapter II

Standards of Knowledge Communities

Ironically, the sector that was expected to define and lead the global economy into the new growth era of the new millennium would be the first casualty of a global economic slowdown and a diminishing capitalization of new products and ideas at the very beginning of that millennium. This contraction in the information technology sector in 2001 may have created further doubts in the minds of those who are unable to conceptualize the relationship among the rapid development and diffusion of IT, nurturing and interlinking knowledge cells into knowledge communities, and the empowerment of communities in the traditional non-industrialized economies.

However, under ideal circumstances, increasing access to information would enable groups to generate the knowledge that is critical in the transition of individuals, households, businesses, communities, and other levels of human and economic organizations into the global digital and networked economy. Hence, the myriad of connectivity initiatives around the world, which relate to all types of economies. In the advanced economies, these initiatives include the National Information Initiative (U.S.), Smart Communities (California), Singapore One, Connecting Canadians, Smart Capital (Ottawa, Canada), Digital Cities (Europe), Bayern On-Line (Germany), Ennis Information Age Town (Ireland), European Digital Cities, Telematique (France), and other programs in cities such as Stockholm, Seattle, Sacramento, and San Diego among others (Eger, 2001). Connectivity programs in emerging economies include Malaysia's Multimedia SuperCorridor, Hong Kong's Cyberport, and Indonesia's Cybercity. Other transition economies and developing countries are also engaged in designing local connectivity programs, with the support of their development partners in the donor community, foundations, businesses, and special initiatives.

Local and global investments and activities related to bridging the digital divide between the industrialized and non-industrialized worlds have raised the information and telecommunications capacity of many non-industrialized countries to at least a minimal level, despite the known digital divide. A Nielsen//NetRatings study of individuals in 23 countries in April 2001 indicated that the global population of Internet users had climbed to 390 million, and the bulk of Internet page readers may no longer be located in the industrialized economies alone. The Asia-Pacific region, led by South Korea, had become one of the zones of most avid surfers (CNN, 2001, asia.internet.ap/index.html); regional efforts such as the e-ASEAN (Association of South-East Asian Nations) Initiative are attempting to facilitate the transition of these communities into the global knowledge economy.

Latin America and Africa are also making inroads onto the information superhighway: all 54 African countries are now online, and connectivity emphasis is beginning to shift from urban centres to rural areas in some countries (Jensen, 2001). In some African countries, telecommunications operators are required to set up special area codes for ISPs to make all calls to the Internet become 'local calls,' and to enable networks with national coverage at a reduced cost for rural areas. The United Nations Economic Commission for Africa (UNECA) is spearheading the Africa regional connectivity programs through the African Information Society Initiative (AISI) and the National Information and Communications Infrastructure (NICI) initiative.

Several bilateral and multilateral frameworks and programs are also providing developing country institutions with the tools and means to participate in the sharing and application of global knowledge, but reference to any network that the author may be affiliated with is not an attempt to bias the reader toward the initiatives. The Global Knowledge Partnership (GKP), for example, is an informal partnership of public, private, and not-for-profit organizations that are committed to sharing information, experiences, and resources to promote access to, and effective use of, knowledge and information as tools of sustainable and equitable development. The Global Knowledge Partnership emerged from the cooperation of several organizations that sponsored one of the first conferences to consider global knowledge sharing for development through the Global Knowledge 97 conference: the GK97 conference, which was dubbed "Knowledge for Development in the Information Age," convened in Toronto, Canada, in June 1997. The World Bank also initiated and continues to support connectivity for several knowledge sharing programs, including: the Information for Development (infoDev) program, which funds connectivity programs across the developing world; the Development Gateway Foundation (DGF) that is expected to develop a database containing more than

300,000 development activities around the world; the Global Development Network (GDN) that is concerned about generating knowledge through strengthening the capacity of knowledge institutions to undertake policy-relevant research; the World Links for Development (WorLD) program that would link students and teachers in at least 1,200 secondary schools in 40 developing countries by the year 2000; and the Global Development Learning Network (GDLN) that provides the medium to deliver courses, seminars, and global dialogues through the multimedia Distance Learning Centres (DLC) of the participating nations. The U.N. Secretary-General has also established an ICT Task Force that aims to find new and creative means to spread the benefits of the digital revolution. The United Nations Development Programme (UNDP), in partnership with Accenture, and the Markle Foundation have also established the Digital Opportunity Initiative with the aim of identifying the roles that information and communication technologies can play in fostering sustainable economic development and enhancing social equity. The G8 nations have also begun identification of the manner in which they could participate in bridging the digital divide among nations: the Kyushu-Okinawa Summit of the G8 head of states in July 2000 (G8, 2000) created a Digital Opportunity Task Force (DOT Force) that would translate their Okinawa Charter on the Global Information Society into action. The DOT.Force deliberated on these issues, gathered public input, and made recommendations to the G8 head of states at the subsequent G8 Summit in Genoa, Italy. Bilateral development agencies have also established several connectivity programs for knowledge sharing to address key barriers and opportunities for ICTs in achieving development targets. They include the Bridging the Digital Divide program, joint initiative of the U.K. Department for International Development, The Netherlands' Ministry of Foreign Affairs, and the Swiss Agency for Development and Cooperation; the Acacia Initiative of Canada's International Development Research Centre; and the Leland Initiative of the United States Agency for International Development, among others.

These connectivity initiatives, regardless of the capacity of the economy, conceptualize a connected community as one in which the majority of businesses and residents within a geographic space become linked to a local data network to obtain information about government activities, community events, and critical social services such as disaster preparedness, health information, and education, among others.

A smart community could be imagined as an environment in which members could make knowledge deposits and withdrawals toward building their own future. The community's currency would be knowledge units such as ideas, databases, individual and institutional networks, tools, investment capital, and other knowledge resources. The community, as a knowledge bank, would have visionary portfolio and fund managers who can take calculable risks to maximize gains to the investor and the firm. The virtual community would also have expert planners or knowledge brokers to process raw information into value-added assets prior to deposit or withdrawal to achieve a maximum dividend to the depositor; thus financial planners would become knowledge processors. The better the broker or planner, the higher the dividend to the client. The attributes of the value-added, and the efficiency of utilizing the accessed knowledge would determine the reward to the client and other stakeholders. There would be no withdrawal fees, but the penalty for misappropriation of the accessed knowledge units would be the retardation of those whose actualization the transaction was supposed to facilitate. Knowledge and funds will be housed in the air around each individual, and these resources could be accessed *via* modern tools of communication that are now able to fit into the palm of toddlers. The more powerful the information and knowledge processors, the more efficient the client and portfolio managers would be in manipulating and interacting knowledge and funds. The more knowledgeable the group, the wiser it would become in the use of accessed knowledge and funds. The more such knowledgeable members a group has, the more collective social, economic, political, and technological advances would ensue in their community.

The potential of communications as virtual networks to enhance the capacity of institutions and communities is an issue that affects developing nations more than industrialized nations. If the Information Society is to enable sectors of economies to increase their capacities and efficiencies, then institutions in developing countries that have the least capacities in the global economy could benefit tremendously from virtual network resources to respond to the needs of their dependents. Sectors such as health and population growth, education, agriculture, food, nutrition and the environment, governance, private sector and businesses, technology, and infrastructure need to make quantum leaps in their capacities and efficiencies. Thus the ability to create virtual networks could make greater impact in developing nations than in more efficient economies. There is no other plausible route to quickly raise the capacity of institutions in the developing world to an appreciable state without these institutions being part of knowledge networks. Research in health sciences, medicine, and pharmaceuticals, for example, could not suddenly reach an appreciable level in an African country to enable the population to enjoy improved lifestyles comparable to any of the industrialized or transition economies in the foreseeable future under the current regimes. However, the local health industry, being a member of a global health knowledge community, could almost instantaneously benefit from global advances in medical research and knowledge.

Considering these expectations about IT, it appears that the enthusiasm with which groups and institutions, including the financial markets, embraced the concept that connectivity and smart communities could spur economic growth has not been matched with models to measure the impact of introducing IT. The most significant outcomes of *smart community* initiatives have therefore been the establishment of Internet portals containing an arrangement of institutional and individual profiles, business activities, products for sale, white papers, and technical briefings about government policies, and similar documents that could be accessed by the enquirer in a passive manner. Consequently, crude measures of the impact of an Internet portal or a Web page are based on the number of 'hits' (the number of times that Web surfers accessed the Internet page), and a rush to identify the next word that could be preceded by 'e.' Some program and proposal reviewers are sceptical about academic components of building knowledge networks, and even have "serious doubts as to the practical applicability of 'intellectualized' indigenous knowledge employing IT" (Anonymous, personal communication, December 2000) when knowledge drives the activities of the humblest of livelihood means.

Measurement of the impact of connectivity initiatives that would succinctly produce the generalizations of the relationship between the introduction of definite amounts of knowledge networking tools and resources, and concomitant changes in the social and economic attributes of the host environment, are yet to be generated. A large amount of data and other observations that can fully characterize the impact of connectivity and knowledge flows are required prior to formulation of theories about the impact of IT on development outcomes, or the identification of 'best practices' in the establishment and nurturing of knowledge communities. Kuhn referred to this type of measurement in discussing Lord Kelvin's dictum: "If you cannot measure, your knowledge is meagre and unsatisfactory" (Kuhn, 1977: 178). Quantitative methods are an integral part of advances in the physical sciences, and Kuhn suggested that the 'measurements' implicit in Lord Kelvin's assertion are the logical intuitions, statements, and laws that underlie numbers. Therefore, the number of hits is an observation and not by itself the basis of the laws that governed the relationship between IT and the prosperity of those who 'hit' the Web site, although such observations may be necessary to establish these laws; these observations by themselves do not explain the impact of knowledge flows on development.

The measurements that are sought for the Information Society would be the establishment of the laws that may govern the criteria of reasonable agreement between knowledge resources and expectations about digital opportunities. Formulation of these laws needs to include the perspectives of both the impact communities and external development agents; an open process of data generation is required to develop the laws and statements that may become the criteria of reasonable agreement so that all stakeholders involved in the deployment of information and communications technologies to address needs would understand which elements in the model they could optimize in their unique environments to enhance development outcomes. This flexibility and creativity in operationalizing IT in local domains are necessary in light of the different technological, economic, and human potentials of the various communities that seek to use the same tools.

The qualitative studies that may be required in the development of the generalizations regarding input-output functions of knowledge communities would relate to the social, cultural, and philosophical bases of the host environment, and the adaptations to, and applications of, the introduced communication tools. Essentially, the impact of introducing IT into a community would depend on the manner in which the tools are integrated into the local economy, the adoption and adaptation trends, the local intellectual capital, and the needs and opportunities of the elements of society that the tools could be applied. Consequently, the imaginations and perspectives of the host environment are crucial and would influence the standards that are acceptable as empowerment that is the result of utilizing knowledge resources.

Agreeably, knowledge communities could not evolve by some *de jure* standard formation (Mansell and Wehn, 1998: 182); nevertheless, it is critical to understand as humanly possible, some of the factors that may be essential in determining the functional relationships between communication tools, and the evolution and growth of knowledge societies. Some universal standards could be developed to ensure that the development, acquisition, deployment, application, evaluation, and sharing of best practices of tools and processes would nurture knowledge communities. The knowledge communities could then be evaluated by the efficiency with which the group generates or utilizes knowledge, and whether such activities and outputs are able to confer security to the community members and the natural environment.

The productivity within knowledge economies, due to the same tools as inputs, would also demand the same level of returns on investments, but the types of outputs could vary: Angola, Mozambique, and Kosovo, for example, could employ Geographic Information Systems (GISs) to identify the location of land mines, while other communities may employ the same tools to map out the natural resources of the local environment and to monitor the effects of management systems on these resources; some groups could employ networking tools and imaging systems to create a team of integrated health care professionals to monitor pregnant women in rural communities as part of a safe motherhood campaign, while other communities could use the same tools to host the local segment of television reality shows. It may suffice for some communities in developing nations to provide mobile phones as voice-only messaging systems for the user to determine commodity prices, without an access to knowledge-enhanced inputs such as improved crop varieties; safe environmental management techniques; efficient methods of production, processing, and distribution; or the realization of new opportunities. The acceptance of these standards may also be influenced by awareness about alternate methods of applications of knowledge resources. The differences in output components would be a factor of the local value systems and other attributes of the communities, such as ability to absorb and utilize technologies, and the social, economic, and philosophical aspirations.

The principal tools of the knowledge economy are invariably similar, are produced by a few companies, and often without discount in cost to underprivileged groups. These tools may actually cost more in deprived economies due to local excise laws, cost of connectivity, inability to make optimal use, or lack of strong competitions within the local telecommunications sector. Moreover, investment capital has become universal, and all types of economies are expected to compete for investment funds from the same global pool. Labour, an important aspect of the knowledge economy, has also become global, migrating toward the community with the most attractive living environment and working conditions. The outputs of information and knowledge flows in education, for example, are measured according to the same rules—all prospective students of graduate schools in the U.S. are ranked by the same standardized tests, without adjustment for the country of origin of the applicant. The human development index that is used by the United Nations (U.N.) to rank nations has the same expectations about all nations: it compares each against all others, using some presumed universal aspirations about the quality of life, assuming falsely or rightly that each nation would aspire to those qualities. It is therefore not in the interest of developing nations that they should have lower expectations about the returns on investments in connectivity and knowledge resources.

At the core of modern challenges in developing countries is the vacuum in which communities and institutions operate: the lack of intellectualization of local knowledge systems, and disproportionately high foreign technology input into local economies often as finished goods. These weaknesses have resulted in a high cost of engineered tools and inability of institutions, households, and communities to fully access modern knowledge and its outputs. This has created poor institutional capacities in many sectors of developing country economies, including production, processing, distribution, research, planning, technology, and governance, among others, and rendered the livelihood attainment and income generation of their average citizens to insecure states: the available data on sub-Saharan Africa indicate that there are 160,150 farm tractors in use, about 5,000 harvesters-threshers, and about 460 milking machines available to the region's 380 million agricultural workforce (FAO, http). This implies that almost all crop cultivation is by the hoe technology. Besides, the knowledge from plantation agriculture in cash crop production (rubber, cocoa, coffee, tobacco, etc.) has not impacted small-scale food crop and local fruit-tree farming systems. Generally, in spite of the proliferation of 'technology transfer' and 'appropriate technology' schemes, there is very little evidence of technology transfer between various sectors of a developing nation's economy itself.

The knowledge vacuum has reduced the majority in the developing world to continue to derive all their inheritance from the land: they hunt for mushrooms from the wild-like diamond gems, crack palm kernels on rocks, sharpen machetes on rocks, employ the hoe-technology in cultivation, grate vegetables on rocks, drink water that is the source of many of the diseases that shorten life spans, and women give birth anywhere and often bleeding to death. The majority continue to search for new lands to grow their 'primitive' crop cultivars, hardly replenishing the land; their young have joined militia groups that kill, maim, and rape girls for the sake of bread and butter; and the scourge of the human immunodeficiency virus and Acquired Immune Deficiency Syndrome (HIV/AIDS) has compounded their challenges. Poor nations also consume imported technology inefficiently, creating some of the world's most polluted cities.

Globally, there is an increasing pressure on production and other aspects of economies to adapt to new technologies, and communities and organizations are searching for more intelligent methods to address the increasing complexities of production to enhance the quality of life, to intensity the search for new knowledge for human interaction with the environment to be safer, for synergistic and mutually beneficial interaction of global capital with local economies, and for productivity to be more efficient, among others. Individual nations, organizations, units, or households may lack the ability to resolve problems that are becoming more complex and global in nature.

The industrialized nations are in need of innovation for their own security as well. The intensification of industrialization of food production, processing, and distribution, for example, has become a public health and safety concern. While farmers in the industrialized economies are becoming more technologically sophisticated, their ability to absorb new technologies efficiently would require beyond cursory introductions to the new methods. As farmers and others in the food industry adopt new biotechnologies and other tools that are developed in distant laboratories, issues of chemical and genetic pollution for instance are becoming more important to the industry's professionals and the public. Today, animals are bred on one farm, reared in another, processed in a different country, and consumed in yet another country; human beings and other goods are similarly in a flux, from one region of the world to another. Bioengineering and other scale-up mechanisms are enabling bulking up and blending of biological products from different sources. Thus a tiny amount of infected product could travel great distances and become incorporated in the food chains of a large number of communities that may be separated by oceans. The rapid innovations in agricultural biotechnologies demand that agro-business professionals interact continuously with the institutions that are spearheading the innovations in this important sector to learn the new ways of performing their tasks. The interaction of technology researchers and those who employ these innovations is necessary both to increase the rate of technology adoption for increased productivity and efficiency, as well as for the health and safety of producers, consumers, and the natural environment.

The recent outbreaks of foot-and-mouth disease, and mad cow disease in the European animal and feed industry, the hole in the Ozone Layer, the general evidence of a global warming trend, and inability to quickly resolve these insecurities indicate the complex production systems and processes that human activities have created. There is an obvious limitation of local groups to extricate themselves from such complexities due to the global influence of local activities and *vice versa*. Animal diseases such as swine fever and foot-and-mouth are endemic in some regions, and British veterinary scientists thought contaminated meat from one of such endemic foot-and-mouth areas found its way into the diets of British pigs. Therefore, solutions to such crises of global nature might require collaborations among nations. For example, while the U.K. cattle industry was the most severely impacted community of the recent outbreak of *bovine spongiform encephalopathy* (BSE) or mad cow disease, it was a group of scientists in Switzerland who first developed an antibody to recognize the infectious particles of protein (prions) that spread diseases such as BSE. Scientists, prior to the Swiss discovery, were unable to distinguish between proteins that are normally present in the body, and the malignant form that causes the disease (BBC, 2001). The same knowledge partnerships could address the causes of these diseases and many others in the developing world as these regions also play a role in the lifecycles of these diseases.

The volatility of energy cost, most recently the high cost of energy from the fall of 2000 through the winter of 2001, was another reminder of the need to find cleaner and reusable energy sources that would propel the knowledge economy (CBS, 2001). The computer industry is partially responsible for an increase in energy consumption; the number of domestic appliances that require year-round power supply in homes and institutions has increased significantly due to the advances in computerized electronic goods, from toasters to laundry appliances. Furthermore, there is a growing awareness of the dangers of dirty fuels, industrial wastes, and household garbage generation on the global environment, the climate, and human health. These are issues that networked institutions could address as common concerns.

These complex challenges that are the result of interconnectedness of communities, complex production, processing, and distribution chains, and their effect on the natural environment, also require networks of brainpower originating from divergent sources to generate a sustainable system. Diverse groups could converge into knowledge clusters or blocs to generate the critical knowledge base for the design of holistic solutions since no individual element within a sector, economy, or community possesses the full model of sustainable growth. Knowledge flows have therefore become critical, and IT has been heralded as the power to integrate solutions for human insecurities.

IT, presumably, would create the interacting spaces for groups to collect, process, utilize, and share knowledge. Innovation and problem solving are therefore the hallmarks that are demanded of smart communities.

The market contraction experienced in 2001 by major actors of the IT sector and the effects on businesses, investors, and economies therefore demand an analysis of the extent to which IT impacted problem solving. Perhaps, the contraction was a rebuke of the industry for the inability to contemplate communications contents alongside the new and imaginative telecommunication tools and products, or failure to increase efficiency and to capture new markets. Another plausible cause of the telecommunications-led market contraction was the over-capitalization of some components of the network economy model and undercapitalization of other components. The ensuing 'digital divide' is not only between technology haves and have-nots, such as different economic regions and nation-states, but also within an organization and within an economy. Acquisition of information and knowledge technologies without application in the entire activities of the organization or community could create a blockage in the deliverables of the organization, leading to overcapacity and undercapacity among the various units of the organization. Sector-wise, as one aspect of the technology sector enjoyed the confidence of investors, it alone amassed the capital that was dedicated to the deliverables of the entire sector.

Businesses that are related to the development of IT infrastructure did not foresee that their own continued relevance depended on the ability of the other components to utilize the infrastructure, and that their products and services needed to generate increased wealth across sectors. This lack of integrated deployment of telecommunications has caused the entire information technology sector gravely. The inability of knowledge economy players to create the watershed effect within organizations and economies, and lack of models to predict the output that could result from acquiring information technology infrastructure, have wrecked havoc on individual investors, businesses, and economies. Dataquest and International Data Corporation reported that unit shipments of PCs fell in the second quarter of 2001 compared to the same period one year earlier, the first time the industry had contracted on a year-over-year basis in at least 15 years. In spite of the price war between PC makers, second-quarter unit shipments in Japan dropped nearly 20 percent from the first quarter, and down 8.1 percent in the U.S. By the time of this decline, about 75 percent of homes and 95 percent of U.S. businesses had been equipped with PC units, and further upgrading of these units would require more than price cuts (CNN*fn*, 2001, technology/pcs). Perhaps, there are other potential participants in the telecommunications revolution, who are yet to be identified and empowered to utilize the tools in contributing to personal and institutional advancements.

The technologies that were supposed to determine the wealth of nations could not predict their own worth over time. The sentiments of an intelligent Western investor in technology stocks in 2001 revealed the failure and consequences of technology and economic growth models to significantly link information technology infrastructure to national economies, the performance of the industry itself, and the effect on investment capital management. This investor recalled the accolades that were bestowed on the management of telecommunications firms, and the investment advice that emanated from *The Street*, noting that 20 out of 21 analysts had recommended 'strong buy' ratings on the stock of his interest. The Street would become dangerous, murky, and wild within a very short time for this and other investors, and the entire information technology sector: "And then two weeks later, it was a complete 180 degrees. I'm stunned. I'm stunned at the way this has been handled all around. There are not a whole lot of people going 'we really messed up'; there hasn't been any retraction by any reporter" (Dixon, 2001: A17). But investors can be gullible: as the advances in the IT sector were contributing to the longest economic expansion and increasing productivity in many other sectors, investors paid very little heed to the possibilities that 'irrational exuberance' could unduly inflate the value of assets, as Greenspan (1996) conjectured about four years before the fall of technology stocks. Instead, some investors and businesses may have latched on to the thought of infinite economic expansion or stayed with the stocks, knowing that 'you win some, you lose some.'

Market analysts and brokerage houses are beginning to face the consequences of some of their lapses. Merrill Lynch, the number one U.S. brokerage house, agreed to pay US $400,000 to a former client as a settlement of a civil case that was initiated by the client with the New York Stock Exchange. The plaintiff claimed losses of about a half-million dollars from alleged misleading calls made by one of the technology stock analysts of the company in a possible conflict of interest matter. The analyst was alleged to have maintained a 'buy' rating on the stock of a wireless and broadband services provider, despite the stock's decline, with the motive to enable a lucrative financial deal for Merrill Lynch (CNN*fn*, 2001, merrill_bloget). The attorney for the plaintiff indicated that similar claims would be filed against an Internet and telecommunications analyst at Morgan Stanley Dean Witter and Company, and at Salomon Smith and Barney. These issues related to circumstances and reports in which brokerage firms and their analysts may be urging investors to look favourably to companies for whom these firms may be providing other services, or companies in which analysts may own personal stocks (Blackwell,

2001). These developments further the argument that the market performances during the technology-led expansion could have been artificially inflated.

The knowledge economy would be flawed from inception if it could not measure progress and identify the possible sources of failure with more precision and accuracy than luck alone.

REFERENCES

BBC. (2001, Feb. 23). No borders for meat trade. *The British Broadcasting Corporation*. [Online]. <http://news.bbc.co.uk/hi/english/uk/ newsid_1186000/1186559.stm> [2001, Feb. 25]: See also: Foot-and-mouth outbreak: On the trail of the virus. *The British Broadcasting Corporation.* [Online]. <http://news.bbc.co.uk/hi/english/static/in_depth/uk/2001/ foot_mouth/trail/default.stm> [2001, Mar. 14]; Infected swill was likely cause. (2001, Mar. 13). *The British Broadcasting Corporation.* [Online]. <http://news.bbc.co.uk/hi/english/uk/newsid_1218000/1218025.stm> [2001, Mar. 18]; Scientists close in on mad cow test. (1997, Nov. 5). *The British Broadcasting Corporation.* [Online]. <http://news6.thdo.bbc.co.uk/ hi/english/uk/newsid_23000/23452.stm>[2001, Mar. 8].

CBS. (2001, Jan. 12). Natural gas prices erupt. *CBS News*. [Online]. <http:// cbsnews.com/now/story/0,1597,260539_412,00.shtml>[2001, Jan. 13]: "In Denver, angry consumers told Colorado's utilities commission that they could not take another rate increase: 'People will die. The blood will be on your company's hands.' It was worse for industries, compared to households; companies could literally see their profits go up in flames, and there are no quick remedies to the crises."

CNN. (2001, May 25). Asia leads the world in Internet activity, study says. *Cable News Network*. [Online]. <http://www.cnn.com/2001/TECH/internet/05/ 25/asia.internet.ap/index.html>[2001, May 25].

CNN*fn*. (2001, July 20, merrill_bloget). Merrill settles complaint; No. 1 broker pays client $400,000 over 'misleading' call by analyst Blodget. (2001, July 20). *Cable News Network Financial News (CNNfn)*. [Online]. <http:// cnnfn.cnn.com/2001/07/20/investing/merrill_blodget/>[2001, July 21].

CNN*fn*. (2001, July 20, technology/pcs). PC sales drop in 2Q; Surveys show global deliveries off 2 percent in 2Q; Japan, U.S. markets hit. *Cable News Network Financial News (CNNfn)*. [Online]. <http://cnnfn.cnn.com/2001/ 07/20/technology/pcs/>[2001, July 21].

Dixon, G. (2001, June 16). The Stock, the shock, and an irate investor. *The Globe and Mail*, Toronto, p.A1 and p.A7: Tim Leslie was reacting to a radio broadcast concerning the huge second quarter loss that had been announced by Nortel Networks on June 15, 2001. The company announced a projected loss of 19.2 billion U.S. dollars, the second largest quarterly loss by a Canadian firm at that time. Leslie, an airline pilot, had purchased 5,600 shares of the company, in stages, to the tune of 350,000 Canadian dollars, but the value had been reduced to 84,950 Canadian dollars as the company's stock value fell.

Eger, J. M. Smart communities. [Online]. The World Foundation for Smart Communities. <http://www.smartcommunities.org/links.htm> [2001, March 30].

FAOStats agriculture data. [Online]. United Nations Food and Agriculture Organization. <http://apps.fao.org/page/collections?subset=agriculture> [2001, May 16].

G8. (2000). G-8 pledges to overcome international digital divide. [Online]. U.S. Department of State, International Information Program. <http://usinfo.state.gov/topical/global/ecom/00072401.htm> [2000, July 24]. Also, see: Addressing the global digital divide. [Online]. Digital Opportunity Task Force. <http://www.dotforce.org/> [2001, Sep. 30].

Greenspan, A. (1996, Dec. 5). The challenge of central banking in a democratic society. Annual dinner and Francis Boyer Lecture of the American Enterprise Institute for Public Policy Research, Washington, DC. [Online]. The Federal Reserve Board, U.S. <http://www.federalreserve.gov/boarddocs/speeches/1996/19961205.htm> [2001, Oct. 17].

Jensen, M. (2001, May). The African Internet—A status report. Homepage. [Online]. Association for Progressive Communication. <http://demiurge.wn.apc.org/africa/afstat.htm> [2001, June 15].

Kuhn, T. S. (1977). *The Essential Tension*. Chicago: The University of Chicago Press.

Mansell, R. and Wehn, U. (1998). *Knowledge Societies: Information Technology for Sustainable Development*. Oxford, UK: Oxford University Press.

Chapter III

Nurturing Knowledge Communities

A distinguishing factor in IT-led knowledge for development models could be the concept of nurturing knowledge communities versus knowledge management, as advocated by Denning (2001). Knowledge management essentially implies the structural arrangement and aggregation of information or information sources while the nurturing of knowledge communities would include the psychology and philosophy of enhancing the civilization of the impact community, and the application of knowledge tools and resources to actualize those values. Knowledge management, by inference, is an important element in nurturing knowledge communities, but this practice in itself would not constitute the core activity that can transform an organization or a group into a smart community. Considering the permutations of words that could cover the vast field of sustainable development and communications, for example the challenges, assets, and opportunities of the impact community, it would be quite a challenge to arrange all development information entries and sources into subtitles that could be held by one or a few organizations for equal and user-friendly access by all in the community and globally. While such an arrangement of information is desirable and perhaps technologically feasible, the information revolution is ideally concerned with teaching people about how to find information and how to generate data about a community's attributes, access complementary information from elsewhere, utilize that information, mine knowledge from the information and application, and generate innovative solutions that would enhance the attribute concerned; data could be spread on several Internet hosts, but technology can splice them into relevant information for local applications. Moreover, the realignment of the psychologies, philosophies, and other values of individuals, institutions, communities, and the nation-state toward application of IT as knowledge tools could determine the outcome of information and knowledge flows to a larger extent than knowledge management.

Nurturing knowledge communities to the extent that these communities can be secure and prosperous demands access of the community to information, development of ideas regarding the quality of the community's attributes, validation of the ideas, building networks and partnerships for the mobilization of intellectual and technological resources as capital inputs, and generation of prototype solutions. The validation of ideas is now more intense since Listservs can pool talents from various spaces and themes into a virtual evaluation team.

Denning also suggested that nurturing knowledge communities could be visualized as gardening; the Internet Encyclopedia of Philosophy observed that few retreats could be more favourable to philosophy than a garden; and, indeed, the *Academia* founded by Plato was originally a public garden that was planted with olive and other trees. Plato possessed a small garden within this enclosure where he opened a school to receive those who were disposed to his instructions that became the precursor of the modern university (IEP, 2001; Keyes, 1996).

THE CORN INDUSTRY AND NURTURING KNOWLEDGE COMMUNITIES

The new learning environment that is afforded talent grooming by the revolutions in telecommunications is here conceptualized as a field of corn (*Zea mays* L.) regarding the constitution, operations, and productivity of the farm. Corn has been impacted by nanotechnologies in biology, like communications have been impacted by nanotechnologies such as microwaves in engineering. Corn is grown across many latitudes, unlike many crops whose cultivation is delineated by latitudes, and the crop is used in a variety of ways depending on the local culture; similarly, modern telecommunications are ubiquitous, but the use to which they may be put is subject to local values and abilities. The corn industry in the U.S. has had a major impact on agriculture and crop improvement in general. The genetic aspects of conventional crop improvement programs were deduced largely from corn breeding schemes, and corn plays a role in the feeding of the hungry around the world in humanitarian programs; similarly, the telecommunications revolution in the U.S. and the other industrialized nations have impacted many aspects of today's society and economy, and the development agencies are also involved in connectivity programs in their impact regions. The hybrid corn industry in the U.S., where the crop has undergone the most transformation into a reputable industry, therefore provides an example of nurturing a garden through processes that maximize productivity by manipulating the genetic attributes of the species and the environmental conditions that enable full expression of the genetic potentials in a defined and nourishing environment.

The single-cross hybrid corn industry involves the development of several inbred lines that are highly specialized and reliable (pure) for the desirable features, the combination of two individuals that are divergent in the expression of the trait, and identification of the two inbred parents that combine to produce progenies that exhibit the greatest synergies in the desirable attributes of the species. This scheme is highly environment-specific. Similarly, IT can create highly specialized researchers in several disciplines of poverty alleviation, who could be integrated into a knowledge machine or team. The two inbred lines that are selected as 'parents' in the hybrid corn industry are mated to produce the seeds that are marketed to farmers for cultivation; similarly for IT, expert panel outputs and computer applications are synthesized and disseminated to target communities. These parents combine in very definite ways to produce seeds that give rise to plants of definite features and outlooks, for example seeding rate, nutrient requirements, reaction to stimuli (sunlight intensity and duration, disease and insect pest populations, and moisture), growth stages, and yield. The uniformity among the progenies is important: the farmer could plant the entire field within a narrow timeframe, provide the same nutrients to all plants at the same time, be assured of the same harvest window for all plants in the field, and could predict the yield of the field, among others.

The investigations to identify the specific crosses that would result in the best performing progeny are specific to localities. The growing environment could therefore be optimized for the specific progeny type and would involve quantitative doses of sunlight, moisture, weed control, and insect and disease management practices. The requirement for a carefully controlled environment in an erratic climate causes severe distortions when an element deviates from the prescribed regime; yield would be significantly affected when any of the input factors is not optimized, or when a plant variety developed for one locality is transplanted into a different environment. This illustrates the need to involve the knowledge about the impact zone in development frameworks, however the laws in IT are not yet advanced to the point that a certain amount of a defined communication tool would generate a particular amount of productivity for various types of communities.

The relationship between diversity and problem solving is another aspect of the corn industry that is relevant to knowledge and development schemes. All the corn plants in a farmer's field might originate from the same parents or parents with close genetic backgrounds, and many farmers in the locality often cultivate the same varieties. The possibility exists that the narrow genetic base and the monoculture of the industry might not buffer the plant community against changes in the environment. The survival of species, on the other hand, is based on variability in the genetic constitution of the species, so that some individuals within the species would react differently to unexpected changes in the environment and enable the species to adapt and survive. It is feared similarly that proliferation of IT could clone minds and obliterate minority cultures that are not represented in the mainstream media of global reach. Moreover, the artificial environment—particularly the application of insecticides, pesticides, and chemical weed-control—that is required by elite hybrid varieties has become a contentious issue between those who oppose monoculture and the use of chemicals to confer tolerance to biotic stresses in agriculture, and other actors such as the biochemical industry. Another major drawback of the single-cross hybrid industry is that farmers would have to buy new seed from the laboratory for each planting season, as the unique genetic combinations would segregate in the succeeding generation crosses. IT and knowledge for development programming could avoid this drawback by creating the interacting spaces that would enable local groups to behave as innovative communities and generate their own solutions on a continuum, without the need to depend on external sources for all its knowledge needs all the time.

Other methods to combine parents to produce non-single-cross hybrid seed exist, with their advantages and limitations, but perhaps of value to sustainable communities. The progenies of these alternate seed production systems may be more varied in their genetic constitution, and more buffered and flexible in reaction to changes within the environment or due to other stressors since the different genetic backgrounds within the community would enable some genotypes to compensate for others in the event of unforeseen stresses. However, these progenies lack the uniformity that is characteristic of single-cross hybrid plants: the plants would not be as uniform in input requirements, growth and developmental stages, reaction to stimuli, harvest window, or productivity. The yield or output levels of these types of plant communities could also be lower than in the single-cross hybrid system, hence these types of crosses do not fit in the present model's production practised by the mainstream grower.

Similarly, the development of human resources and institutional capacity-building programs in an IT-led nurturing of knowledge communities could vary by economic region, however the general patterns of networks include training of highly specialized individuals, and the combination of such individuals into 'task teams' to perform defined functions. The coherence among the differently specialized individuals or units within the institution and the influences of the local environment would determine the quality of the product of the team and their yield in terms of market niche that the institution commands as a result. These requirements for unique combinations of talents and the provision of tools, resources, and an enabling environment that could allow group genius to flourish imply that various knowledge communities might require customized tools and interfaces according to the level of their sophistication and opportunities. It is also likely that the relocation of individuals from one team to another might not produce the same synergies regarding outputs, although relocation of human resources is a hallmark of many economies.

The specific combining ability of experts in team building and group outputs within organizations are often modeled around competitive and market niches of organizations, and perhaps for a specific challenge or growth opportunity. With such specificities, the unique combinations of talents would segregate over time, as the composition of the team changes, and the input-output functions would change accordingly. A unit leader in an industry may be considered highly successful in one firm, but when moved to another firm of the same industrial sector could fail to meet expectations, all things being equal. Hence, communities that do not have the internal capacity to produce their own talents or products could borrow ideas from external sources, but it is essential that the imported idea is bred into the local system, like the corn breeder in an environment could obtain seeds of corn varieties from colleagues and institutions globally for incorporating the desirable genetic attributes into the local varieties through breeding programs but not as seed to grow the following season's crop.

Institutions and businesses are aware that production inputs and consumer behaviours are dynamic. This situation requires an adaptive organization that is able to foresee trends and take advantage of market shifts. Hence, many organizations and communities are in the process of defining the optimal human organizations, business and institutional processes, the resources that could stimulate group genius, and the customization of solutions to the specific entity. It is becoming more apparent in this regard that individuals within an institution should have multiple peaks in their training and expertise so that they would have the lateral ability to understand the role of their organization in the global marketplace. The ability of individuals with highly specialized and narrow expertise to become competent in multiple capacities requires a commitment to continuous learning. Multitasking, especially during economic down turns, tight budgets, and layoffs should be distinguished from multiple intelligence. Multitasking, in which corporations assume that a few can be made to do the work of many, could actually be counterproductive, as the time costs can increase with the complexity of the chores; it has been reported that subjects in multi-task schedules are unable to concentrate for tens of minutes at a time, as it may take a longer duration to switch between tasks, and could cost a company as much as 20 to 40 percent in potential efficiency loss (Rubinstein, et al., 2001; Anderson, 2001).

The knowledge economy is therefore one in which institutions and local communities would search for how best to groom talent, retain it, and derive the best outcomes for the individual, the team, the entire organization, and the local economy. These features may not be achieved for each type of organization in a wholesale program; each sector, organization within sector, and perhaps teams within an organization may require their own solutions. This then is one of the mechanisms through which the knowledge economy could create new opportunities, including new jobs.

What is more, knowledge drives every activity, including those of hodmen, or people who carry bricks and mortar for a mason (Stiglitz, 1999). Therefore a knowledge community would be one that provided the nurturing environment for all groups within the community to utilize timely and comprehensive information and ideas in the entire spectrum of economic and socio-political functions. The imaginative ways in which members of communities—individuals, households, and institutions of all sectors—apply networking tools would determine the outcomes of knowledge community initiatives. That IT is revolutionary implies its wide and dramatic effects, but the sustaining ability of IT in economic growth may be deduced from ability to create the nurturing environment for continuous learning and reinvestment of knowledge gained into downstream activities and reformulation of the initial production steps.

The need for research and technology outputs by the economies that cannot generate all the necessary inputs into a knowledge-based system by themselves should not place these nations and their agents in conflict with international regimes that cover knowledge properties. Médecins sans frontières (MSF), Oxfam, and other non-governmental development agencies have been campaigning for access of the developing nations to vital drugs; notably, these groups and the U.N. supported the South African government position in the court battle between the government and pharmaceutical companies regarding access to generic drugs for HIV/AIDS care, with the drug manufacturers insinuating a breach of patent laws (Capella and Meikle, 2001; Oxfam, 2001; MSF/Oxfam, 2001). The leaders of poor nations, the development community, and civil society organizations consider the knowledge assets of the biotechnology research industry as public good on ethical grounds while the industry has the legal rights to the protected knowledge. This situation demonstrates some of the needs in the developing world to which the global development and donor communities could devote attention in nurturing knowledge activities in the developing world.

The pharmaceutical industry or other business sectors could be pressured by civil society to make knowledge products available to the word's poor, but they could provide inferior quality products: although the pharmaceutical companies such as GlaxoSmithKline agreed to allow local non-profit, low-cost, generic versions of three of its anti-aids drugs to be manufactured by a South African company, critiques contended initially that the versions of the products licensed were not the latest versions of drugs available; in some cases, activists claimed that the full combination of cocktails were not being provided to the poor communities that are unable to afford the full cost.

The authors of a U.N. report observed that developing countries could undertake generic drug manufacture under the compulsory licensing mechanism, a principle in international commerce that permits countries to 'use patents without permission of the patent holder in return for a reasonable royalty on sale.' They referred to the precedence set by advanced economies in which Australia, Britain, Canada, Germany, Italy, New Zealand, and the U.S. benefited from this right of compulsory licensing. Canadian consumers, for example, saved $170 million in drug costs in 1991-1992 prior to joining the North American Free Trade Agreement (NAFTA). More recently, the Canadian government admitted that it broke its own drug-patent rules in a rush to protect Canadians from the threat of anthrax bioterrorism in the aftermath of the September 11, 2001, terrorist attacks against the U.S. and the spread of anthrax spores to some targets. The Canadian government ordered 900,000 tablets of the antibiotic Cipro (ciprofloxacin) from Toronto-based generic drug manufacturer Apotex Inc. at about one dollar, although the government had granted the German pharmaceutical giant Bayer AG, which holds the patent on Cipro through 2003, the right to the Canadian market; the error was attributed to a government employee, who had failed to seek approval from the country's patent commissioner to circumvent the act (Laghi and Scoffield, 2001). The government subsequently reached an agreement with the two drug companies: Bayer AG would supply the drug to the Canadian government at a reduced cost, and Apotex did not charge the government for leftover stock. The U.S. government was also determined to obtain a substantial reduction on the cost of Cipro supplied by Bayer AG to less than one dollar, or the administration was prepared to go to the U.S. Congress and ask for some support to obtain the drug from other sources (CNN, 2001, cipro.thompson). In the end, the U.S. paid Bayer 95 cents a pill for Cipro, down from the previously discounted price of $1.77 per tablet. It was therefore suggested that developing nations could strengthen their national laws in order to enable local production of cheaper, lifesaving AIDS drugs (Macan-Markar, 2001).

While invoking this clause might be essential as a matter of urgency, many countries in Africa and similar economies would not be able to take advantage of this nature of opportunity; they do not have the manufacturing ability, and the cost of procuring the generic version is also unaffordable by themselves, and they would still need funding from the nations whose business patents are to be circumvented. The knowledge outputs of the research and development programs of the private sector in the Western economies such as the pharmaceutical industry are partially funded by the public, including the investments of governments, parents, and students in the development of human resources through public universities. Hence, the major drug manufacturers are obliged to provide the health sector of the industrialized nations at any cost, or their workforce would become weak, but to extend these privileges to communities that may be considered to be outside the institution's traditional resource base may be perceived as a matter of humanitarian assistance. A sustainable approach for access of poor nations to enhanced knowledge products could be the mechanism that assisted such nations to establish critical knowledge bridges for partnerships and integrated local networks for local innovations and problem-solving methods to flourish locally. The development and donor community could contribute to and invest up front in the processes of finding knowledge solutions and products, and to procure such knowledge on behalf of the societies of their concern. Without the foresight of the development community to identify potential knowledge products to invest in or support up front, it would be difficult to realize some of the ideals of globalization, including that of knowledge as a public good.

The assistance from other domains toward the development of the knowledge culture of poor communities should, however, not perpetuate the state of dependency, exploitation, or other forms of unbalanced relationships either. Globalization, if it is a virtue worth pursuing, could therefore be viewed from a perspective that is broader than the performance of private capital markets alone; development has also become a global issue. The development community has also been investigating how it could transform itself to respond better to globalization. Many of the multilateral and bilateral agencies have been attempting to transform themselves and their impact communities into knowledge communities. Dumelie suggested that the transformation of traditional development philosophy from 'international development' to 'global development' could become the next major contribution to development philosophy; international development is based essentially on a donor-recipient model, compartmentalization of nations, and the transfer of capital and projects vertically between these nations, while global development is based on partnerships, knowledge sharing, and networks in which communities anywhere could relate to another elsewhere (Roger Dumelie, Canadian International Development Agency, personal communication, July 25, 2001). Connectivity for global development would aim toward building and supporting such knowledge networks.

The industrialized nations could make bold initiatives to develop knowledge channels with and within developing nations as part of the transformation of their international development assistance programs into global development perspectives. Canada, for example, is a member of the G7 Nations; its global position is built on developing social safety nets for its citizens, protecting brokered peace among warring factions around the world, and feeding the hungry. The Canadian economy is now largely service-sector driven, but Canada has traditionally depended on the management and exploitation of its rich natural resources like some endowed nations in the developing and transitional economies. In the Information Age, the weapons in Canada's arsenals to keep the peace and undertake emergency relief actions could change to averting ethnic strife, preventing hunger, and spreading its knowledge about natural resource exploitation and management. Indeed, a Canadian Government task force identified that the sharing of the knowledge that underlies Canada's economic and social development could become a stronger component in Canadian partnerships and trade relationship with countries that are now attempting to evolve their human and environmental sustainability models (IDRC, 1997).

The current market corrections and restructuring of the business of information technologies provide an ideal opportunity to determine if knowledge for development programs of the traditional donor nations intended to refocus the Information Society toward knowledge-based economies in an open-learning system as the new academy. This academy would be the interacting spaces, where information and knowledge tools converge and engender the various elements of society. This IT-led knowledge empowerment of humans and institutions, if self-actualized, could be central in nurturing knowledge economies.

The initial wave of projects regarding telecommunications and knowledge flows in developing nations focused on access to the tools, hence, ISPs, website managers, Web page developers, school connectivity, and training of institutional leaders. The assessment of these nations' readiness in the knowledge economy consequently has focused on infrastructure such as number of units, type of hardware, bandwidth, number of Web pages, and Internet traffic in general. These assessments were weak in the conceptualization of the impact of connectivity that involved identification of knowledge needs, and development of content and interactive tools for problem solving.

FACILITATORS OF KNOWLEDGE NETWORKS

An important attribute of a knowledge community is the role of facilitators who spur, guide, and ensure access to the spaces to increase the ingenuity of the community and the realization of opportunities by all members. Essentially, at the advent of the modern Information Age, organizations established new units dedicated to network management. These units have been primarily concerned about procuring the tools (hardware and software) for their institutions and divisions, training personnel on how to use the tools, and providing technical assistance for the smooth flow of information. The content aspects of the knowledge economy also require dedicated units that would integrate the knowledge inputs-outputs of their domains and identification of how these elements interact with the global economy. ISPs and technical managers could not necessarily assume the role of knowledge facilitators, who should have thematic expertise and ability to provide lateral or cross-cutting perspectives. The expected outputs of knowledge facilitators and brokerages would be problem-solving tools that would make the contents relevant to the community's needs and facilitate relevant 'search' outputs in information-on-demand; they could be essential in the generation, organization, processing, and dissemination of information locally, and in identifying the talents in the local communities that could speed up the generation of functional outputs.

It is evident that both the North and South are seeking imaginative solutions to the complexities that arise from human activities, and to extend human civilization into the next frontier. Homer-Dixon defined ingenuity as ideas that can be applied to solve practical, technological, and social problems, consisting of a set of instructions to help arrange the world in a defined manner (Curtis, 2000; Homer-Dixon, 2000). As societies are racing into the future, they create complexities in every field; the difference between a society's desire for ingenuity and the uncertainty of supplies could be referred to as ingenuity gap.

The response of many businesses to the ingenuity gap in their operations is the wave of mergers and acquisitions that have become common occurrences, as many businesses are unable to define their market niches in the rapidly changing nature of business operations; consequently, these businesses seek strategic partnerships and alliances in order to re-orient their activities to the Information Age. Some of these mergers and acquisitions may benefit the businesses involved through greater opportunities in economies of scale and reduction in production costs, with the assumption that IT has increased the boundary of business operations before the scale of diseconomies begin to come into play.

Mergers and acquisitions on the other hand are often followed by redundancies of personnel and business units, and may also be creating market hegemonies rather than the proliferation of entrepreneurial spirits, growth of small businesses, or increased diversity of products that the information revolution was supposed to herald. The merger between America Online (AOL) and Time Warner was celebrated as a new business model in the Information Age, with the traditional media acquiring the capabilities of the new media business; less than two years after the completion of that merger, the incoming chief executive officer of the AOL Time Warner empire needed to address the problems at the struggling online division, and also explain how it fits together with the old Time Warner businesses, including cable and publishing (La Monica, 2002); shares of AOL Time Warner had slipped more than 60 percent since the merger.

Some firms and businesses may be greedy, acquiring firms that may be their competitors, and in the process could over-extend themselves even in a weakened competitive market while being unable to deliver to the public and investors on the potential of their market shares and performance expectations. Basically, the field of technology and innovation is wide, but the talent and outputs may be weak; many of the firms that swallow up their competitors are often unable to make significant returns on the amount of pooled capital assets that they would have mobilized from the high growth economy and the public, and the market does not take kindly to those who renege on business performance outlooks.

Even as different types of media—print, broadcast, and Internet—converge under the same business group, there is little evidence that information emanating from these conglomerates is more substantive than before. During the 2001 Solo Spirit balloon circumnavigation flight attempt of Steve Fossett (Solo Spirit, 2001), many of the cable television news channels that blurted out 'news' about the flight could not provide the audience with any reference to the historic and successful circumnavigation of the Breitling Orbiter 3 team of Swiss psychiatrist and pilot Bertrand Picard and British co-pilot Brian Jones in 1999 (BBC, 1999), granted that the Fossett attempt was a solo effort.

Developing country economies though may be able to take advantage of mergers and acquisitions within the local economy to acquire capabilities regarding modern telecommunications. This need becomes apparent when the adoption of networked tools and processes are compared between the private sector and the public sector. The public sector in Africa for example may lag behind the private sector in IT adoption while the public sector may be an effective catalyst of IT adoption and utilization in the private sector.

Roberts (1997) suggested seven core attributes for stimulating group genius that may enhance the transformation of businesses, institutions, and communities into knowledge-based societies. These include body of knowledge, process design and facilitation, education, environment, technology, project management, and venture management. The body of knowledge component urges institutions to recognize that the collective knowledge and experiences of a team within the institution are its most valuable resources. Organizations should therefore assess this body of knowledge, determine where such knowledge may reside, and ensure that each element within the organization is aware of this knowledge to avoid duplicating efforts and to build team dynamics. Organizations could also find out how creative processes and pathways that often happen by accident occurred, in order that the internal processes may be cleared of obstacles, instead of the tradition to dictate how things are done. Moreover, as learning is a continuous process within organizations, groups should discover the processes by which they gather information or explore new ideas, and the physical and psychological work environment should support creativity and collaboration. Roberts also observed that while technology could enable an organization to leverage its creativity, it could also be a false 'quick fix' that will simply magnify and accelerate flaws that remained in the creative processes, hence technology should be customized to the institutional needs and systems; project management should endeavour to manage the environment and not the people, and facilitate the creativity of the team. It is also important for the organization to set strategic goals and modify daily activities and processes to realize them through maintenance of organizational health, preservation of functional aspects, and searching for new, more effective, and creative systems.

Finding ingenious ways to realize the knowledge economy is a daunting task; neither the advanced nor developing economies can boast of an error-proof method to identify talent and groom ideas into products through knowledge networks. This is the opportunity for developing countries to make significant gains in economic development, hence leapfrogging.

Knowledge Facilitators and Expert Systems

The knowledge for development philosophy includes finding the unique ways in which knowledge channels could be distributed, interactive, with content that is relevant to local needs. Developing nations could not acquire the efficient human resources to manage their transition into efficient knowledge-based production systems without contemplating new learning systems. Considering the level of knowledge hunger and the poor knowledge channels and tools that currently exist in these economies, traditional learning systems could not yield the intelligent human capital locally. Knowledge for development programming requires more than using information technology tools as a marginal enhancement of the status quo; people and institutions should not be resistant to change but look for creative, innovative approaches to new opportunities; they should not try to 'save the theory,' stick fast to old methods, or look for old solutions to new problems (Morrison and Twigg, 2001).

Knowledge management as aggregating information sources alone may not create the desired impact of investments in IT infrastructure and expert teams. At present, the amount of knowledge that could be shared among various units and personnel of the most efficient knowledge-based organization is less than 20 percent of the potential knowledge that might exist within the organization or a knowledge community. According to estimates by the Delphi Group, about 88 percent of an organization or a community's tacit knowledge—voicemail, E-mail, employees' minds, meeting notes, and informal discussions—is not retrievable by others or available for sharing through keyword searches. This 'knowledge sharing problem'--such as not finding the person who has the information, doing what has already been done but not knowing where to retrieve the information, keep answering the same question or sending the same information to different people within the same organization repeatedly when one cannot find the information needed at the time it is needed, or the vacuum created when an employee leaves the organization--is expected to cost Fortune 500 companies alone about $57 billion in the next two years (AskMe, 2000). The Best Practices LLC observed that although nearly every company practises some form of knowledge management, very few are able to fully leverage knowledge to drive bottom-line results, and suggested that much of this failure stems from the inability to identify and leverage pre-existing knowledge communities. IT-led knowledge for development would require the design of interfaces that can generate solutions to customized queries, beyond the arrangement of information sources.

Knowledge network facilitators could therefore play an essential role in making passive information portals become active by integrating the human aspects of information flow with electronic aggregations of information sources. Tools are being developed to assist such knowledge brokers in brainstorming and generation of solutions for the needs of clients, but some schools of thought may frown at the relevance of artificial intelligence to increasing the knowledge quotient of development practice. As the Information Society is understood more clearly, the component of artificial intelligence that relates to knowledge discovery and data mining would become the essence of empowerment of institutions and communities in developing nations, as many as these tools are relevant for institutions and communities in the industrialized economies.

The industrialized economies have been developing their templates for these expert tools and systems in response to the knowledge-sharing problem; several expert systems are being developed for specific applications such as accounting, engineering, and biology (PC AI, http). AskMe Enterprise™ and Practicity (True Source) for example provide methods to capture employees' expertise, catalogue it, transfer it to those who need it when they need it, and store that valuable knowledge for future use A U.K.-based group is also developing a 'Brainstorming Toolbox.' Many of these expert tools and their variants are tailored to the corporate entity and not specifically designed for the uniqueness of developing nations.

The contents from which expert tools determine solutions for the information-seeker would determine the relevance of outputs from these tools. Comprehensive problem solving through interactive spaces therefore require availability of information that is pertinent to the environment of the user, and outputs that are customized to local needs. Ideally, if an information pool with a comprehensive entry in the thematic areas of interest could be established, problem-solving toolkits could be developed to facilitate interactivity from the perspective of the user. In order to create a comprehensive solution, the knowledge society would first generate as much information related to the subject.

The expert tools could then splice contents from various databases to generate a functional output, just as nanotechnologies in biology, for example genetic engineering protocols in the identification of functional genes from sequences that may include non-coding elements, and in gene therapy.

The nature of the Information Society requires that various sectors of economies—health, education, research, business, government, and the development community to develop their own unique ways to use the advances in communications to increase their efficiencies and deliverables. While the global development community employs modern communications, perhaps at a level comparable to other sectors of economies, the development community acquires these tools and applications as the general user population. The development community though is unique, as its central operations are based in the industrialized economies, but the core of its programming pertains to communities far removed. The global development community therefore needs to champion the development, acquisition, applications, evaluation, and exchange of knowledge network tools and platforms for the concerned communities. Only a few of the experts systems that are currently being developed target the special needs of the development community or its clients, for example the work of Stamper toward MEASUR (R. Stamper, University of Twente, The Netherlands, personal communication, 2000).

The global development community needs to conceptualize the future of convergent communications and stimulate the development of tools that would impact its activities and help to meet the needs of its clients. These expert systems could identify the challenges of livelihoods attainment, the causes of insecurities, and best practices in resolving these challenges through the splicing of information from local and global knowledge domains. Since the primary impact communities have very little information about themselves (not the views of others about them) in existing databases upon which Internet portals are being created, the application of expert tools to current information in databases would not be able to generate functional knowledge solutions for many local communities. The Global Gazetteer (1998), for example, provides maps for 2,880,532 world cities, towns, and small communities, including Woadze. This community of about 800 people in the Volta Region of Ghana is not depicted on most printed maps, but is now visible to anyone anywhere at any time, online. The Global Gazetteer states the geographic bearings of Woadze, but other pertinent information about the community that is required to depict the opportunities and challenges of this community in the global information pool, and information that may be included in 'search' outputs, is not available online. Information about such communities around the world is supposedly included in the descriptions of the 'average' rural community in a region or country. This situation leads to development of 'one-size-fits-all' programs that may or may not be representative of many communities. A worthwhile exercise in IT-led knowledge for development programming could be the inculcation of a digital culture among local oral communities so that they can generate information about themselves.

Activities toward relevant problem-solving spaces such as information gathering, data mining, and pattern identification should therefore be viewed as major and viable components of local knowledge economies and creation of local opportunities. Opportunities could be provided in local capacity-building programs in developing countries for design of templates that could facilitate the ability of communities and indigenous professionals to document their own principal features and major transitions toward creating visibility about themselves. This would impact knowledge discovery and data mining, monitoring community health, providing targeted development ideas, and identifying opportunities by the individual, institution, or community to generate online information for development planning. Detailed information about the microenvironment (the community, household, and individual) is essential for targeted development practice, especially to inform development planners, who may be located far from the impact areas, about local knowledge features; creating such community profiles with regular feature updates would be done most effectively by the communities themselves.

Digital documentations of indigenous practices could serve as teaching material to students in the international development and research communities, and for those who have a general interest in development knowledge flows. The substance of documentation about the developing world should however highlight how the majority meet their livelihood challenges, considering that the wildlife of the Safaris in East Africa and Southern Africa have attracted significant capital investments in multimedia documentation. E-tourism and eco-tourism promotion could become important in environmental knowledge and management, and as sources of revenue for the destination economy while enhancing the quality of life of the tourist; however, digital documentations should also highlight the means by which the poor practice and earn their living in a secure manner. This is essential because the poor are actually the custodians of the environment. Wildlife parks exist most commonly in the communities of the poor; the rich may patronize the natural reserves, but the meek tend the ground just as The Beatitudes observed more than 2,000 years ago. Human activities significantly affect the health of wildlife, and the marginalization of the majority, who are poor, further intensifies the human effects on wildlife and ecosystem health. Some of the greatest dangers to animal and plant habitats in the developing world occur in the basic activities of the poor, such as cultivation of new lands in agriculture and the trapping of animals for food and other products. Knowledge about improved and environmentally sound agriculture alone could have a significant impact on wildlife health and security. In other words, providing for the security of human communities would reduce human-induced pressure on animal and plant habitats.

IDENTIFYING TALENTS

Another essential feature in nurturing knowledge communities is the ability to identify talents and ideas, and to groom them into products for the benefit of the possessor and the community of origin. Many institutions and communities of all scales and abilities, from the sports courts and fields to the multilateral development institutions, demonstrate weaknesses in assessing talents and ideas to their own detriment. A notable case was the early departure of Joseph Stiglitz from his post as vice-president and chief economist of the World Bank. Stiglitz explained his action thus: "Convincing people at [one institution] of [his preferred approaches to assisting the developing world, particularly during the Asian financial crisis] proved easy, but changing minds at the [sister organization] was virtually impossible" (Stglitz, 2000: 2). Less than one year later, Stglitz would share the 2001 Nobel Prize for Economics with George Akerlof and Michael Spence for their work in the 1970s, which laid the foundation for a general theory of markets with asymmetric information in which actors on one side of the market have better information than those on the other side (Nobel Foundation, 2001). The Laureates established modern information economics, with applications in fields ranging from traditional agricultural markets to modern financial markets. The contributions of Stiglitz shed light on the type of market adjustment, where poorly informed agents extract information from the better informed, and further provided the key to understanding many observed market tendencies, such as unemployment and credit rationing. Had Stiglitz found the principal actors in development policy receptive to his ideas and stayed on, the World Bank would have been delighted to share in his glory, especially as another multilateral development agency, the United Nations, and its Secretary-General Kofi Anan were the recipients of the Nobel Peace Prize in the same year. It is not an easy task to identify where resistance to change originates in large organizations: in the case of Stglitz, whether the reluctance of the institutions to accept his ideas emanated from the board that is appointed by finance ministers from the advanced industrial countries and that approves all loans by the IMF, or from the staff.

Another example of missed talents and opportunities was in play during the championship series of the National Basketball Association's (NBA's) professional league in 2001, which pitted the Los Angeles Lakers against the Philadelphia 76ers. The 76ers' head coach, Larry Brown, duelled with the Lakers' Phil Jackson. Much earlier in his coaching career, Jackson had applied to be an assistant coach to another team that had Brown as head coach, but Jackson would not be offered the job. Jackson went on to win six NBA championships with Michael Jordan and the Chicago Bulls in eight years (1991-1998 seasons), followed by his seventh title with Shaquille O'Neal, Kobe Bryant, and the Los Angeles Lakers in 2000, and was vying for his eighth win, this time against Brown, who was still winless in the championship title category. Jackson and the Lakers beat Brown and the 76ers.

Stiglitz was already an accomplished professional by the time he went to work for the World Bank, having taught at Oxford University, Massachusetts Institute of Technology, Stanford University, Yale University, and Princeton University, and held other posts, hence he knew what to do—move on. Coach Brown was also an accomplished professional by the time he lost to Jackson, but for the young, career dreams are nipped in the bud when they are unable to express their potentials due to restrictive work environments. Talent identification and talent grooming toward a knowledge community should therefore give priority to the future, by enabling the young to be curious and assist them in grooming their ideals into careers.

Students at the Ralph Bunche School in Harlem (New York, NY), as an example, have done research on the life and contributions of Ralph Bunche. The school comprises Grade Three to Grade Six and a mini-school referred to as the Computer School for Grades Four through Six. Four pupils (Lisa Glenn, Amber Stewart, Nicole Geohagen, and Azuka Anunkor) wrote about the life and contributions of Ralph Bunche in *Who Was Ralph Bunche?* on the Internet, regarding the 1950 Nobel Peace Prize winner and how their school got to be named after him. Lisa Glenn was one of these pupils and wrote: "Ralph Bunche was a champion of peace because he helped to settle the disagreements in the Holy Land between the Arabs and Israelis. In 1950 Ralph Bunche won the Nobel Peace Prize for helping end the war in the Holy Land. Our School P.S. 125 has the honor of being named the Ralph Bunche School ... [through a contest] after he died in 1971. Ralph Bunche wanted peace in our world. So the children at P.S. 125 should keep peace." Such an interesting project and publication may have disappeared from the Internet for any reason, but hopefully not because the child authors were undervalued. In another case, eight nine-year-old school children (Elvis Majozi, Portia Khumalo, Mickey King, Zandile Mkhize, Nomthandazo Sishi, Amahle Gumede, Howard Mngoma, and Amanda Mkhize) of Durban wrote their stories when they were all nine years old in South Africa's KwaZulu-Natal province have co-authored a book, *Voices of Eight*, to share their experiences as children of mostly disadvantaged backgrounds with other children in the province. Three-thousand copies of the book have been distributed to 60 disadvantaged schools in the Durban area to address the language problems faced by Zulu-speakers in an English-medium school system (SABC, 2001).

These and other children are aware that education is the key to success and a weapon in the socio-economic development of any winning nation, but their contribution to national economic performance would depend on the opportunities that are available to groom their ideas into functional outputs. The curiosity of children may lead to some research and development at universities and in industry, however, there are few mechanisms to institutionalize processes that could tap ideas from this generation and contribute to their own prospects in society. The eight South African pupils, and the children of the Ralph Bunche School may have already expressed some career paths that they could pursue; these children could be guided into the activities of the U.N. and its specialized institutions such as the United Nations Educational, Scientific and Cultural Organization (UNESCO), the Department of Peacekeeping at the U.N., or other programs that place these young talents in permanent touch with the activities of relevant organizations to further their growth.

Children are major users of modern information tools, and this is causing a great deal of anxiety among their less computer-savvy parents as to what these children might be accessing on the Web. The solutions currently offered to parents hinge on parents using technology to block access to undesirable Internet sites and televisions programs, which the children could circumvent. The imaginations and activities of children, however, could be guided to employ their IT skills toward personal development and career path building; these tools could also increase the awareness of young people at an early stage about other cultures, and how to groom their common future.

The inability of any economy to identify talents and to provide the nourishing environment for growth has caused frustrations that increase talent migration from homes of origin.

The industrialized economies are not immune from this lack of talent identification and nurturing either: Canada for example would now be the wealthiest country in the world, had skilled labour kept pace with technology advancements (At Guelph, 2001). Canadians already are among the world's most connected at work, school, or home. However, participation in the Information Society and the knowledge economy requires more than access to gadgets; people's lives, institutional outputs, communal health, and national economies need to be positively impacted by the new tools of communication. Canada, with 0.5 percent of the world's population, produces about four percent of the world's scientific publications, ranks sixth among the world's major producers of scientific knowledge, and fifteenth in research and development innovations among countries of the Organization for Economic Cooperation and Development (OECD). However, Canada's share of direct foreign investment in the 1990s was reduced from four percent to 3.5 percent worldwide and from 15.6 percent to 7.6 percent within NAFTA, while the U.S. increased its share of worldwide direct foreign investment from 16 percent to 40 percent (Industry Canada, 2000). These observations imply that a large proportion of new knowledge and technologies are generated outside Canada. Canadian firms, consequently, rely more heavily on foreign technology for new product development than their counterparts in any of the other G7 nations—by six-fold, compared to U.S. or Japan for example. While international research collaborations involving Canadians are increasing, the mechanisms by which Canadians access foreign knowledge are a disadvantage to small and medium-sized enterprises (SMEs). SMEs however, make up the bulk of Canada's businesses, accounting for 96 percent of Canada's one million businesses, 60 percent of the total private sector employment, and 60 percent of new job creations. This important sector spoke of the 'real need for intelligence' or value-added information, and access to the intelligence of knowledge developments that are occurring elsewhere in the advanced economies, which would be of real service to the industry.

In spite of the knowledge needs of SMEs and other communities in Canada and the developing regions that are impacted by Canadian internationalism, there are few opportunities and processes of grooming others into independent positions within existing university structures. Post-doctoral research programs, for example, have not been restructured to meet the expected increases in knowledge demands; these programs are currently not serving as transitional programs between graduate studies and substantive careers, but have become careers in themselves for a growing number of doctorate holders, often first-generation or new immigrants, who are unable to find substantive employment. As for undergraduate degree holders, the joke is that their expensive education is just to enable them to 'flip hamburgers; what a waste of talents and resources of governments, parents, the educational system, and the meagre earnings of students themselves through hard labour in the summer when they may mow lawns in the heat of the summer. Similarly, a young Argentine woman yelled: *I want to work!* during the economic meltdown of that nation's financial system in 2002 after four years of economic recession, and ensuing presidential resignations; unemployment was running at 18 percent in Argentina at the time.

University enrollments in North America on the other hand are expected to increase dramatically as a result of an increase in the number of 18- to 24-year olds in Canada and the U.S. and their quests for degrees. A study of enrollments and faculty recruitments at Ontario universities revealed that this Canadian province alone would need more than 15,000 professors over the next decade to meet the expected rise in enrollments, and as replacement for a wave of faculty retirements. The University of Toronto, for example, would need to hire one faculty member a day for the next few years, while Carleton University in Ottawa would need one new faculty member a week until 2010 (Rushowy, 2001).

Universities are aware that the quality of faculty would impact the quality of programs and attraction to prospective students in an era of increasing competition among educational institutions. However, a society could not command talents without investing in grooming talents. Many universities are not flexible enough to realize new opportunities in knowledge generation and realization of economic dividends. Thus many doctoral holders spend infinite periods in post-doctoral situations without integration into current university structures; students are graduating through pipeline education without benefiting from individualized learning systems and talent grooming, especially in the environment of poor student-professor ratios. As a result, students may be very knowledgeable about issues as background, but may lack the capacity to synthesize solutions. Furthermore, the occasional interaction of first- and second-cycle schools, and the general public with a university's defined perimeter may not be suitable in the knowledge-based economy; provision of continuous interactive spaces beyond passive websites may be required, but university professors alone may not be able to supervise research, teach courses, engage in outreach, and actively facilitate the transition of the local businesses and institutions in the local environment into knowledge-based communities. These issues indicate the communities from which to draw knowledge facilitators for nurturing knowledge communities.

If such is the state of talent grooming into productive membership of knowledge economies or development of ideas into knowledge products in the industrialized nations, the situation in developing nations could only be imagined as being deplorable.

Furthermore, the inability of many university graduates to employ their horned skills in gainful employment perhaps endears them to be a force in the protests that have followed global leaders around the world since the Seattle convention of the World Trade Organization (WTO) in December 1999.

The policy positions of global institutions could benefit tremendously through provision of channels and mechanisms to collect views from wide consultations, especially on university campuses, and feeding such ideas into global knowledge databases. Current initiatives on virtual consultations are devoid of serving the career interests of the contributors and are therefore not what is suggested here. Many more students and young people could have been active participants in major virtual discussions that are convened by the development community around issues of global importance, but these groups often participate in virtual consultations as passive listeners or surfers, as the list of registered participants and the active contributors to the forum would reveal.

A learning society of all, and provision of resources to translate learning into knowledge products in all facets of the knowledge economy, including the poor and their practices, should be the ultimate goals of nurturing a global knowledge community.

REFERENCES

Anderson, P. (2001). Study: Multitasking is counterproductive. *Cable News Network* [Online]. <http://www.cnn.com/2001/CAREER/trends/08/05/multitasking.study/index.html> [2001, Aug. 6].

AskMe. (2000). Solutions that drive bottom-line business benefits: Why companies under-perform. [Online]. AskMe Corporation. <http://www.askmecorp.com/solutions/default.asp> [2001, Mar. 16].

At Guelph. (2001). Technology driving growth, but lack of skills keep it moderate. *At Guelph* [Online]. University of Guelph, Guelph, Ontario, Canada. <http://www.uoguelph.ca/mediarel/01_01_10/technology.html> [2001, Jan. 10].

BBC. (1999, Mar. 20). Balloonists soar into history. *British Boradcasting Corporation* [Online]. <http://news.bbc.co.uk/hi/english/special_report/1998/11/98/great_balloon_challenge/newsid_300000/300106.stm> [2001, Aug. 30]: "The pilots of the Breitling Orbiter 3 balloon have crossed into Africa and a place in history—after their 20-day 26,600 mile (42,197km) journey. A cheer went up at Breitling mission control in Geneva as the two-man crew crossed the finish line over northern Mauritania shortly before 1000 GMT on Saturday."

Best Practices. Knowledge alliances: Driving sales, service and innovation through communities of practice. [Online]. Best Practices, LLC. <http://www.best-in-class.com/research/communities/index.html> [2001, Mar. 16].

Blackwell, R. (2001, July 21). Merrill pays settlement in plugging of Net firm. *The Globe and Mail*, Toronto, p. B1.

Capella, P., & Meikle, J. (2001, Feb. 21). UN backs use of cheap generic anti-AIDS drugs. *The Guardian* [Online]. <http://www.guardian.co.uk/Archive/Article/0,4273,4139390,00.html> [2001, Feb. 21].

CNN. (2001, Oct. 10). U.S. set on getting Cipro for under $1 a pill. *Cable News Network* [Online]. <http://www.cnn.com/2001/HEALTH/conditions/10/23/cipro.thompson> [2001, Oct. 23]. See also: U.S. buying 100 million doses of anthrax antibiotic. *Cable News Network* [Online]. <http://www.cnn.com/2001/HEALTH/conditions/10/24/anthrax/index.html> [2001, Oct. 24].

Curtis, J. (2000, Oct. 21). Stop. Look. Think. [Review of *The Ingenuity Gap* by T. Homer-Dixon]. *The Globe and Mail*, Toronto, p. D8.

Denning, S. (2001). Share knowledge or die—Experiences from the World Bank. In Thurnheer, K. (2001). *Knowledge—A Core Resource for Development*. (pp. 18-19). *Helvetas* Documentation on the Swiss meeting on global knowledge sharing and information and communication technologies, Berne, Switzerland, (2001, Mar. 20); also available online. <http://www.helvetas.ch/km/workshop/papers.html> Helvetas. [2001, Mar. 20].

Global Gazetteer. (1998). Woadze, Ghana page. [Online]. *The Global Gazetteer*. <http://www3.calle.com/info.cgi?lat=6.7167&long=0.3333&name=Woadze&cty=Ghana&alt=784&zoom=0> [2001, Apr. 15].

Homer-Dixon, T. (2000). *The Ingenuity Gap: How Can We Solve the Problems of the Future?* New York: Alfred A. Knopf.

IDRC. (1997, Mar. 14). Connecting with the world: Priorities for Canadian internationalism in the 21st Century (task force report). [Online]. International Development Research Centre, Canada. <http://www.idrc.ca/strong/eintegra.html> [1999, Aug. 17].

IEP. (2001). The Academy. In *The Internet Encyclopedia of Philosophy*. [Online]. University of Tennessee. <http://www.utm.edu/research/iep/a/academy.htm> [2001, July 18].

Industry Canada. (2000, June). Advisory council on science and technology, Canada. *Reaching Out: Canada, International Science and Technology, and the Knowledge-Based Economy*. [Online]. <http://www.acst-ccst.gc.ca>. Report of the Expert Panel on Canada's Role in International Science and Technology. Industry Canada.

Keyes, B. (1996, April 16). Atlantis: Plato. Homepage. [Online]. The Active Mind. <http://www.activemind.com/Mysterious/Topics/Atlantis/plato.html> [2001, June 15]: "Plato (circa 427-347 B.C.) was a student of Socrates. After the death of Socrates (399 BC), Plato traveled extensively, including journeys to Egypt. He returned to Athens in 387 BC and founded the Academy, a school of science and philosophy that became the model for the modern university. Aristotle was probably the most famous student of the Academy whose teachings have had tremendous impact on philosophy through today. Many of Plato's works, including The Republic, have survived till today as a result of safekeeping of the materials by the Academy."

Laghi, B., & Scoffield, H. (2001). Ottawa pays twice for Cipro. *The Globe and Mail, Toronto* [Online]. <http://www.globeandmail.com> [2001, Oct. 23].

LaMonica, P. R. (2002). AOL Time Warner phase II: Addressing problems in the online division will be new CEO Richard Parson's main task. *Cable News Network* [Online]. <http://money.cnn.com/2002/05/15/news/companies/aol/index.htm> (2002, May 15).

Macan-Markar, M. (2001, July 10). UN report sees green light for generic AIDS drugs. *Inter Press Service* [Online]. <http://www.oneworld.net/ips2/july01/22_25_031.html> [2001, July 17].

Morrison, J. L., & Twigg, C. (2001). The Pew Learning and Technology Program initiative in using technology to enhance education: An interview with Carol Twigg. *Technology Source* (May/June) [Online]. The Michigan Virtual University. <http://horizon.unc.edu/TS/default.asp?show=article&id=859> [2001, June 30]: "For the most part, ... we are using information technology tools as a marginal enhancement of the status quo. ... We are resistant to change and rarely look for creative, innovative approaches to new opportunities. In the same way that scientists try to 'save the theory' (Thomas Kuhn), we ... stick fast to ... the ... method and look for old solutions to new problems."

MSF/Oxfam. (2001, Mar. 5). Joint MSF/Oxfam press release: 39 drug companies versus South Africa: People die for lack of affordable drugs as inhumane industry ignores reality. [Online]. Médecins sans frontières <http://195.114.67.76/msf/accessmed/accessmed.nsf/html/4DTSR2?OpenDocument> [2001, Mar. 7]: The agencies noted that during the same week of the court case, the five biggest companies involved in the trial would have sold $2.2 billion worth of medicines and made $560 million in profits.

Nobel Foundation, The. (2001). The Bank of Sweden prize in economic sciences in memory of Alfred Nobel 2001. [Online]. The Nobel Foundation. <http://www.nobel.se/economics/laureates/2001/press.html> [2001, Oct. 30]; The Nobel Peace Prize 2001. (2001, Oct. 12). [Online]. The Nobel Foundation. <http://www.nobel.se/peace/laureates/2001/index.html> [2001, Oct. 30].

Oxfam. (2001). *Cut the Cost Campaign*. [Online]. Oxfam. <http://www.oxfam.org.uk/cutthecost/index.html> [2001, Mar. 5].

PC AI. Expert systems. *PC AI Magazine* [Online]. <http://www.pcai.com/pcai/New_Home_Page/ai_info/expert_systems.html> [2001, Mar. 16]. Other examples of the communications industry trends toward bots include tools and services of Infinite Innovations Ltd., and True Source (Practicity): Brainstorming Toolbox. (1999). [Online]. Infinite Innovations Ltd. <http://www.brainstorming.co.uk/toolbox/brainstormingtoolbox.html> [2001, Mar. 16]; Practicity 4.1 Today. [Online]. True Source, Inc. <http://www.truesourceinc.com/html/tsi_practicity.html> [2001, Mar. 16].

Ralph Bunche School, Harlem, New York, U.S.A.: Students at the Ralph Bunche School (Lisa Glenn, Amber Stewart, Nicole Geohagen, and Azuka Anunkor) wrote about the life and contributions of Ralph Bunche in *Who Was Ralph Bunche* [2000, Nov. 4]. The websites were <http://ralphbunche.rbs.edu/bunche/frame.html>, <http://ralphbunche.rbs.edu/index.html> or <http://csd5.org/ps125m/ps125m.htm>, but may have become unavailable.

Roberts, P. (1997). Eliminate the blockages and you enable 'group genius.' *Fast Company,* 11, p. 212; also [Online]. <http://www.fastcompany.com/online/11/domains.html> [2001, Jan. 15].

Rubinstein, J. S., Meyer, D.E., & Evans, J. E. (2001). Executive control of cognitive processes in task switching. *American Journal of Experimental Psychology: Human Perception and Performance,* 27(4), 763-797. See also [Online]. <http://www.apa.org/journals/xhp/press_releases/august_2001/xhp274763.html> [2001, Aug. 6].

Rushowy, K. (2001). Hunt on for 15,000 professors. *The Toronto Star,* (Jan. 15), A1 and A12.

SABC. (2001, May 16). Child authors lead the way in education. *South African Broadcasting Corporation* [Online]. <http://www.sabcnews.com/SABCnews/south_africa/education/0,1009,14918,00.html> [2001, June 20].

Solo Spirit. (2001, Aug. 17). Solo Spirit mission ends: Fossett in good health. [Online]. Washington University in St. Louis. <http://solospirit.wustl.edu/news.asp> [2001, Aug. 30].

Stiglitz, J. (1999, Dec.). Scan globally, reinvent locally: Knowledge infrastructure and the localization of knowledge. [Online]. The first conference of the Global Development Network, Bonn, Germany, Dec. 5-8, 1999. The Global Development Network. <http://www.gdnet.org/pdf/226_GDNfinal.PDF> [2000, Jan. 15]: The former Chief Economist of the World Bank, citing the work of Keynes (1936, 383) in his keynote address, noted: "We in the ideas business should never forget the power of ideas. Keynes put this forcefully when he said that: 'Practical men, who believe themselves to be quite exempt from any intellectual influences, are usually the slaves of some defunct economist. Madmen in authority, who hear voices in the air, are distilling their frenzy from some academic scribbler of a few years back.' In the same vein, the early 19th century poet Heinrich Heine (1797-1856) pointedly remarked: 'mark this, ye proud men of action: ye are nothing but unconscious hodmen of the men of thought who, often in humblest stillness, have appointed you your inevitable work.'"

Stiglitz, J. (2000, Apr. 17). What I learned at the world economic crisis—The insider. *The New Republic* [Online]. <http://www.thenewrepublic.com/041700/stiglitz041700.html> [2001, Oct. 30].

Chapter IV

Splicing Modern Knowledge and Ancestral Wisdom

Communications channels with and within the developing world, hence, should be considered in light of the transition of such economies into knowledge societies. The transition from abject poverty to humanly secure is getting shorter, and the tools to foster brain convergence in development planning have become significantly more powerful, more user-defined, more flexible, more abundant, and cheaper. Canada became a country only 133 years ago, and Malaysia and Ghana only in 1957. Yet, at the time of Canada's 133rd Birthday on July 1, 2000, the United Nations had ranked Canada as the nation with the highest quality of life for the seventh consecutive time (Globe and Mail, 2000). And although Malaysia and Ghana became independent from Britain in 1957, today the two nations are not at the same level of human security. Providing human security relates to optimization of multiple factors that interact nonlinearly; therefore nations in comparable agro-ecological zones that would have been ruled by the same colonial authorities might not achieve the same development status upon being granted political independence; the environment may be suitable for the cultivation of the same crop species, but land management and other inputs and farm practices would determine the yield that each obtained. However, a common feature among nations that have evolved a higher quality of life is probably the development of strategic national goals that are based on increasing the knowledge component of economic and socio-political attributes, and the design of mechanisms to implement and continuously monitor strategies and their effects on society.

Some developing nations have demonstrated the ability to learn from other civilizations, and such learning has translated into improved economic and human security in their local economies. When there are many nations similarly capable within a geographic region, they could constitute a regional bloc with local prosperity and ability to compete more strongly at the global level, as in the case of South east Asia. In line with this, developing countries strive to establish horizontal knowledge channels to learn from each other's experiences and connect to the industrialized economies to refine their models, but these schemes have often not translated into the expected advances in the local economies. Africans, for example, express dejection at the fact that earlier efforts toward development and formation of a united Africa at the beginning of continent-wide independence were unrealized. However, the tools for development and regionalization at that time were poorer, less available, unreliable, and unaffordable while the political environment was a turbid stream of ideological experimentations; corruption further weakened the young institutions and their weak human resources, thereby creating the current human insecurities in that region.

The environment is now more conducive, as the tools that would empower people to know and learn about themselves and the rest of the world to improve their own security are now more available, cheaper, and more powerful. What is required now is for developing countries to fill their knowledge vacuum in a systematic manner—to digitize their oral cultures, mine knowledge from their own civilizations, recognize the complementary and critical knowledge from global centres of excellence and other knowledge domains, process all the spliced information and knowledge into functional states, building knowledge networks and partnerships to capitalize the translation of the ideas into products that would meet their peoples' needs. The matrixes and energy to develop the required information linkages to integrate local and external knowledge systems are contained in IT.

The information linkages, or Digital Bridges, could be constructed through a global project similar to the International Space Centre project, except that the project would be concerned about the ground on which life is known to exist. It is acknowledged that investments in space research have also contributed to the accelerated development of communications of nations on earth. The quest by space scientists to understand the origin of the earth (see for example, Stenger, 2001), could similarly be mirrored in local communities of developing nations by searching for the unwritten wisdom and knowledge that have nurtured these non-industrialized societies. Timid and weak efforts in developing nations' connectivity programs would crush their poor more than other failed programs. Those who use the poor telecommunications infrastructure and technological laggard states of the developing world to suggest that the advances in IT are not relevant to solving the problems of the poor need to be more imaginative and receptive to new thoughts and possibilities.

The advent of the Information Society could be an opportunity for governments, policymakers, intellectuals, global specialized institutions, and the development community to redeem themselves from the subjugation of the world's majority to the state of atavism and penury. Partners of developing countries in the Information Age should endeavour to simulate best practices in development communications by designing prototypes of information and knowledge flows and the partnership arrangements that may be required to develop these prototypes and other outputs and solutions; these prototypes are essential in convincing policymakers and venture capitalists about the efficacy of knowledge networks in creating prosperous and secure communities in the developing world. For basic communities to rise from the depth of knowledge hunger, the knowledge networks should touch the ground, like the energy in a hurricane touches the ground, to manifest the power of knowledge flows. That ground would be the communities and institutions from which the majority in the impact community obtain their livelihoods.

In the expectation that access to global knowledge could improve human and environmental security, the challenges of the developing world provide the ideal environments for optimization of communications tools, and for evolving sound ideas in connectivity. The technological and knowledge states of most of the developing countries are conducive to test the hypothesis that modern tools and knowledge networking could engender economic, political, and social prosperity.

The advent of convergent communications has given rise to new development paradigms; a *New African Renaissance,* for example, was envisioned by African leaders and the region's development partners such as the U.S. administration:

> *"Challenges remain, but they must be to all of [us] a call to action, not a cause for despair. [We] must draw strength from the past and energy from the promise of a new future. My dream for this trip is that together we might do the things so that 100 years from now, your grandchildren and mine will look back and say this was the beginning of a new African renaissance." (GNA Bulletin, 1998).*

Within two years of this vision, however, there would be indications that the challenges could forestall the realization of this new revival due to the region's share of explosions of civil warfare, a slow move towards democratization, the HIV/AIDS scourge, famine, and hunger (Wright, 2000). The transition from insecurity to a secure state, however, could not occur without establishment of a vibrant information and knowledge infrastructure, but it is prudent to continuously monitor and question the paths upon which these poor nations are travelling, so that the hope that connectivity could lead to local prosperity can become a reality for the majority.

The realization of sustainable communities in the developing world would occur when such nations are able to design their Information Societies in a manner that is different from the establishment of schools and modern institutions in their earlier attempts at nation-building. The initial phase of the rise of developing countries from slavery and colonialism was the independence movement era that culminated in their *freedom* from domination. However, establishment of schools and modern institutions did not result in the expected actualization of these nations. The euphoria that ensued with *independence* was soon replaced by ideological wrangling; ineptitude; depravity in high places; corruption; lack of critical thinking; alien theories of development; blind replication of ideas that had been formulated for societies with very different social, technological, and philosophical states; and externally conjured and imposed economic reforms. In that era, schools, colleges, universities, national bureaucracies, research, industry, banking, commerce, transportation, the judiciary, among others, sought a strange world for the new countries based on replication of models of nation-building that did not have any legitimacy in the indigenous philosophies of the majority in these nations. The human tragedies that have consequently befallen the developing world, particularly the rural and urban poor, are well known in the living rooms of citizens of the world.

It is necessary to view convergent communications as the tools with which to build knowledge communities in an approach that would enable learning to relate to the needs of the majority, and to stimulate critical thinking as the basis of all activities. The challenge would be to develop knowledge networks that include the indigenous institutions of local wisdom so that such knowledge, which has sustained these communities for centuries, even if not glamorously in the wake of modern challenges, could become heritable—not local knowledge by itself but rather building bridges between indigenous and modern scholarship and experience. It is no longer acceptable for developing countries to adopt wholesale models from outside their spheres as an approach toward nurturing their local economies in the networked era. These designs should not be based entirely on the local modern institutions either, since such institutions have not reflected clear linkages to the assets, practices, needs, and opportunities of the majority.

In the virtual world, indigenous institutions also can be linked to the global knowledge grid, directly or indirectly, for systematic knowledge creation and institutional capacity-building schemes. Strategic policy frameworks with imagination, innovation, and futuristic perspectives should be at the core of the design and transition of developing country economies to knowledge-based and solutions-driven economies. As developing countries are confronted with the scourge of HIV/AIDS, for which their modern institutions could be questioned by future generations as to their failures to build firewalls to contain the initial outbreak, Africa and its development partners for example have suddenly turned to the wisdom in the region's indigenous healing mechanisms. A few indigenous healers are now invited to major regional meetings and conferences concerning HIV/AIDS. But such an approach seems an *ad hoc* measure that could produce false results, considering that the capacity of indigenous institutions has not been improved for so long, and that few indigenous healers are within the bandwidth of knowledge flows through rudimentary communications with the medical and pharmaceutical research industries of their countries, let alone through communications afforded by modern communications such as e-mail and the Internet. The transformation of institutions within the concept of knowledge societies requires not only a single dose of 'knowledge,' but continuous interactivity with other groups within the intelligent sphere. Therefore, some have pointed out that the 'cures' touted by indigenous healers might be references to the treatment of opportunistic infections, but not HIV/AIDS.

Current poor telecommunications in these regions should not limit the imagination of the designers because leapfrogging is an obtainable objective. Should developing countries fail to contribute to the designs, others would do so for them; and being less knowledgeable about their realities than the developing country intellectuals, uninformed designs would send these countries back into economic bondage. The developing world needs to develop a cadre of IT champions, people whose intentions are to develop local brainpower from governmental, academic, commercial, local, and individual spheres. Moreover, these designs should invest in the future, the children, so as to begin the process of leveraging with the advanced civilizations.

The needs for sustainable communities in the Information Age and globalization are access to state-of-the-art convergent communication tools to avoid costly and frequent upgrading that developing countries could not afford; new forms of learning as opportune by the IT industry; knowledge processing for Internet content development that reflects the strengths and needs of the end-users, which would be as important as the physical infrastructure; genuine and long-term partnerships among knowledge sources such as learning and research communities, formal and informal sectors, and funding; and investment sources for optimizing the potential of the new communication tools.

Ideally, connectivity for health, or *telehealth,* in indigenous communities could mean national preventive health care that recognizes the principles and practices of indigenous health systems in developing an accessible flow of health information with external centres such as the World Health Organization (WHO) and the Centers for Disease Control and Prevention (CDC). This knowledge flow would include the science of traditional birth attendants (TBAs), who constitute the highest level of obstetrics among the majority populations, and indigenous healers who act as health officials for 80 percent of most communities in Africa, and not just the local modern institutions of health. University studies in medicine and pharmacology similarly would include knowledge of twigs, barks, roots, and social support systems. Technical and engineering institution linkages would include second-cycle technical and vocational institutes and knowledge of indigenous tool smiths and rural artisans, who are the indigenous engineers of rural technologies, for example, agricultural implements such as hoes. Hypothetically, such linkages would result in the design of hand-held solar energy-dependent motorized-hoes to replace the quintessential hoe and machete as primary tillage tools, with some components being produced in local foundries. Business studies and management curricula would include modern financial institutions that are cognizant of both the indigenous social capital systems and the values and mechanisms of indigenous marketing structures in the design of e-Commerce schemes. Agricultural studies would feature indigenous rural agricultural practices, provide weather charts and tracking of disease epidemics with Geographic Information Systems, and knowledge for cultivation of mushrooms instead of hunting for them from the wild. Yet another highly desirable outcome would be the ability to strengthen indigenous civil society, the pinnacle of which is the indigenous governance structure that is the repository of the indigenous knowledge system, and the basis for mobilization and the survival of rural communities of these regions.

GENERAL DEVELOPMENT KNOWLEDGE NEEDS OF RURAL COMMUNITIES

The shift in development philosophy from aid toward partnerships in knowledge for development is in response to the knowledge gap that has continued to exist between the industrialized nations and the rest of the world, notwithstanding the amount of resources that have been poured into 'development' assistance from the industrialized nations. This knowledge gap is notably in technology and innovation, as about 100 nations, mostly in Africa and Latin America, have not benefited significantly from global advances in science and technology partnerships, innovations, and knowledge flows. These nations also have a poor capacity to generate their own scientific knowledge, and accounted for less than one percent of the world's scientific publications, research and development (R & D) expenditures, and patents (de la Mothe and Dufour, 1995). Africa as a whole has 0.36 percent of the world's scientific potential (Galliard and Waast, 1992), 0.4 percent of the world R & D expenditure (de la Mothe and Dufour, 1995), and produces 0.3 percent of scientific papers that are published in mainstream science journals (Eisemon and Davies, 1992).

These statistics of knowledge generation are revelations of the state of their humanity; they also serve as indicators of the knowledge hunger, human insecurity, and a reflection of need identification at the basic level in the communities of developing nations. The statistics reflect the ability of the community in the principal components of knowledge creation through research capacity, application, and exchange of best practices through peer-reviewed publications. These depictions should not be misconstrued as the denigration of these communities or those involved in development programming for these communities. On the other hand, the refusal to admit their sad state of insecurity further intensifies their predicaments and constitutes the defamation of these communities. However, the underlying causes of the statistics and the implications in humanistic terms are required alongside the data to give meaning to IT-facilitated knowledge for development planning.

The human security indicators of developing countries reveal a high incidence of pregnancy-related deaths among rural women. Rural women sometimes give birth outside the home: on farm roads, at marketplaces, and at commuter stations. The most affected communities are in Africa. Africa has about 10 percent of the world female population, but about 40 percent of all pregnancy-related deaths occur in this region, including 22,000 deaths from unsafe pregnancy intervention procedures (PAI, 1998). One of the underlying causes of this high rate of maternal mortality stems from a neglect of the institutions that serve the pregnancy-related health needs of women. As the educated became nurses and staffed modern clinics, there was no scheme to link the traditional birth attendant with the modern clinic. Women in the villages who work the land, produce, process, and market food sometimes give birth with the assistance of traditional birth attendants and leaders of their faith-based organizations. They depend on their indigenous knowledge during childbirth, but complicated cases are referred to hospitals after exhausting the indigenous methods, often too late. This could be one of the reasons that Africans associate hospitals with death (Zwalen, 1996). This is the picture that the statistics of a high incidence of maternal deaths during childbirth connotes.

Rural people and domestic animals in many of the developing countries drink and bathe in the same creeks and ponds as if it were in The Garden of Eden, but that paradise was long lost. Consequently, about 80 percent of diseases such as diarrhoea, malaria, guinea worms, bilharziasis, and river blindness that plague them are of water associations (Ayensu, 1997). Meanwhile, petroleum or gas stations are cleaner than the location of food vendors who are often close to gutters that are filled with raw sewage and stench, but KFC Corporation, formerly Kentucky Fried Chicken, began at a petrol station. Today, "the world's most popular chicken restaurant chain serves nearly eight million customers every day, around the world, with the same great taste Colonel Harland Sanders created more than a half-century ago; KFC is part of Tricon Global Restaurants, Inc., which is the world's largest restaurant system with nearly 30,000 KFC, Taco Bell, and Pizza Hut restaurants in more than 100 countries and territories" (KFC Corporation, http). Consequently, a large number of people, particularly children, are prone to infectious diseases. These infectious diseases are often the underlying causes of the staggering rates of death among children in these regions; that figure is 95 deaths per thousand childbirths in Africa. Some speculate that those who live and survive under poor sanitary environments in developing nations would have immune systems that are much stronger than others who visit the communities from elsewhere, on the grounds that residents of such environments would have been naturally immunized against the pathogens of the environment. This could be the case possibly. However, the build up of these pathogens and their associated diseases reaches critical stages within the individual and at the community level, and causes morbidity or death in a large segment of the local population, which may partially explain the short average life span in these communities.

Small-scale farmers in these regions use hoes, machetes, and other similarly simple implements as primary tillage tools. These tools could be considered as ancestral tools; they were bequeathed to them by the technological advances of their forebears and have not undergone innovation for centuries, while the massive tractorization schemes that were launched by their educated leaders and formal institutions have been expensive failures. Odhiambo (1997) estimated that the tools, processes, and primary mechanisms by which the majority attain their daily livelihoods have not evolved for 500 years, in the case of Africa. The Stone Age technologies of the regions mean that their farmers 'sharpen' agricultural tools on rocks while others elsewhere employ Global Positioning Systems and Geographic Information Systems in precision farming. Many farmers in Africa and similar technological states do not engage in significant replenishment of the agricultural land; their practice is usually shifting cultivation. However, the high rate of population growth in these regions, and the poor capacity of the soil to regenerate itself have resulted in a reduction of the fallow period and a reduction in arable lands. The situation has caused an increase in the encroachment on previously uncultivated lands, and awakening of agents that may harbour or cause strange diseases such as Buruli ulcer (WHO, 1997). Reliance on rain-fed agriculture has also meant erratic harvests, with accompanying food crises. Many irrigation schemes have failed; there are few successful water resources that are under any form of management, unlike the irrigation successes of the Incas and Mayas. The Chimu culture, for example, was one of the civilizations that thrived along Peru's coastal region prior to the ascent of the Incan Empire; they had a highly sophisticated network of irrigation canals that enabled them to harvest crops on tracts of land that today are little more than barren sand (ILAS, 2001).

Environmental management knowledge is also of critical importance to developing nations to enable people in local communities to meet their basic needs of life, without negatively impacting the environment or the personal health of individuals. These nations also depend on old technologies that may cause health hazards to their citizens. Old technologies in the automobile industry and factories in general are responsible for creating some of the world's heavily polluted cities in some developing nations, and this situation could get worse as the environmental impacts of earlier industrialization schemes in these regions were not carefully considered. Many rivers, lakes, and cities exhibit symptoms of environmental decay, and some water bodies may have become syrups of raw industrial and household sewage. Rural people also carry their agricultural produce on their heads and walk several miles to markets, some damaging their vertebrae permanently. The hard labour to which rural people in developing countries have been subjugated induces hernias in many, and machete wounds have left permanent scars on the legs of many.

The ingenuity of indigenous engineers is evident in the number of old model vehicles that ply developing country roads. Often, these vehicles are too old to be found in other regions of the world except as antique vehicles that are more of hobbies than necessities. However, such ingenuity has not benefited from global knowledge in machinery or tool manufacturing and maintenance. The tools of the local fitter mechanic are primitive and are unable to provide proper diagnosis of the imported machinery and processes; revenues from commercial vehicle operations are meagre, but the cost of replacement parts and fuel are as high as in the industrialized world, where these parts are produced, hence owners are unable to meet maintenance costs. Thus rickety vehicles ply the roads in these regions, endangering the lives of the operators, passengers, and pedestrians, and the ensuing road accidents further weaken the resources of the health care system. The same engineering ingenuity is demonstrated in the manufacture of agricultural implements in which the blacksmith in the village makes all the hoes for agricultural activities while formal education, including at the university level, does not teach students about the hoe or contribute modern engineering knowledge to village foundries that manufacture the hoe and other implements. Therefore, blacksmiths have remained the manufactures of all the affordable agricultural tools for the majority, who are small-scale farmers, despite the global engineering advancements.

The children of the poor that have the opportunity to receive the highest level of formal education, for example university degrees, are also those who are most removed from the physical and cultural realities of rural livelihoods. This is not to insinuate that developing country intellectuals have not made contributions in other terms: many of the educated, whether they work inside or outside their countries of origin, contribute financially to their communities, but there has been no significant knowledge flow between their learned careers and village livelihoods. Children of the poor are unconsciously educated out of the villages, intellectually.

Resolving the knowledge gap-induced challenges of the developing world demands formulation of continuously innovative schemes with feedback mechanisms between advanced knowledge and the ancestral knowledge systems. Knowledge and ideas coded into technology and innovation, according to the *new growth theory*, more than the Adam Smith factors of business (land, labour, capital and entrepreneurship), are the engines of national economic growth (Wysocki, Jr., 1997). Science-based knowledge of human, society, and nature, and the concepts, theories, metaphors, and global views emanating thereof has become the most strategic asset in development (Soedjatmoko, 1989). However, organization of knowledge and ideas, in concert with a defined national economic vision, is a prerequisite for knowledge to translate into economic growth. An effective knowledge and ideas economy would involve an intricate web of infrastructure and policy decisions to splice modern knowledge and ancestral wisdom into relevant knowledge for local applications in critical sectors, including infrastructure, education, research, manufacturing, commerce and banking, management, and social behaviour.

Currently, developing nations are largely excluded from sharing in global science and technology, a situation that frameworks in globalization aim to reverse by creating equity in access to global knowledge and capital. In negotiating such frameworks, developing nations should demand and contribute ideas toward effective mechanisms that would enable them to tap into these global resources with high efficiency. They would need to attract a significant amount of knowledge and capital, and develop knowledge processing systems that can achieve the maximum for those who are the most in need. These conditions are a prerequisite for development knowledge to make any significant impact on human security improvements in these regions.

Global knowledge exists to model sustainable communities; however, it is generally agreed that communities would be unable to leapfrog in whatever form without the active participation of local groups. The participation of local groups in the development programming should emphasize the role of their local knowledge and resources in the processes and deliverables of the new frameworks. The most appropriate form of innovation for these communities would be based on what is available locally and affordable, with minimal assistance from external knowledge systems. That would be the cheapest, most reliable, and most critical inputs into sustainable development frameworks. But local experts and communities lack the necessary information to make the right decisions, hence the need to form strategic alliances with other civilizations. Both the local and external institutions that are responsible for orchestrating development programs, especially science and technology policy, for these regions should be open-minded about the indigenous technological values in order to develop policies that do not increase the marginalization of the majority.

The development of functional knowledge, or the splicing of indigenous and external knowledge systems to create enhanced local knowledge, may seem a daunting task, but operationalization of the Information Age in these nations would provide the energy that can drive the process to completion.

Indigenous knowledge has also become the subject of other sectors, apart from the development community.

GLOBAL BENEFITS OF INDIGENOUS KNOWLEDGE

The industrialized economies are able to recognize and translate specific aspects of local knowledge from any civilization into economic gains and to enhance their own quality of life. Western medical and pharmaceutical industries are among the sectors that are exploring the role of indigenous and local knowledge in their product development and corporate philosophies. Health food stores and alternate herbal medicines that are increasing in appeal in the industrialized world are often derived from indigenous cultures around the world. Body Shop, the skin and hair care retailer, markets products whose designs are based on the cosmetic knowledge of cultures around the world (Body Shop, http).

The eating habits of some poor communities gave rise to Western medicine's hypothesis that high-fibre diets may reduce the incidence of colon cancer in men and also lower blood cholesterol levels (BBC, 1999). Similarly, Western scientists have hypothesized that the barks, roots, and gums of plants that the *Maasais* of East Africa snack on might be responsible for the low incidence of heart conditions among the ethnic group, whose diets are high in saturated fatty acids (Judge, 1998). An investigation into causes of Alzheimer's disease by Hendrie et al. (2001) at Indiana University that compared members of a Nigerian community to Americans in Indiana is revealing some of the non-genetic factors in the development of the disease (Aisen, 2001). It is also generally agreed that the cure for some of the diseases that haunt all humanity may be found in the forests of the South. American society is now accustomed to the phrase "it takes a village" (Clinton, 1996) to raise a child and to protect and advance a community's civilization, which is also a philosophy of poor communities of the South. In rural Africa, children are left under the care of grandparents and others in the extended family system while parents go to the fields. The Ghanaian *kente* fabric has also become a global culture, especially among the African-American culture; the fabric is increasingly being used in non-traditional circumstances, such as the design of church choir robes. Indigenous spiritual and cultural symbols of arts and crafts have also become the heritage of some of the most renowned museums in the industrialized nations, for example

Ghana's Ashanti Golden Stool, Nigeria's Benin Bronze, and Egypt's Sphinx's Beard, among others (Ross, 1998).

In spite of these desirable features of indigenous knowledge, rural development programming in these regions was for too long dependent on outside ideas, outside goals, outside implementation, outside supervision, and evaluations of alien origins (Atteh, 1992). Development planning for these communities hardly emphasized knowledge enhancement; instead they were modelled to devote their energies and disproportionately large amounts of their resources to the extraction of natural endowments as cheap export commodities. Often they apportioned the most fertile lands to the production of crops of little domestic use, without equal regard to human capacity development. Such primary commodity export-oriented economic development models were fabricated on unequal terms, hence these countries have not been able to generate sufficient export revenue to import the goods that they would have been unable to produce locally; corruption and inefficiencies also affect the little revenue that could be generated. Obviously, attempts to substitute indigenous knowledge and ideas with alien theories in the development process have been expensive failures.

There has been renewed optimism that the chronic human indignity, economic malaise, and environmental degeneration of the poor are about to be reversed because the revolutions in IT would provide a stable theatre within which economic growth could occur. Therefore, it is important to continuously ponder if current connectivity programs in these nations are creating the enabling environment for development to blossom. For that to occur, it is presumed that global knowledge as capital would enable communities to govern themselves, build the human resource capacity needed, improve rural occupations and practices, prevent and resolve crises, and increase the efficiency of utilizing and managing the natural environment. These could be attained by developing an informed society, one in which all decisions are arrived at after considering all the possible options, by integrating information about the past, the present, and the future of the local community, as well as awareness about global development. Such circumstances require the development of 'information-affluent' cultures, a term eloquently used by Samara (1999).

Indigenous knowledge is archived, accessed, and disseminated chiefly by oral methods, with a predisposition for decay, misinterpretation, and loss. The information society will enable developing nations to digitize their oral repositories and information access methods. This digitization would enable the identification, documentation, quantification, processing or value-addition, and exchange of knowledge equitably. Moreover, the capacity to communicate is expected to become a human rights issue (d'Orville, 1996), and the ability of a community to collect, process, synthesize, disseminate, and utilize information through modern information and communication technologies, and to communicate with itself and with other communities locally, regionally, and globally, will determine the potential to develop coping mechanisms against challenges of livelihood means (d'Orville, 1996; Njinya-Mujinya and Habomugisha, 1998). Hence, the 1995 Copenhagen Declaration on Social Development recognized the need to facilitate access by poor peoples to convergent communication technologies for social development (U.N., 1995).

Indigenous scholars have also realized the need for documenting their values, and some have expressed dejection at the poor capacity of their communities to create modern literature about themselves. Akotey, for example, in his prelude to Akafia's novel—*Ku Le Xome* (conveniently translated as *Death Originated from the Home*), which was a textbook of choice of schools and as leisure reading among the Ewe ethnic groups in Ghana and Togo—expressed his wishes for a local literary community:

> *"Excuse me! It is a special honour for me to write the forward to a novel that has the power to motivate humanity. What endeared me to do this is the desire that is burning with vigour within the author toward a viable Ewe literary world, in an era that the old books, which were written for us by the white missionaries, are disappearing. If this desire would burn among other young men and women, then I am hopeful that it would not be long before there will be an abundance of such important literary products in the Ewe community." (Akotey, 1970:1)*

Developing country intellectuals could take advantage of the opportunities presented by the global development community to dedicate attention to the connectivity and knowledge needs of developing, and contribute their knowledge about the local values in the modelling of multimedia visions for their communities.

Indigenous knowledge is also being valued in military and peacekeeping efforts, for example a group of indigenous hunters known as the Kamajor in Sierra Leone were transformed into an effective fighting force as part of the civil defence forces that were in partnership with regular armies in the restoration of peace in that country. Samuel Hinga Norman, who is Sierra Leone's deputy minister of defence, is also the head of the Kamajor militia, and is credited with the transformation of the hunters into fighters and peacekeepers. The Kamajors came to the defence of President Ahmad Tejan Kabbah after his democratically elected government was overthrown by rebels and renegade soldiers of the Revolutionary United Front, led by Foday Sankoh in 1997. The authorities in Guinea also recruited 1,300 traditional hunters to back the national army in the government's fight against rebel insurgents (Sierra Leone Web). The Kamajor draw on magical and religious beliefs that they are invincible in battle or resistant to bullets, based on Kamajor practices that date back to their traditional role in the Mende tradition, which identified and assigned the Kamajor hunters as community founders, protectors, and providers (IRN, 2000). These practices indicate the relationship between hunters and the security of the community.

In peacetime though, hunters in Africa are toward the bottom of the economic ladder, as animal herds have dwindled, and it is not obvious that there are any programs aimed at integrating the Kamajor and their contemporaries across Africa and other regions into environmental specialists.

Developing nations often attempt to emulate the industrialized nations, but these are most notable in the political arena, for example the impeachment trials of the presidents of the Philippines and Indonesia following the impeachment trial of U.S. President Clinton (Ressa, 2001). Similar successes of developing nations learning from the industrialized nations for local application are less significant in other sectors.

Knowledge for development programming would recognize hunters for their knowledge about flora and faunae; they are among the most knowledgeable about herbs, the migratory patterns of animals and birds, bush trails, damages to fields due to insects and pests, and knowledge about natural resources such as the changes in the volume of streams and creeks that should be considered as vital to environmental health; hunters are the managers of environmental health in indigenous communities.

A systematic knowledge splicing for local impact would require establishment of the communications policies and infrastructure to build knowledge networks, but it will require a new form of partnership arrangement between the North and the South, between political leadership and civil society, between formal and informal sectors, between formally literate and illiterate, and between urban and rural communities. It requires a judicious blend of technological advances with indigenous cultures and peoples, as well as a balance between human activities and the natural environment.

The compartmentalization of society into urban versus rural, literate versus illiterate, formal versus informal, old versus young, among others, could be misleading, and should be considered only as a matter of convenience and academic. For, in many developing economies, all of these 'classes' may reside under the same roof and in insecure states. For example, one of the two parents of a household may be an illiterate; one may be in an urban environment and the other in the countryside, one may be employed in the formal sector while the other labours in an informal occupation, and so on, but on average neither is isolated from the insecurities that characterize their world. Therefore, nurturing knowledge communities in such communities should embrace the entire spectrum of 'classes.'

Most rural communities are not physically removed from modern civilization; people in rural areas are aware of the lives of the people of the city, except that they cannot afford such living conditions, as many who sojourn to the cities soon realize. Generally, people from rural areas have populated modern urban centres in developing nations in search of employment opportunities, especially as a result of the industrialization schemes of post-independence governments. The industrial and seaport city of Tema, in Ghana, for example, was populated after Ghana's independence in 1957 during the industrialization scheme under the country's first post-colonial administration.

Effective knowledge splicing could also feature the possibility that IT would enable developing nations to tap into their own learned groups, who have relocated beyond the physical borders of their countries of origin. Presumably, accessing such knowledge pools would mean access to the human resources and institutional capacities of the communities that these individuals now serve. This model would annul the brain drain in a unique brain enrichment scheme. For Africa, this could also be an opportunity to tap into the communities of descendants of those who were forcibly removed from the continent, and whose emancipation in distant lands has brought the reawakening of the need for reconnecting to the land of origin. The various groups of Africans are eager to develop their shared values. Such a bond is necessary especially in a world that is becoming more and more globalized, where one's identity could be lost if not in a coalition.

As has been mentioned widely, content is an issue that needs to be critically assessed in contemplating the Information Age in the developing nations. Considering the knowledge needs of these economies, so painfully described, the content of development communications programs should emphasize how to develop productive tools for drought-prone environments and marginal agricultural lands, minimize the rapid rate of population growth, prevent scourges such as HIV/AIDS, and provide career opportunities for the youth. The myriad of knowledge needs suggests that distributed learning through connectivity would be more effective as digital and knowledge bridges than coaching African students on passing test scores, such as for the Test of English as a Foreign Language (TOEFL) to gain admission into foreign universities, as guidebooks already exist for these test scores. Hence, virtual education programs concerning the developing world, such as the African Virtual University, should focus on substantive goals. Prospective students might need to know about emerging fields of study that they might not have been exposed to in the limited curricula and research themes in their home countries; they may also need to understand the implications of such disciplines on their local economies, and how to use the period of overseas education to create networks that they could interact with upon returning home. A mad rush to over-simplify the Information Age, and to emphasize parochial programs such as how to pass the

Test of English as a Foreign Language (TOEFL) over knowledge sharing and systematic learning, would be another folly in development practice. A small proportion of the people in the developing world are already copious consumers of goods and services produced elsewhere, with grave economic consequences for the majority in the local environment.

Developing countries also need to learn quickly from the mistakes identified in more advanced economies so that they can avoid repeating the same errors. China, for example, has made a significant progress in technology acquisition and innovation, and has assisted many developing countries to develop their infrastructure. The Tanzam Railway that links landlocked Zambia to the Tanzanian seaport city of Dar es Salaam for example was undertaken with Chinese technology and capital in the mid-1970s (Dar Es Salaam.com, 1999). Sadly, however, such innovation has not eliminated the insecurities that characterize the majority, who may be residing in the countryside, compared to the fledgling commerce and improved lifestyles in the urban areas. It has been estimated that about 100 miners across China's impoverished countryside die each week at old mines that lack adequate safety features while searching for livelihoods means at illegal and abandoned mines, despite the rapid economic growth that has been occurring in that country. Industrial and transport-related accidents kill many more Chinese; about 47,000 people were killed in the first six months of 2001 alone (Cernetig, 2001). The case in which the Chinese Government admitted in mid-2001 that it faced a serious AIDS crisis in its central Henan province may be similar to cases that had occurred more than a decade earlier in some of the industrialized nations, where contaminated blood was used in transfusion. According to the accounts of Chinese villagers and news reports from the affected Chinese province, more than half a million people may have become infected while selling their blood to local government-run blood banks in the mid- and late-1990s. Blood was reportedly taken from several people at the same time and pooled in one container; after the removal of the blood plasma, the remaining blood was injected back into the donors' bloodstreams. This, combined with the unsanitary method such as unsterilized equipment and the re-use of needles, may have given the disease an easy access into the local population (BBC, 2001).

SOME FEATURES OF INDIGENOUS KNOWLEDGE

The efficiency of a society may be evaluated by the ability of its people to obtain the basic necessities of life—food, shelter, clothing, and education. Indigenous knowledge systems, more than all the formal education abroad, and all of the technological imports by developing nations, have been able to provide the means for their dependents to meet the basic needs of life, even if not in a glamorous state today. Indigenous peoples have domesticated their own crop species, and developed systems in crop and animal husbandry. They invented their own pharmaceutical and health care systems, technologies, engineering, and architectural designs; they produce their own textiles and clothing, and their own styles of furniture, kitchen, and household utensils. Indigenous knowledge systems have also developed and maintained their own arts and humanities that include language (script and oral) systems, philosophies and value systems, culture, and socialization, among others. Indigenous knowledge has been able to impart wisdom, heal the sick, resolve disputes, and provide moral guidance to the practitioners for generation after generation (Anani, 1999; Brokensha et al., 1980; Chambers, 1979; Warren, 1995). Children of these communities also make their own toys from wood, rubber latex, or discarded aluminium and tin cans. Ethnicity, deriving from indigenous cultures of the developing world, has been erroneously perceived as the basis of conflicts, for example the Rwandan massacre, instead of the contribution of indigenous knowledge to the sustainability of primary cultures for several centuries. The 'ethnic wars' in many of these communities are often the outcomes of selfish modern political manipulations that attribute poverty among local groups to undue diversion of imaginary national resources to the 'other' ethnic group.

Indigenous knowledge and idea systems were invariably aware of agriculture's role in the progress of human civilization. Therefore these knowledge systems ensured access to land, and designed tools and cultural practices around agriculture. The indigenous *Ewe* calendar, for example, is based on the farming seasons and weather-associated phenomena—when to burn the bush (because the primitive tools cannot clear the tall Guinea grass easily), prepare the land, plant yams, and the season of showers. Social capital methods were evolved to guarantee optimum production levels for the individual household through group strength for labour requirements in agriculture, provision of shelter, and other basic necessities of rurality, and such knowledge could have formed the basis for an effective micro-credit or rural banking scheme in modern administration. Indigenous knowledge systems were also conversant of environmental security: in the indigenous African knowledge system for example, a piece of the forest was set aside and mythologically assigned as the place of worship of the gods and nothing was extracted from that land; fruit trees such as oranges and coconuts were also planted in the name of a newborn child. These practices predate modern environmental conservation and management programs, and could have been integrated into agro-forestry systems in combination with child nutrition programs aimed at preventing common diseases such as cholera and diarrhoea from drinking contaminated water.

Indigenous knowledge stipulated the average spacing between childbirth; in most African societies, women space childbirth by two to three years, and derogatory terms are used to describe those who might give birth too frequently. Following the delivery of a child, specific diets and other forms of care are provided to the nursing mother to minimize post-delivery complications. Female relatives assist in the performance of household chores, and almost all households in small communities would fetch water from streams and firewood from the fields as presents to the new mother. These mechanisms were designed to enable post-natal recuperation of the nursing mother before she resumed performing such chores.

Indigenous knowledge has also achieved some engineering marvels, such as a community that is built to exist physically, economically, socially, and spiritually on a body of water: Ganvié for example, a community of about 30,000 inhabitants that is located about 25 km from Cotonou, Benin, was founded in about 1717 on Lake Nakoué and is accessible only by boat, as it is situated entirely on water. Ganvie has a floating market, schools, a church, and is a cultural and tourist attraction (ESMT, 1999). The children of Ganvie could be viewed as candidates in connectivity programs that aim to build on the architectural engineering knowledge of local communities, assuming that they were interested in pursuing career objectives that are based on the sustainability of their communities. The curiosity of these children might also pertain to the design of bridges and water transport systems in their region.

Indigenous knowledge systems also established socio-political frameworks, for example the supervision of laws and taboos that bind the members, and the mobilization of indigenous communities are under the jurisdiction of indigenous leaders—councils of elders, chiefs, and queen mothers. There are no village mayors, police posts, post offices, or health clinics in many rural communities in Ghana and much of rural Africa. The indigenous governance system recognizes the unique talents, resources, and capabilities among the various clans, and it distributes roles accordingly—some would be chiefs or queen mothers, others linguists, herbalists, smiths, spiritualists, and so on.

Indigenous knowledge is pervasive in the developing world, and within each indigenous society the knowledge system covers all aspects of human associations and human-ecosystem interactions, hence, the holism of indigenous knowledge systems.

Significantly omitted, whether by intent or oversight, in almost all aspects of national strategy in development programming in the modern states of the developing world has been the potential of local knowledge systems and a clear manner in which such knowledge could be harnessed and systematically integrated into development frameworks. Instead, indigenous knowledge was denigrated, perceived as primitive, and declared a target that must be conquered. However, development 'experts,' in their search for alternative models in development, have rediscovered the importance of local and indigenous knowledge. Panels and roundtables on aspects of development, poverty alleviation, and human security now include the role of indigenous knowledge in their frameworks.

Several development initiatives now contain, at least, references to indigenous knowledge, because that knowledge system is available as a community's own heritage (Atteh 1992)--it is cheaper, proven to be effective, and can link local and national interests as well as be blended with outside knowledge.

Splicing modern knowledge and ancestral wisdom, however, requires a systems approach because indigenous knowledge is more complex than the simple and linear formats that they have been reduced to in scholastic pursuits, such as traditional healing, cattle grazing and animal husbandry, or cropping system, or convenience of indigenous components in formal frameworks during crises.

Several groups have initiated the documentation of indigenous knowledge systems, and elements are being incorporated into mainstream programming. These initiatives that seek to mainstream indigenous knowledge are positive developments in the recognition and utilizing local knowledge, however, elements of indigenous knowledge, taken in isolation, may not achieve the desired function.

Essentially, connectivity for development knowledge generation and sharing of best practices for rural development in the developing world would utilize indigenous knowledge as the template upon which modern knowledge is situated; to include indigenous knowledge in a program, as just another item, might not create a watershed effect or a sustainable impact.

Indigenous communities rely on storytelling to impart values and wisdom on to the successor generation. Development experts from both the North and South could recall their experiences to each other in stories. In so doing, they may stumble upon some elements that are common between their local experiences and perhaps be able to add value to the practice by relating their experience to similar practices elsewhere. Indigenous festivals about the weather are used to illustrate this scenario: weather forecasting is critical in agriculture, and indigenous knowledge has its weather scientists. Changes in global climatic patterns, some attributable to global warming and Ozone Layer depletion (NRC, 2001), might not have been taken into account in the centuries-old indigenous calendar systems. The indigenous weather forecasting methods may appear to depend on superstition, hence indigenous weather scientists have been described in external media as sorcerers: "Each year, sorcerers from Niger and neighbouring countries converge at the village of Massalata for a grand ceremony referred to as *arwa*. The practitioners invoke spirits in the prediction of weather patterns for the drought-prone region, and discuss issues of faith, and culture" (Globe and Mail, 1999). The media report about this practice did not provide the basis upon which the 'sorcerers' make their predictions. The sorcerers apparently look for a rodent that is dissected to reveal the types of food the animal may have consumed. This would indicate if the rodent were preparing for a long period of hibernation or other forms of tolerance to adverse weather patterns (Abdoulkarim Soumaila, Chef Departement Telecommunication, Niamey, Niger, personal communication, during the Rural Com'99 conference in Cotonou, Benin).

Similar philosophies of indigenous weather prediction are known in North America folklore, such as Groundhog Day in Canada and the US; the Old Farmer's Almanac for example has published information for people in various walks of life for more than three centuries—tide tables for those who live near the ocean, sunrise tables and planting charts for farmers, kitchen, and general weather predictions (Farmer's Almanac, http).

Groundhog Day occurs about midway in the cold and long winters of Canada and U.S. Legend has it that some groundhogs (*Marmota monax*) are able to predict the duration of winters. On Groundhog Day, the venerated animal would be awakened early in the morning, and if the animal looked around and could not see his shadow, there would not be another six weeks of winter. The tradition stems from an ancient Celtic belief in which the winter season was divided into two halves; if the midpoint of winter is sunny and clear, there will be two winters in a year. The practitioners claim that their groundhogs have been accurate about 90 percent of the time in some cases, but scientific studies show groundhogs are accurate only 37 percent of the time (O'Malley and Buiza, 1999; CBC, 1999). In any case, the tradition is part of attracting tourists and generating local revenues while providing levity; North American farmers in reality do not rely on the shadow of groundhogs to predict climatic patterns, but are aided by Global Positioning Systems and Doppler Radars.

Knowing these similarities, North American overseas development planners would not minimize the role of indigenous weather forecasts in the economic and social development of rural communities of Africa and elsewhere; these occasions could be promoted for their economic and cultural benefits even if not valuable to agricultural productivity directly.

YAM AND OIL PALM IN HOLISM OF INDIGENOUS KNOWLEDGE

The holism and conceptualization of blending indigenous and modern knowledge systems are exemplified in the cultural significance of yams (*Dioscorea species*) and oil palm (*Elaeis guineensis*).

Yams have cultural, political, and socio-economic attributes, apart from their principal use as tuber crops. Some yam species are also the source of diosgenin, a female hormone precursor that is used in the manufacture of contraceptives (MacNair, 2001). In West Africa, Yam festivals are more than signals of the beginning of the harvest season; they provide the main annual traditional durbars of chiefs and people of many communities during which the wealth and values of the community and its people are displayed in music, dance, games, community gatherings, decision-making, and planning for the following year. Also, yam festivals draw urban-dwelling children back to their villages to participate in discussions about village development goals. Often, such festivals provide the only opportunity for the head of the national government to interact with indigenous leadership and local communities; they are also featured in national tourism promotion and country guidebooks. The cultural significance of yams in West Africa is vividly described in the literary works of Achebe (1958, 1964).

Yet the production of yams is one of the most labour-intensive cropping systems, and it represents one of the most bio-physiological challenges to the rural farmer, who depends on ancestral production systems and tools. It is the ability to overcome production challenges, from making yam mounds and building yam barns, until the farmer realizes a barn full of yam tubers as harvest probably explains why festivals have been created to celebrate a successful production year. There is no indigenous festival for cocoa or coffee; yam is the king of crops in West Africa. A lazy farmer does not own a yam farm, because the size of the field, and the quality of tubers would reveal a lazy person's sloppiness. In some cultures, the farmer digs the ground to a great depth and then makes a huge mound over it, using the 'hoe technology.' The prize for the farmer is a large tuber size that could weigh more than 10 kilograms. Therefore in most cases, the crop grows as a huge vine that must be supported by a high and strong stake to expose the leaves to sunlight. This architecture is necessary to develop the required engine of photosynthesis to produce the storage nutrients in tuberization of that magnitude. Yams are therefore the first crops in the crop rotation so that they can grow under the most fertile conditions, especially in a system of poor land replenishment programs. Yams also require about 1,000 mm of total precipitation, but the farmers operate within a rain-fed agricultural context. The large size of yam tubers also demands caution during the harvesting process, as bruises serve as breeding grounds for pathogens that shorten yam barn life.

Yam improvement programs therefore feature modification of the canopy structure by plant physiologists with the aim of reducing it from the giant foliage that must be staked to one of short stature, in combination with an improved photosynthetic engine. The small plant stature would require less input and minimize some of the production challenges.

It has been postulated that if plant breeding could reduce the size of yams into smaller tubers, the land preparation method for the crop would then be reduced to mere ridges, similar to potato seeding (E.V.C. Doku, former dean, Faculty of Agriculture, University of Ghana, personal communication, 1983). This would also lend to mechanization of both seeding and harvesting. Presumably, breeding methods that have been perfected in corn could be employed in yam breeding to combine small plant architecture and small tuber sizes with the culturally acceptable nutritional qualities of edible cultivars. But the edible yams seldom flower or produce seeds. Root and tuber crops of such cultures have been developed traditionally and the genetic constitutions of the desirable local varieties were fixed or cloned through vegetative propagation methods; yams are consequently planted as cuttings or pieces of the tubers. However, application of nanotechnologies in biology could impact the process of yam improvement: small-size tuber genes could be identified through techniques of molecular biology such as quantitative trait loci (QTL) mapping, characterization of the putative genes that pertain to the desirable features of the crop PCR techniques, and embryo rescue techniques in the transfer of the these traits to adapted yams. The role of crop biotechnology in sustainable agriculture is not yet resolved, but ongoing research could address some of the issues that are yet to be resolved.

The oil palm is another crop of multiple uses that is tied to the cultural, economic, and nutritional values in indigenous cultures. The fronds of the palm are used in making many household items such as baskets to carry foodstuffs from the farm, fishing gear, mats to dry cocoa and coffee beans, hencoops, sheds for gatherings such as funerals, and the leaves as feed for domestic animals. The fruit of the palm is prepared as soup and processed into the red palm oil and palm kernel oil that is used for cooking and as industrial ingredients in the manufacture of margarine and soap. Several attributes of palm oil make it desirable in the food and manufacturing sectors. Palm oil has a high level of the tocols or Vitamin E (which are powerful natural antioxidants), low concentration of linolenic acid, a moderate proportion of linoleic acid (the most readily oxidized components of oils), an exceptional resistance to rancidity, and an excellent stability at high temperatures that make palm oil desirable as frying oil in large-scale food processing (MOPGC, http).

However, not all varieties of oil palm elicit a desirable edible taste. Indigenous systems, in West Africa for example, therefore evolved elaborate processing methods to confer culturally acceptable tastes; they add various spices, such as ginger, in the processing of the fruit into oil, for example *dzomi* of the Ewe, a product that is now commercially available in the metropolis of the industrialized nations for the West African Diaspora market. Moreover, the sap from the tree trunk is the infamous *palm wine* that is important in traditional gatherings such as marriages, funerals, and clan assemblies. Palm wine is also used as restitution for an offence against another member of the community, and in pouring libation or invocation of ancestral spirits at the opening and closing of gatherings. Although there are mills to extract pulp from palm fruit, the services are more oriented toward commercial-scale preparations and not affordable within the capacity of the small-scale producers or in household applications.

The preparation of palm kernel oil is even more tedious. Households and small-scale producers crack the hard shell of the kernels with stones, one kernel at a time. There are small mills to assist this practice as well, but the extra production cost at the mill would not be affordable by people producing to feed themselves.

New varieties of oil palms that are seedless and exhibit shorter plant habits have been developed, but the cultivars that abound in many African fields are of the older types and not the modern types that are found in plantation agriculture and adapted for commercial applications.

Malaysia's oil palm industry, however, demonstrates the efficacy of intellec-tualizing indigenous practices and adapting them toward higher income generation. The Malaysian oil palm industry, unlike the industry in Africa, has undergone intensive research to a level that varieties employed in that economy contain the desirable attributes of palm oil. The oil palm, however, originated from West Africa and was a major trade commodity prior to the colonization of these nations. Oil palm was introduced to Malaysia in 1870 as an ornamental plant and its use as a crop was not developed until 1917. The Malaysian government embarked on a massive programme of agricultural diversification in the 1960s and as a result, the oil palm is the leading agricultural crop in Malaysia today; oil palm covers about two million hectares (a third of the global cultivated land dedicated to oil palm) in Malaysia, and the country currently accounts for 51 percent of world palm oil production (MOPGC, http).

The success of the Malaysian oil palm industry derives from strategic policy positions, research and development, and local investment capital and human resources.

Connectivity could enable knowledge for development programs to design the flow of research information and knowledge that would assist scientists in develop-ing countries to perform the necessary domestication of knowledge in their local research systems. These programs could also employ multi-dimensional reasoning in line with the holism of indigenous knowledge. Thus the entry points of the Information Society into development programming should include the impact on education, health, agriculture and the environment, governance and democracy, girl-child education, women, households and communities, producer groups and rural occupations, trade, investment and economic planning, statistics, knowledge networks and institutional linkages, institutional capacity building and reform, culture (music, computer graphics and animations, arts and crafts), the media, legal reforms and human rights, and infrastructure development (hard-and soft-ware development and deployment).

REFERENCES

Achebe, C. (1958). *Things Fall Apart*. London: Heineman Educational Publishers;

Achebe, C. (1964). *Arrow of God*. London: Heineman Educational Publishers.

Aisen, C. F. (2001, Feb. 13). News releases 2001, article listing: African-Americans develop Alzheimer disease and other dementias at twice the rate of Africans. [Online]. School of Medicine, Indiana University. <http://www.medicine.indiana.edu/news_releases/archive_01/nra01.html>[2001, Feb. 15].

Akotey, Y. E. (1970). Prelude. In Akafia, Y. S. (1970). *Ku le xome*. Accra, Ghana: Bureau of Ghana Languages; and Akafia, Y. S. (1970). *Ku le xome*. Accra, Ghana: Bureau of Ghana Language: *"Excuse me! It is a special honour for me to write the forward to a novel that has the power to motivate humanity. What endeared me to do this is the desire that is burning with vigour within the author toward a viable Ewe literary world, in an era that the old books, which were written for us by the white missionaries, are disappearing. If this desire would burn among other young men and women, then I am hopeful that it would not be long before there will be an abundance of such important literary products in the Ewe community."* [translated to English]

Anani, K. V. (1999). *The Pursuit of Politics of Sustainable Livelihoods: Focus on Governance in Ghana*. Doctoral thesis, University of Guelph, Guelph, Ontario, Canada.

Atteh, O.D. (1992). Indigenous local knowledge as a key to local level development: Possibilities, constraints and planning issues. *Studies in Technology and Social Change*, No. 20. Iowa State University, Ames, Iowa.

Ayensu, Edward S. (1997). The status of science in the service of sustainable livelihoods in Africa. Paper presented at the workshop of the United Nations Development Program International Working Group on Sustainable Livelihoods. Pearl River Hilton, New York, November 19–21, 1997.

BBC. (1999, Jan. 21). Eating fibre won't prevent cancer. *British Broadcasting Corporation News* [Online]. <http://news2.thdo.bbc.co.uk/hi/english/health/newsid_259000/259638.stm> [1999, Feb. 1]: "High-fibre diets have been recommended by doctors since the 1970s after scientists noticed that bowel cancer in Africa—where vegetables and grain is the staple diet—was rare."

See also: Diet change can ward off cancer (1998, Dec. 11). *British Broadcasting Corporation News* [Online]. <http://news2.thdo.bbc.co.uk/hi/english/health/newsid_232000/232371.stm> [1999, Feb. 1]; and Fibre slashes bowel cancer risk. (2001, June 22). *British Broadcasting Corporation News* [Online]. <http://news.bbc.co.uk/hi/english/health/newsid_1402000/1402906.stm>[2001, June 24]: "A diet rich in fibre can reduce the risk of developing bowel cancer by as much as 40 percent, according to results from the biggest ever study of diet and cancer. The study, conducted by the European Prospective Investigation of Cancer and Nutrition (Epic), involved 400,000 people in nine European countries. The authors of the report dismissed some studies in the U.S., which suggested that fruit and vegetable consumption was not important in reducing the risk of colorectal cancer, as those studies were based on homogenous groups with very similar habits."

BBC. (2001, Aug. 9). China admits AIDS crisis. *British Broadcasting Corporation News* [Online]. <http://news.bbc.co.uk/hi/english/world/asia-pacific/newsid_1481000/1481542.stm> [2001, Aug. 9]: "Chinese official statistics indicated that there were 23,905 reported HIV/AIDS cases at the end of March 2001, but some experts said the number could be more than 600,000, and the United Nations has estimated that China will have 10 million or more HIV/AIDS cases by 2010 if decisive actions were not taken. The news echoes cases in France, Iran, Portugal, Italy and Canada where contaminated blood was used in transfusion, predominantly to haemophiliacs, who then contracted the virus."

Body Shop. Company profile: How we do 'business as unusual.' (1999). [Online]. The Body Shop International PLC. <http://www.thebodyshop.com/usa/aboutus/profile.html>[2001, Aug. 11]. The Body Shop states that its goal is to: "Help build livelihoods and to explore trade-based approaches to supporting sustainable development by sourcing ingredients and accessories from socially and economically marginalized producer communities. Through this programme, The Body Shop sources raw materials for inclusion in some of its best-selling products, from cocoa butter in Cocoa Butter Hand & Body Lotion to babassu oil used in White Musk Body Lotion, as well as accessory items including massagers from India and baskets from the Philippines."

Brokensha, D. W., Warren, D. M., & Werner, O. (eds.) (1980). *Indigenous Knowledge Systems and Development.* Lanham, MD: University Press of America.

CBC. (1999, Feb 2). The Tradition of Groundhog Day. *Canadian Broadcasting Corporation News* [Online]. <http://tv.cbc.ca/witness/weather/wepredict.htm> [2001, Aug. 7]: "Wiarton Willie of Wiarton, Ontario,

Canada, and his successor draw about 20,000 tourists each year to the small town of Wiarton on Groundhog Day; Willie passed away in 1999 but has been replaced." Some of the other notable groundhogs include Shubenacadie Sam (Nova Scotia), Punxsutawney Phil (Pennsylvania), Brandon Bob (Manitoba), Staten Island Chuck (New York), Balzac Billy (Alberta), Gary the Groundhog (Kleinburg, Ontario), and Phoenix Phil (Arizona).

Cernetig, M. (2001). Peasant miners die for the glory of China. *The Globe and Mail*, (Aug. 4), Toronto, A1, A10.

Chambers, R. (1979). Rural development: Whose knowledge counts? *Special Issue of Institute of Development Studies (IDS) Bulletin*, (10)2, University of Sussex.

Dar Es Salaam. (1999). Dar Es Salaam.com. [Online]. <http://www.daressalaam.com/right.htm> [2001, Oct. 18].

de la Mothe, J., & Dufour, P. (1995). Techno-globalism and the challenges to science and technology policy. In the quest for world order. *Daedalus: Journal of the American Academy of Arts and Sciences,* (124) 3, 1995, 219-235.

d'Orville, H. (1996). Tackling information poverty. In d'Orville, H. (Ed.), *Beyond freedom: Letters to Olusegun Obasanjo*, pp. 483-494.

Eisemon, T. O., & Davis, C. H. (1992). Universities and scientific research capacity. *Journal of Asian and African Studies,* 17(12), 68-93.

ESMT. (1999, Dec. 6). En vedette: Ganvié. *Bulletin du Forum*, numéro 3, RuralCom'99, Cotonou, Benin, December 2–7, 1999. [Online proceedings at: <http://www.esmt.sn>. Ecole Superieure Multinationale des Telecommunications (ESMT), Dakar, Senegal]: "Construite en 1717 par un seigneur de guerre, la cité lacustre de Ganvié, située sur le lac Nakoué à 25 km de Cotonou, compte aujourd'hui 30.000 habitants. Avec deux communes, un marché flottant, un cemetière, plusieurs écoles et églises, c'est un pôle économique (pêche), culturel et touristique non négligeable où le téléphone n'arrive pas encore."

Farmer's Almanac. Who are we? [Online]. The Old Farmer's Almanac. <http://www.almanac.com/aboutofa.html> [1999, Mar. 6].

Galliard, J., & Waast, R. (1992). The uphill emergence of scientific communities in Africa. *Journal of Asian and African Studies*, 17(12), 41-67.

Globe and Mail, the. (2000, June 29). Canada, for the seventh consecutive year, ranks as the best place to live in the world, says the United Nations Development Report. *The Globe and Mail*, Toronto, p. A2. See also: *Human Development Report 2000*. [Online]. United Nations Development Program. <http://www.undp.org/hdr2000/home.html> [2001, July 29].

Globe and Mail, the. (1999). Sorcerers forecast rain. *The Globe and Mail*, (Mar. 6) Toronto, p. A16.

GNA. (1998). Speech by President William Jefferson Clinton at a durbar held at the Independence Square, Accra, Ghana. *Ghana News Agency* (Bulletin). (Mar. 23), See also: Clinton reaches out to 'new' Africa. (1998, Mar. 24). *The Globe and Mail*, (Mar. 24), Toronto, A9.

ILAS. (2001, May 21). Resources for teaching about Latin America on Native Cultures: Ancient and contemporary. [Online]. The Teresa Lozano Long Institute of Latin American Studies (ILAS), University of Texas at Austin. <http://lanic.utexas.edu/ilas/outreach/resources/native.html> [2001, July 7].

IRN. (2000, Jan. 8). Sierra Leone: Diamonds fuelled conflict, report says. *Integrated Regional Information Network* [Online]. U.N. Office for the Coordination of Humanitarian Affairs. <http://www.reliefweb.int/IRIN/wa/weekly/20000114.htm> [2001, Aug. 7].

Judge, M. (1998). Maasai's miracle high-fat diet. *The Globe and Mail*, (Oct. 24), Toronto, D5.

KFC Corporation. About KFC. [Online]. KFC Corporation. <http://www.kfc.com/about/default.htm> [2002, May 2]. This is not an endorsement of the products or practices of this business.

MacNair, T. (2001, May 2). Progesterone creams based on extracts of wild yam. *British Broadcasting Corporation* [Online]. <http://www.bbc.co.uk/health/ask_doctor/hrt_wildyam.shtml> [2001, Aug. 12]: "Creams containing extracts of Wild Yam are a type of progesterone (a type of female sex hormone, and one of the main components of hormone replacement therapy or HRT), currently available without a prescription, over the counter as a treatment for menopause. But there is very little reliable scientific evidence about how effective cream versions of progesterone are, how safe they are and even whether they are properly absorbed through the skin to reach the rest of the body."

MOPGC. Versatility and technical advantages of palm oil. [Online]. Malaysian Oil Palm Growers' Council. <http://www.mpopc.org.my/abtegfu3.htm#> [2001, July 15]. See also Malaysian palm oil at a glance. [Online]. Malaysian Palm Oil Promotion Council. <http://www.mpopc.org.my/abtegfu2.htm> [2001, July 15].

Njinya-Mujinya, L. & Habomugisha, P. (1998). The third millennium, information banks and publishing in Africa. In Habomugisha, P., Asafo, D. R., & Njinya-Mujinya, L. (Eds.). *Now and in the Next Millennium 1990s-3000 CE: Assessing Africa's Scholarly Publishing Needs and Industry*. 146-154.

NRC. (2001). Committee on the science of climate change. *Climate Change Science: An analysis of Some Key Questions*. [Online]. National Academy

Press, National Research Council, U.S.A. <http://www.nap.edu/catalog/ 10139.html?onpi_newsdoc060601> [2001, June 10]: "There are different opinions regarding global warming, but these disagreements derive largely from the method by which global temperatures are obtained—disparities between the surface temperature and upper-air temperature. While surface temperature measurements have indicated a rise in the Earth's temperature, data generated by satellites and balloon-borne instruments since 1979 suggested that little warming trends had occurred in the low- to mid-troposphere. A committee of the National Research Council (U.S.), made up of 11 of the top climate scientists in the U.S. including members of the National Academy of Sciences, and a Nobel laureate recently considered global warming trends over the last century, what may be in store for the 21st century, and the extent to which warming may be attributable to human activity. They concluded that despite the differences in the way the Earth's temperature was obtained, there has been a real warming trend in the global mean surface temperature during the past two decades, and this trend is substantially greater than the average rate of warming in the 20th century. They also concluded that the Earth's surface has warmed by about one degree Fahrenheit in the past century; evidence for this warming trend includes retreating glaciers, thinning arctic ice, rising sea levels, lengthening of growing seasons for some regions, and earlier arrival of migratory birds."

Odhiambo, T. R. (1997). Research and knowledge: Natural and physical sciences. Paper presented at the research and the production of knowledge in Africa conference. Center for the Study of Cultures, Rice University, Texas, November 7–8, 1997.

O'Malley, M., & Buiza, R. (1999, Feb. 2). Wiarton Willie still dead, long live Wiarton Willie! *Canadian Broadcasting Corporation News* [Online]. <http://cbc.ca/news/indepth/background/wiarton_willie.html> [2001, Aug. 7].

PAI. (1998, May 3). Press release—Africa at the turning point: Development hinges on success in population. [Online]. Population Action International. <http://www.populationaction.org/programs/afpop/afpop_pr.htm> [1998, May 10].

Ressa, M.A. (2001, July 30). Asia's power women: Indonesia's Megawati and the Philippines' Arroyo. *Cable News Network* [Online]. <http://www.cnn.com/ 2001/WORLD/asiapcf/east/07/30/arroyo.megawati/index.html> [2001, Aug. 3]; President Clinton comments on end of Senate trial. (1999, Feb. 12). *Cable News Network* [Online]. <http://www.cnn.com/ALLPOLITICS/ stories/1999/02/12/clinton/transcript.html> [2001, Aug. 3].

Ross, V. (1998). Victims gaining in tug of war over antiquities. *The Globe and Mail*, (July 18), Toronto, A12.

Samara, N. (1999, Oct. 25). Speech by Mr. Noah Samara, chairman and CEO, World Space Corporation. [Online]. Africa Development Forum, United Nations Economic Commission for Africa, Addis Ababa, Ethiopia. <http://www.un.org/Depts/eca/newweb/html/1025address_noah_samara.htm> [1999, Nov. 25].

Sierra Leone Web. (2000, Dec. 27). News Archives, *Sierra Leone Web* [Online]. <http://www.sierra-leone.org/slnews1200.html> [2001, Aug. 7].

Soedjatmoko. (1989). Education relevant to people's needs. *Daedalus: Journal of the American Academy of Arts and Sciences*, 211-219.

Stenger, R. (2001, June 30). NASA probe poised for trip back to the future. *Cable News Network* [Online]. <http://www.cnn.com/2001/TECH/space/06/29/map/index.html> [2001, June 30]: "The Microwave Anisotropy Probe (MAP) launched by NASA will compose a full-sky montage of radiation from the edges of the physical universe, thought to be remnants of the immediate aftermath of the theoretical Big Bang."

U.N. (1995, Apr. 19). *Report of the World Summit for Social Development*. [Online]. The World Summit for Social Development, Copenhagen, Denmark, March 6-12, 1995. United Nations. <http://www.un.org/documents/ga/conf166/aconf166_9.htm> [2001, June 15].

Warren, D. M. (1995). Indigenous knowledge for agricultural development. Keynote speech for the workshop on traditional and modern approaches to natural resource management in Latin America. Technical environment unit, Latin America and the Caribbean region, The World Bank, April 25-26, 1995.

WHO. (1997). Global Buruli Ulcer Initiative. [Online]. World Health Organization. <http://www.who.int/gtb-buruli/initiative/index.html> [1998, June 27].

Wright, R. (2000). 'African renaissance' hailed by Clinton now a distant memory. *Los Angeles Times*, (Aug. 25).

Wysocki, B. Jr. (1997). How to make an economy grow. *The Globe & Mail*, (Feb. 15), Toronto, p. D5: "Forget land, machinery and capital, says economist Paul M. Romer. Ideas are the driving force behind economic growth, and they can be created or reproduced at almost no cost at all."

Zwalen, R. (1996). Traditional methods: A guarantee for sustainability? *Indigenous Knowledge and Development Monitor*, 4(3), December 1996 [Online]. <http://www.nuffic.nl/ciran/ikdm/4_3/articles/zwahlen.html> [1998, June 8].

Chapter V

Digital Bridges and Digital Opportunities for Developing Nations

"When it comes to ending hunger, economic growth is not enough. [Developing nations] need growth with equity. Hunger will not be overcome just by growth in GNP or in food production; poor people and poor women in particular must have access to food. We need to invest in people—in their good nutrition, in their health, in their education—to invest in ways that improve their lives. Freer markets and a strong place for the private sector are also crucial. But they are not enough. We need to invest in farmers, not just in farming." (Statement by Catherine Bertini, Executive Director, World Food Programme at the FAO Regional Conference for Africa, Addis Ababa, Ethiopia, February 19, 1998)

Multidimensional frameworks have been advocated in knowledge for sustainable livelihoods programming. Connectivity for development and poverty alleviation would also endeavour to be a convergence of themes, institutions, tools, and resources. Some of the multiple factors that may be included in such IT-led knowledge for development models are discussed in the following sections; they are not to be viewed as discrete elements, as these factors interact in complex forms.

THE DIGITAL DIVIDE

It is agreed that the existing teleconnectivity in many developing nations could actually be poor. As of January 2000, Ghana and Uganda, with about six Internet hosts per one million people, were among the least connected countries, compared to Senegal (32) and Sri Lanka (63); there were about 1.5 PCs per 1,000 people in Ghana and Uganda in 1998, compared to nine, 15, and 47.4 in Zimbabwe, the Philippines, and South Africa, respectively (WDR, 2000). Sub-Saharan Africa, excluding South Africa, has only 0.48 telephone lines per 100 people, but the region's rural people, about 70 percent of the population, share only 228,000 telephone lines (d'Orville, 1996). In Ghana for example, there are 0.31 lines per 100 people nationally, but about 40 percent of the nation's population of 18 million share 3,800 telephone lines, or 0.06 lines per 100 people. The Ghana Government's Telecommunications Policy for an Accelerated Development Programme 1994-2000 seeks to meet short-term demands in telecommunications by providing 100,000 new lines, but businesses are the priority of that program (MTC, http). Overall telephone demand is estimated at 300,000–500,000 and the government has acknowledged that network growth of about 35 percent per annum would be required to meet even the lower end of demand estimates; that is, a network growth rate of almost two times the level achieved by some more advanced economies is required. The government's connectivity target for rural Ghana would mean one public telephone in each village of 500 people, which is far less than the modest five lines per 100 populations recommended by the International Telecommunication Union. Considering that the investment cost in telecommunications in Ghana is about $1,500 - $4,200 per line, the expectation of majority access to IT would be unrealistic without devising innovative applications of the tools.

However, these statistics soon become obsolete due to the increasing activities of programs and activities at different levels of development organizations, national governments, civil society groups, and the advances in wireless telecommunications.

THE STATE-OF-THE-ART TECHNOLOGY

What is needed is a poor person's connectivity system that would enable an entire community to utilise a few units of the convergence of television, radio, telephone, Internet, CD-ROM, and print media, to offer new prospects in the delivery of sophisticated information to predominantly oral cultures that are currently considered as 'uneconomic' regions of the world. However, this poor person's connectivity system should not imply deployment of the lower end of communications or inefficient tools. Without the appropriate tools, the notion that IT and knowledge flows can lead to sustainable development everywhere may not be realized.

It is vital for today's poor nations to have access to the same high-quality communication tools in order to compete successfully and have equity with the rest of the world. There is no technological basis in modern communications to justify the existing digital divide. Issues of geography, physical barriers such as mountains, poor infrastructure, and Internet language should not be bases to prevent deploying the full power of IT in developing countries; technology has 'been there and conquered that.' Moreover, a low teledensity should not be an excuse for lack of access, although telesaturation should be a necessary effort. In acknowledging the current low teledensity in the developing world, and the need to provide access to the majority, some groups conceptualized vehicles equipped with convergent communications (mobile information vans) to travel the 'last mile' between district centres and which can act as the purveyors of information on rural routes until fixed communications arrive in rural communities.

However, advances in wireless telecommunications are presenting the possibilities that developing countries can quickly connect their rural majority to the global communication circuit. Wireless telecommunications are increasing globally and could benefit developing nations that do not have extensive communications cables. Wireless communications and access to data reached a new height with the launch of the Freedom Of Mobile multimedia Access (FOMA) by Japan's NTT DoCoMo as a commercial wireless operation in October 2001 (NTT, 2001). FOMA is a third-generation (3G) wireless telecommunications that is expected to provide a maximum downlink speed of 384 kbps, some 40 times faster than conventional wireless data communications, and facilitate the smooth access to large-volume data such as video images, with unprecedented voice clarity and the freedom to access multimedia content without restrictions in time and place. The 3G mobile networks can support a lot more subscribers and increase the speed of downloading of data. In addition, the Wireless Application Protocol (WAP) Forum, which released its first specification (WAP 1.0) in 1998, announced a second version (WAP 2.0) that could address interoperability of its tools, with the addition of various features in response to changes in market requirements and improvements in networks, devices, and new technologies; the forum has 10,000 WAP sites from 95 countries, about four million WAP-readable pages, and 40 million WAP-enabled handsets in circulation worldwide, especially in Asia where wireless devices were seven times more abundant than personal computers (Goldman, 2000).

Developing nations with a low teledensity could make themselves as candidates for testing advances in wireless telecommunication tools and applications in order to take advantage of the possibility that they do not have to make investments in old technologies before embarking on the modern generation of communications. These wireless telecommunications could be coupled to indigenous communication methods, which utilize the *gong-gong*, drums, and other musical instruments, as well as linguists that communicate interactively between indigenous leaders and their communities. Often this is the medium to call villagers to gather and listen to national government memoranda through the indigenous leaders. All major announcements and mobilization for communal duties could be affected by the *gong-gong*.

Connectivity projects in developing countries should ensure that they do not lend to the widening of the digital divide; there should not be *any* connectivity as leapfrogging, a cornerstone in communications for development in these economies, cannot be realized in a rapidly evolving telecommunications market if recently obsolete gadgets are assigned to communities that can least afford the required frequent upgrading.

As knowledge for development is defined more clearly, 'access' to communications would be discussed in terms of broadband connectivity and the full potentials of multimedia. There is already an increasing evidence of bandwidth saturation in some institutions in the U.S., although most of these institutions were connected to the Internet only within the last decade (Stellin, 2001). School districts in the U.S. have realized that as the number of classrooms and schools that share each connection increases, and the number of teachers, administrators, and students who use the system rise, the capacity of the infrastructure and ability to perform certain applications soon become limiting. Some districts are already experiencing bandwidth constraints and find it necessary to migrate to Internet2 systems, the high-speed network that was developed by partnerships among universities, industry, and the government.

Convergent Communications

Convergence of communications is also important, as the information revolution is not about telephony or the radio-set as stand-alone communications. Alexander Graham Bell made the first long distance telephone call 125 years ago; this and Bell's subsequent work are among the precursors of the modern fibre optics systems (Hall of Fame, http). Bell's telephony is still vital but has been enhanced by convergence with motion, graphics, video, text, radio, and other technologies to provide unprecedented methods of communications and information flows. The telephone is now integrated into Internet protocols, although Internet telephony is beset with poor quality due to static, delays, and often third-party services. It is anticipated that new telecommunication products that could make significant quality and feature improvements in Internet telephony will soon be deployed; issues of privacy protection and market competition may be more challenging to the effectiveness of Internet telephony than the required engineering improvements to the devices (Markoff, 2001). The new Microsoft Windows XP operating system features integrated Internet voice chat, online video meeting, data collaboration, recipient tracking, information about the destination such as a restaurant's menu, and improved quality of communications; these features could make Internet telephony superior to standard telephones.

Radio broadcasts have also been important in information delivery since Marconi made the first long distance (299 kilometres) wireless transmission of messages 100 years ago. Marconi was awarded the 1909 Nobel Prize in Physics in recognition of his pioneering work to humanity (CNN, 2001, marconi.01/index.html). Radio broadcasts remain vital in information delivery in developing countries, but the radio alone would not provide the access that is required in knowledge for development programming. The remote control of the radio set in the average home of an industrialized economy does not come with 'rewind' buttons or 'search' buttons, let alone the models that are found in developing nations, and this applies to the traditional television set as well. Moreover, information on demand is rarely an option in standard radio set technology. That is, one cannot choose to access information on television or radio at a desired time and one cannot go 'back' to the message or other related information for an instantaneous retrieval.

The radio technology itself is undergoing changes in response to the new communications. Public radio broadcasting, for example *via* the World Radio Network, reveals that radio broadcasters are aware of the Internet. Radio broadcasters provide their listeners with uniform resource locations (URLs) or Web addresses for following up, contacting the broadcaster *via* E-mail, accessing other messages related to the broadcast (links), disseminating the piece to colleagues as printed matter or as E-mail, and in enhancing storage, retrieval, and processing of the information broadcast into relevant knowledge. Many radio broadcasters, including some developing country stations, now stream their signals over the Web, as the Internet is also becoming the radio's memory bank.

The number of listeners to the traditional short-wave radio broadcasts may have increased, according to estimates of the number of people who tune in to the British Broadcasting Corporation (BBC) for example (Ward, 2001): About 153 million people tune in to BBC Radio broadcasts each week, and this large market has confounded those who questioned the viability of the broadcast service in an increasingly commercial market for news and information. However, the biggest growth in listeners occurred in Africa, Asia, and the Middle East; in the U.S., one-and-a-half-million users access BBC online each month, and twice as many listen to the broadcaster on FM compared to short-wave radio; workers in Zimbabwe are much more likely to hear the BBC World Service over a short-wave receiver than on a home computer (Everett-Green, 2001). The BBC World Service programming has therefore ceased to be delivered *via* the traditional short-wave frequencies to North America, Australia, New Zealand, and the Pacific Islands from July 2001, although North American listeners could receive signals that are directed to Central America and Caribbean regions (BBC, 2001, byford.shtml). The broadcaster has begun to focus on re-broadcasting with partners in the affected zones *via* FM, MW, and online audio outputs in order to adapt to the habits of its listeners. Satellite radio technologies are also making inroads into the convergent communications market, with WorldSpace as a notable player in providing direct-to-receiver satellite audio services for human development.

However, the number of Internet page viewers of the BBC website has also doubled to 40 million, and the BBC and other media conglomerates in the industrialized economies have realized that many people have migrated from listening to the radio for news to surfing for news on the Web.

Furthermore, the traditional radio and television sets as mass media systems impose information while the new media are demand-driven; it is the *netizen* who selects the *cyberlocus* and has the power to reject delivery of messages from unsolicited sources. Moreover, radio and television can be heard and seen *via* the Internet. Therefore, convergent communications are achieved *via* the Internet; the television and radio are subsets of broadband and convergent communications.

The goal in connectivity should be to empower communities in all aspects of livelihoods, including democratization of leadership. The nature of traditional radio broadcast, from one point to mass reception, made its manipulation as an instrument of oppression and undemocratic practices in some developing countries possible, for example the seizing of broadcasting stations and installation of military juntas as government, or in extreme cases to exhort others to commit heinous atrocities such as the Rwandan massacre of 1994.

The critical needs for realizing the Information Age in developing countries are access to tools, relevant content development, building knowledge networks, and financing of communications. By tools, poor nations should advocate for state-of-the-art tools, for development would continue to be unequal unless all groups have equity in access to the tools. If access is unequal and should that be acceptable, the yawning gap in human security cannot be bridged.

Telecentres and Area Networks

The practice of sharing that is characteristic of communities in developing countries is conducive for public information and telecommunications access points commonly referred to as telecentres. Telecentres are now a common sight in the capital cities of developing nations such as Nairobi, Kenya, and Accra, Ghana. The services of these access points could be different from the *Web Café* and other types of public communication terminals in the industrialized economies; for example, they process outgoing and incoming E-mail messages on behalf of technologically challenged clients. These centres are usually privately owned and operated under emerging market conditions of competition. Busy Internet Café in Accra has about 100 flat-screen terminals in a spacious and inviting environment, provides private Internet-ready offices for clients who require office-like work environments at the telecentre, and offer training sessions for the public at affordable rates. Mega Surf is another telecentre in Accra, located directly across from Busy Internet. The quality of customer service and the value-added of these centres would dictate their competitive market niche.

The necessity of providing connectivity within the framework of telecentres should not deny the clients the confidentiality of communications. Telecentre operators could inform customers about their connectivity privileges, for example, any citizen of the developing world who has access to the Internet might as well have a personal free-of-charge E-mail address such as Hotmail and Yahoo. A growing number of patrons of telecentres are now using such personalized E-mail addresses, but many are still dependent on the telecentres' own addresses. In one sense, telecentres could be considered as electronic post offices; when it comes to regular mail that is delivered through the post office system, many individuals in urban areas have their private mailboxes, and communities in rural areas share post office mailboxes. Similarly, with electronic mail, individual and communities could have their private mailboxes; the notion of wholesale broadcast should not crowd the need for customized information.

Telecentres could serve as access terminals and provide a multitude of services, but most centres are currently not involved in value-added services such as content development or training of community members, school children, or local business managers about the utility of the tools. The activities of telecentres could increase the awareness of community members about the applications and prospects of IT. This awareness could stimulate a groundswell of support to create a local demand, and to request their national governments to establish the necessary environment for the local knowledge economy. A groundswell of users of the communication centres would also develop a critical mass of users that could lead to a drop in the costs of connectivity, hardware, and other tools of the knowledge economy that most telecentres currently lack. Many of the telecentres in Africa have poor telecommunication hardware, such as slow computers; the quality of services could also be poor, as in the truncation of messages.

The private sector is largely responsible for the proliferation of telecentres in the developing world, although the development community has also been involved, for example the telecentre initiative of the Canadian International Development Research Centre (IDRC). The relatively strong private sector participation in the telecentre market is also a weakness in provision of rural access points, where Internet the volume of traffic may be insignificant initially. National and local governments, and activities of the development community related to telecommunications and development, could however champion rural connectivity schemes that are a convergence of telephony and Internet connectivity; programs by governments to extend telephone lines to such communities could be combined with connectivity programs that are well defined to impact knowledge-driven development. These stakeholders could set numerical targets, for example, *to every village or community a POP* (communications points of presence) within a defined period, to be undertaken by named entities in a defined manner that includes quality of tools and services, and scale to indicate real intentions.

Most of the telecentres are equipped with low-end telecommunications and lack the convergence of tools and services; applications such as videoconferencing that can link rural communities and institutions to the lecture halls of local universities and global development communities can only be found in elite institutions that are located in urban centres. Teleconnectivity initiatives in knowledge for development ought to be devoid of prejudices that ascribe to some group's less efficient tools. The radio, television, and print media can be integrated, and the most useful interface at present is the computer's processing power in various forms such as desktop, laptop, or palm-held. However, for lack of funds and the notion that some could use less sophisticated technology, token projects with rudimentary gadgets in developing countries may be unscientifically and quickly celebrated as 'success stories.' This practice presumes that the achievements of some countries should be less, although these communities are chastised to adopt the principal features of free-market economics such as competition and globalization. Moreover, no nation that places beyond third is awarded a medal at the Olympic games, regardless of their economic status: the case of the lone African swimmer in the pool during the 2000 Summer Olympics in Sydney, Australia, should be viewed as an aberration, although it depicted individual courage and determination; developing nations should not be joyous about such depictions.

All types of economies can dream and achieve, given the tools and the nurturing environment: the first gold medal at the 8th World Championships in Athletics of the International Amateur Athletic Federation (IAAF) in Edmonton, Canada, was awarded to Ethiopia; by the sixth day of the competition, Ethiopia's overall medal count stood third, behind only Russia and the U.S. (IAAF, 2001). Similarly, the Accra Sports Stadium has a Boxing Hall, which provides training facilities for amateurs, and it is possible that this gymnasium has influenced the quality of Ghanaian boxers who have won world championship boxing matches in certain divisions of the sport, although this is not an endorsement of the sport by this author. Likewise, knowledge halls could be perceived to create an information culture, hoping that knowledge could be distilled into products that would serve communities and individuals in their livelihoods and growth. Africa, presumably, could excel in other fields of aspiration beyond sporting activities, but such goals would require that the knowledge halls, unlike boxing halls, are present in every community, with each node linked to other knowledge halls locally and externally.

The Information Age is about convergent tools that facilitate interaction among intelligent human resources, hence developing countries should opt for nothing less than access to the full potential of IT and global knowledge institutions. In addition, telecentres in developing countries, beyond serving as conglomerations of communication tools, should function as information and knowledge brokerages. An example of such brokerages is the brainstorming CD-ROM kit for rural women entrepreneurs to generate new ideas and business opportunities that was developed as a partnership of the Acacia Telecentre initiative of IDRC in Uganda, and local institutions such as the Ugandan branch of the Council for Economic Empowerment of Women of Africa (CEEWA-U) and the International Women's Tribune Centre (IWTC); the package is reported to include features of voice-activation in the local language of the focus community (Mijumbi, 2001).

Knowledge for development programming requires new methods of institution and nation building to avoid the perpetuation of excluding the majority from advances in living standards. Modern institutions in developing nations and their networks have often proved to lack the resources to adequately respond to the needs of the majority in these economies, While these institutions are critical components of the information flow channels, it would be ideal to empower the majority directly, by providing access to communications through their own indigenous social, political, and economic institutions. But indigenous knowledge and its institutions alone would also be impotent in the wake of circumstances that they were neither designed for originally nor have evolved to match. Local development knowledge hubs could therefore be flexible to allow indirect entry of indigenous institutions to the hubs, through guidance by formal institutions.

Inclusion of indigenous knowledge institutions in the global information infrastructure and knowledge flows would commence with building viable local area networks (LANs) as a necessity to making an effective use of vertical knowledge flows. If LAN systems were not in place, information from external sources or vertical flows would be irrelevant or would lack the necessary local impact envisaged in designing current global information grids, thereby lowering the returns on global connectivity investments in knowledge sharing and development in these regions. The LAN system could be visualized as a direct connectivity of indigenous institutions among themselves, as part of wide-area-networks (WANs) that include national systems and the amalgamation of national systems into sub-regional and regional networks. An advantage of virtual networks is that the neighbouring country in the sub-regional linkage need not be the hostile nation with which a peace-loving nation might share borders. This then is toward a virtual regionalization that could be either geographic or thematic.

An effective LAN in rural communities would first map the communities to determine the most appropriate connectivity nodes that would make knowledge flows to reach the heart of indigenous practices. The mapping process would entail an impartial assessment of indigenous knowledge institutions or practitioners to discern the themes, activities, and the capacity of the indigenous practice. Studies of this nature could reveal, for each type of practice or process, the principal outputs (such as food, medicine, clothing production, or processing methods), the human resources and production capacity, impact level (local, district, national, regional, or global market niches), the networks to which the practitioner may belong (such as indigenous healers' association), and national and global institutions with which the local node could be linked. The LAN map could also include entries into modern institutions in the local area, as well as the ability of local knowledge and IT infrastructure to support telecommunication applications such as videoconferencing, which would allow direct visibility of critical occupational activities to external experts so that they can generate the most realistic development interventions.

DEFINING NATIONAL KNOWLEDGE NEEDS AND NEW COMPETITIVE ADVANTAGES

Developing countries could take advantage of IT tools to begin the process of leveraging human development at the global stage. They could establish themselves, each knowing where it occupies, thereby charting their future, and devising mechanisms to realize such visions in a world in which the forces of globalization might obliterate those who do not form strategic and visible alliances. Africa for instance would mean all descendants of Africa, regardless of space.

Each developing nation or region could understand where it has come from and the knowledge that has guided its evolution in order to find mechanisms that would advance the knowledge system to meet its peoples' needs. With IT, the local knowledge that sustains the majority could interact with the global knowledge network by identifying critical input from external sources for coupling with the indigenous knowledge in all sectors of the economy; democratic institutions could be defined to include the deliverables of knowledge institutions and their machinery that could improve the tools and processes of the rural poor who are the majority, without which the burgeoning political democracies would crumble.

Connectivity in knowledge for development is often discussed from the perspectives of policy and planning, technology, infrastructure, content, and funding opportunities. Realization of an effective Information Age in development practice, however, requires interplay among these elements, supported by viable human resources, reorientation of institutional goals, and capacity building efforts.

An imperative step would be for developing and transitional economies and their partners to define each nation's new competitive advantage in the new networked economy and then operationalize IT infrastructure, content, and financing around the themes to actualize the strategic visions. Individuals and businesses could do as they choose, but for good governance, prosperity, and security at the local and global levels, all actors in the community would need to shape and operationalize the strategic visions. Defining the areas of competitive advantage would lend to identifying key knowledge needs that would indicate the principal impact groups, the partnership arrangements among them, and their knowledge and infrastructure needs.

Rosecrance (1999), in his book, *The Rise of the Virtual State: Wealth and Power in the Twenty-First Century,* classified the economies of sovereign states in the Information Age into head nations and body nations. The former produce intellectual or intangible outputs through investment in education, research and product development, and engage the body nations in the translation of the intangibles into tangible products as manufacturing; the entire process is controlled remotely by head nations. This distributed system of conceptualization and production allows a community that is more knowledgeable in a field to delegate components of the process that require manual labour or automated processes to other domains. However, this delegation of duties requires an assurance that all parties can deliver on their roles within the time allowed.

It becomes essential to ponder what goal connectivity programs in the developing world are toward—head or body nations?

The unique and atavistic infrastructure, and the poor capacity of research and educational institutions, are major challenges for developing countries in the networked word. However, these attributes are also the opportunities for them to create new competitive advantages of the sovereign state, and to develop regionally distributed tasks in the Digital Age. For example, African cities such as Johannesburg (South Africa) and Lagos (Nigeria) could become that continent's financial hub, such as New York, Tokyo, and Frankfurt; Accra (Ghana) could serve as a centre of diplomacy, leadership, and policy visions, such as Washington, DC, and Brussels. Addis Ababa (Ethiopia), which hosts African institutions such as the African Union (formerly known as the Organization of African Unity) and the United Nations Economic Commission for Africa, could serve as the region's conglomeration of global institutions, such as Geneva and New York. Other African cities could become the continent's entertainment, media, and fashion charades, as seen in Los Angeles, Paris, and Rome; the warring countries, such as Zaire, Angola, Mozambique, Sudan, Algeria, Liberia, and Sierra Leone would realize the dividend of peace and emerge from the ashes of war, like Germany and Japan; North Africa and the Niger

Delta could be Africa's energy sources, as in the Gulf Region, while South Africa, The Congo Basin, and Ghana would be research centres for the region's precious metals and mining engineering industries, as are Texas and Calgary (Alberta, Canada). Nigeria and South Africa could serve as Africa's military powers, such as America, Britain, France, Russia, and China; the West Coast of Africa (The Slave Coast) could be Africa's remembrance of the fall of vast African empires and a veneration to the victims of aggressions past against the region, while Dakar (Senegal) could become Africa's judicial centre, as demonstrated by The Hague. Cairo (Egypt) and Tombouctou (Mali) may be the preservations of Africa's previous civilizations, such as Rome and Athens, while Kumasi (Ghana) and Swaziland would become centres that demonstrate features of modern monarchies, as in The United Kingdom and Japan. Liberia, where freed slaves settled, and the homes of Africa's independence leaders and resistance movements from Ghana, Kenya, Zambia, Tanzania, Cote d'Ivoire, Egypt, and Ethiopia may become Africa's Mount Rushmore, The Lincoln Memorial, and Mount Vernon (NPS, http). Cities along Africa's coast, especially in East Africa and the Lake Victoria region could become the region's playground, such as Cancun (Mexico) and Miami Beach (Florida), while Ethiopia could become Africa's land of princesses.

Identifying and exploiting the competitive advantages and sectoral specializations in regions of the developing world are ideal, but there are also some commonalities that are reflected by the needs of their rural communities. These common needs include knowledge to design and manufacture devices such as solar energy-powered, hand-held motorized hoes that are affordable by the target group to assist agricultural productivity; knowledge to convert household waste into organic land replenishment material; water management systems, as irrigation projects have failed to water farmers' fields; knowledge to cultivate mushrooms from simple inputs instead of hunting for mushrooms from the wild; knowledge to process food crops into storable states, and more efficient marketing systems; biotechnology knowledge in the diagnostic and screening of food crops and food products for presence of micro-toxins that cause diseases such as liver cancer from aflatoxins; and techniques such as plant tissue culture for the production of unlimited quantities of high yielding and disease-free planting material of crops, such as cassava, yams, and other root and tuber crops, bananas, and plantains, which are the staple food crops of rural communities and are propagated by vegetative methods such as cuttings, thereby passing latent infections onto new fields.

Developing and transition economies should not lose sight of the IT export either; an illustration of the export performance of developing and transition economies between 1994 and 1998 revealed that some of these economies were able to increase their share in the world export market of IT hardware (computers, electronic components, and telecommunications equipment) in very significant ways. World import demand for IT equipment and components, excluding electrical machinery, was about US$600 billion in 1998, and was expected to exceed $1 trillion by 2005, at a growth rate of about 12-15 percent annually, prior to the contraction in the IT sector in 2001; developing and transition economies' export of IT hardware comprised about $214 billion of the total market, or about 30 percent (ITC, 2001). However, participants in the Executive Forum 2000 invariably concluded that for the majority of developing and transition economies, the emphasis of their export sector in the digital economy should not be on developing capacity to participate in the export market for IT hardware. A participant in that forum remarked: "What is Africa's export potential in ICT? Nil in such a skill-, capital-, and technology-intensive export sector. African firms should concentrate on adding value in those sectors where it has possibilities of being competitive" (ITC, 2001: 20).

It may be quite premature for any economy to relegate itself to peripheral activities of the digital opportunities and world trade. All aspects of the digital economy are still in their evolutionary phases, and opportunities are yet to be explored in several aspects of the global trade in telecommunications and knowledge for development applications, including IT hardware. Had innovation been content with the advent of the electronic typewriter and the facsimile and other communications predating convergent telecommunications, or had the manufacture of word processing been left to the manufacturers of the typewriter alone, the history of communications and human civilization would have been different indeed.

Many countries of the developing world may not be able to amass the critical skills, capital, and innovation to compete in the development and export of IT hardware to a significant level. In Ghana, for example, the total number of dial-up subscription was less than 20,000 customers in 2001 with a high incidence of churning of clients, and an increasing number of ISPs may be competing for this small capacity. However, the IT sector should be viewed as a phenomenon that has permanently shifted the fundamentals of human existence, including economic activities, the wealth of nations, and individuals. In this regard, these economies could consider the regional alliances and franchising systems that are necessary for the development of the critical business capacities in aspects that would enable them to play significant roles in the IT world market.

A partnership among academics and students at the Indian Institute of Science (IIS), and experts from Encore Software led to the development of the *Simputer*, a palm-held Internet appliance that costs less than US$200. The electronics, software, and the industrial engineering for the housing of the Simputer were designed entirely in India. The manufacturers claimed that the portable device had speech recognition in several Indian languages, could be operated by illiterates, and that the demand for the Simputer had reached one million units. After drawing global attention for many months, the Simputer was moving from the drawing boards to the production stage in India (Noronha, 2001; Ribeiro, 2000; Simputer, http).

It may be too early to pass judgment on the capabilities of the Simputer, and any challenges it may pose to the traditional PC market in the local economy or its ability to penetrate the developing world. However, this development could be likened to earlier developments in the automobile engineering industry. The early Japanese automobiles in the world market were ridiculed among some communities in the traditional automobile economies until the Oil Crisis of the 1970s demon- strated the fuel efficiency of Japanese cars; today, Japanese automobile makes such as Honda and Toyota have become 'best models' in North America and around the world. Furthermore, space technology, such as rocket launches, was the reserve of a few nations, but China has been working toward claiming a share of the commercial satellite launches.

Developing and transition economies could become contributors to global economic prosperity, but their IT-led knowledge for development programs would first need to contemplate in far-reaching ways the policies that would enable such economies to contribute to global innovation, as well as to benefit from such advances. These economies should not underestimate their own potential either. The current elements of the IT industry are not the end of innovations, and if developing and transition economies captured a piece of the world trade in this sector, the advanced nations would not be deprived of their economic capacities, as they could metamorphose into other stages of innovation and IT.

With the emergence of Southeast Asia as a major manufacturing zone, communities in the Western economies suffered from the relocation of factories from their environments to the emerging economies, but the losses were soon replaced with new opportunities in other sectors, fostered by the end of the Cold War and deployment of knowledge and products from the relics of that war. Thus communications that were reserved for military operatives were deployed for civilian use, and human activities were permanently changed for the better in most cases, even if it caused an artificial economy in the industrialized nations for several years in which perhaps many people were able to taste what actual wealth entailed.

Partnerships in knowledge for development could lead to defining realistic strategic development goals and finding the means to provide the nurturing environment to realize these goals; imagination in these processes should not be limited by current capacities.

BRAIN GAIN, HUMAN RESOURCES, AND INSTITUTIONAL CAPACITY BUILDING

Efficient institutional capacity and human resources are needed to realize the goals of connectivity. Development of such capacity and knowledge capital hinge on building knowledge partnerships with strategically selected local and global knowledge domains of individuals and institutions to converge as brainpower, as in the assembly of machinery for an engineering project that would involve optimization of several fields through compromises.

Developing nations and their partners have been refocusing development programming on human resources and institutional capacity building. Hopefully, these exercises would examine, question, and scrutinize the fundamentals of partnerships, so that the result would be a re-orientation of these economies toward developing a critical mass of thinking individuals and functional institutions. These capacity building programs would also include quantifiable objectives that would indicate the capacity that the nation concerned would have reached as a result of the exercise. The programs could ponder the niche and the deliverables of the local institutions within the impact areas, the level of expertise, and the resources that would enable the institutions to function at a predetermined or optimal capacity. A strategy of this nature would facilitate the weaning of the impact institutions from a continuous reliance on donor programs.

Knowledge from the external realm and the use of such basis to organize and gauge development in the South, it has been agreed, should be restructured by including the perspectives and active participation of the impact areas—their experts, institutions, formal leaders, community leaders, and practitioners in both traditional and formal economic and socio-political sectors. This interactivity between North and South is made possible by the advances in modern telecommunications. Northern-based development institutions are providing opportunities to collect views from broad consultative processes, especially from the development impact zones; they have also realized that the impact zones of development programs also include the funding source.

The sincerity of these North-South interactions among experts and institutions would require mutual confidence of the thoughts and abilities of each partner to execute its share of the combined operation successfully. But the combination of talents (knowledge) and resources at the institutional and personal levels weighs more heavily in favour of the development community of the North. The external development community is made up of knowledgeable and good-hearted people; however, granting the beggar-status of the development community of the South, equity in program conceptualization and implementation could not be realized except each side pledged to disavow the biases with which they have operated for so long. Considering that many local experts in communities of the South have been trained in the same institutions as their external counterparts, efforts should be made to provide the enabling work environment and conditions to Southern experts in institutional capacity and human resources development programs to engender local productivity. However, no one can hand equity to any group; each partner could use timely and accurate information to make self-assessments, demonstrate its strengths, and seek knowledge and innovation from other parties to enhance local capacity.

This new form of equalization of development resources between the elements of the development community requires development partners to have synergistic capacities that could optimize development programming. These capacities would include ability to diagnose the state of a local community, and identify the challenges, opportunities, and mechanisms to effect desirable changes.

Many jobs and livelihoods in the donor economies are dependent on overseas development programming; about 70 percent of the budget that some developed nations devote to overseas development assistance is returned to the developed nation in the form of jobs, services, and equipment supply from the donor country. The sustainability of developing country institutions may therefore be a threat to those who would not be able to envision the scenario and impact of a mutually beneficial program in knowledge flows between the development partners. The successful outcome of a capacity building program involving a developing nation could benefit the donor nation as well. For example, the impact institutions could acquire the expertise and efficiency of solving problems and be able to participate in generating knowledge that could impact the global community. The impact institutions could be in position to contribute to the search for new knowledge in energy, environmental security, and health, among others--issues that are of global concern. The knowledge and experience garnered by the donor nation in a development partnership could be brokered to businesses in the donor nation so that they can develop and target knowledge solutions for the impact community, and increase their competitive edge over rivals from other nations. It has been amply established that developing countries could make some contribution toward increasing the knowledge quotient of practices in the developed world in this regard.

Development of Human Resources

Developing and transition economies have been suffering from significant brain drain of their local human resources, and globalization could make the situation worse. Labour flows are toward the highest bidder, a scenario in which the non-industrialized economies are unable to compete for their own homegrown talents, let alone attract foreign brainpower in physical terms.

Some communities in the developing world could capture a piece of the evolving information technology market if they could develop some applications or processes that are not yet available even in the industrialized economies. India has been a universal reference of such opportunities, but India's human resources and talents are serving external economies, perhaps more than creating an enabling transition of a significant proportion of local Indian communities from abject poverty to sustainable states. According to the World Development Report (2000-2001), India and Namibia had 23 and 1,174 Internet hosts per one million people, respectively, and Guatemala's 8.3 personal computers per 1,000 people is three-fold the Indian PC possession rate of 2.7 (WDR, 2000). Often, the migration of human resources from a developing nation to the industrialized world is primarily of personal gain to the migrant and institutional gain to the economy of the destination. While the remittances of migrant workers to the extended families could have some trickle effect on the economy of their countries of origin, it is doubtful that the economy of a developing nation can be stimulated significantly by the 'export' of human resources. The relevance of the Information Age to developing economies would lie in creating direct local effects of digital opportunities as local innovative processes and to improve institutional capacities locally. As with other aspects of economies, migration is part of globalization, but no developing nation could be content with models that emphasize grooming talents for export alone.

Participants in an electronic discussion on Reforming Technical Cooperation for Capacity Development considered the problem of brain drain: Baser (2001), for example, referred to the brain drain that has characterized the institutions of developing nations, noting that the percentage of graduates from developing nations living in countries of the Organization for Economic Cooperation and Development (OECD) were staggering: 2.7 percent for India, three percent for China, 7.5 percent for Egypt, eight percent for South Africa, 26 percent for Ghana, and 77 percent for Jamaica. Often, the intellectual component of these migrant populations are integrated into the host nation's human capital pool, and some include graduates from the same elite universities in the West, like some of their counterparts in their countries of origin. Those who constitute the brain drain population when able to gain employment in the West are valued more than their counterparts in their nations of origin. Also, although development programming intends to create equity, development experts are not valued to be worth the same between external brainpower and indigenous brainpower.

Considering these situations, expertise of the same qualifications could be valued at the same level, irrespective of the region that employs them. But under the existing conditions, developing economies could not afford the remuneration levels or the work environments that institutions and personnel in the industrialized economies enjoy. Retaining local experts in their local environments has been the concern of many governments in the developing world, but attempts should be made to improve the livelihoods of the expert through continuous learning and provision of the nourishing environment and not in temporary salary supplementations while engaged in a donor-funded project alone; as Wescott (2001) noted during the electronic forum on Reforming Technical Cooperation for Capacity Development, one reason that development projects are not sustainable is because the salary-supplemented staff may look for new donor projects in order to continue receiving the extra income that is associated with donor projects. However, remunerations and the duties of the developing country expert could be partitioned into salaries and the investments that are required to enable the actualization and deliverables of the local intellectual capital. The provision of resources could be considered as an investment in the capacity development of personnel to meet their production efficiencies. Capacity building schemes that do not address enhancements in job satisfaction among local experts could be doomed to fail from inception.

The poor capacity of institutions in the developing world is a factor of production inputs, including physical and human resources. Most of the institutions and production units in developing countries were designed with foreign consumables in mind; human resource development and the establishment of these institutions therefore did not reflect the philosophical, technical, and material resources in the indigenous infrastructure. Consequently, inputs and outputs did not impact basic livelihoods, and the majority have continued to rely on their ancestral knowledge in production and livelihood attainment; modern factories were not sustainable either, for the same reason that local demand was ineffective and inputs were from external sources that could not continue supplying to nations with poor credit ratings.

The human resources and capacity building components of telecommunications and knowledge for development programs could learn from previous schemes that have benefited other nations: Canada and the U.S. developed a relationship that enabled Canada to develop some of the talents that have been able to make Canada one of the most advanced economies today. A large number of university professors and researchers at Canadian universities were trained in American universities. The calendars of Canadian universities in the 1980s were replete with faculty whose credentials revealed that they obtained their first degrees in Canada, but undertook their further studies in U.S. universities. Their education abroad was combined with the establishment of infrastructure at home that they could employ in translating their new learning into local deliverables and creating local capacities upon their return home. They were able to build on the initial infrastructure to make Canada a member of the G8 Nations.

There are special features of the Canadian-U.S. relationship including a common origin of their modern 'founding' ancestors. As Canada and the U.S. are among the architects of poverty alleviation, globalization, and regional blocs such as the evolving hemispheric Free Trade Area of the Americas, they could recall their own shared development strategies and enable the countries within their hemispheric trade blocs, and others whose development is their concern, to benefit from their own experiences.

The Information Age has the potential to create tremendous opportunities for brain convergence and brain enrichment through networked citizenship, including citizens of non-industrialized economies who have found themselves temporarily located in the industrialized economies. The individual and institutional capabilities of such networked Diaspora groups could create a human capacity level beyond the level that any individual nation would ever have developed alone. These intellectuals of a region, who may be located outside the region's realm, could be networked through communications into the human resource pool of their regions of origin as a digital Diaspora to supplement the local knowledge capital. As Rossman noted, "global distance learning systems should see the urgency of getting educated Africans abroad to work together to help meet needs on that continent; one cannot expect the bureaucrats or the ministers of education to do the creative planning on what learning is needed and how it can best be provided; university presidents and administrators are not going to do it either—they do not have the time, even if some of them might get a glimpse of learner-centred (not professor-centred) education, the kind of learning tailored to each individual and community that we talk about" (Parker Rossman, personal communication, July 2000). For this type of vision, institutions such as the International Organization for Migration, whose activities include the physical repatriation of developing country intellectuals to their homes of origin, could reorient their operations toward a virtual 'return' of talents and the provision of interacting spaces for intellectuals of a region, who may be separated by geography to converge and brainstorm on issues pertinent to the development of their communities.

The digital Diaspora groups have natural abilities to supplement the human resource pool and institutional capacities of their original homes, since it is their siblings, colleagues, schoolmates, and community members who constitute the human resources in these regions. The knowledge of developing country intellectuals abroad, who are conversant of both their heritage and their adopted modern world, could become critical in overseas development agency programming as well; they are located in the nations from which development planning has often emanated, and could be accessible to planners within their homes of origin as well. The digital Diaspora could be equipped to serve as part of the digital bridges between their current foreign institutions and institutions in their homes of origin in facilitating knowledge flows and interchanges. (The perspectives expressed here about indigenous and foreign intellectuals are not a blanket appreciation of all scholars of indigenous parentage, or a condemnation of all external scholars. Some scholars of indigenous origins are not well informed about indigenous knowledge, or may be unwilling to admit to the state of insecurity in their native lands, a situation which resulted from the culturally irrelevant educational system within which they may have been nurtured. On the other hand, many foreign experts are inclined toward the cause of development of poor nations; this discussion is to find the best resolution for goal achievement.)

Significant capital flows between Diaspora groups and their homes of origin also occur, and such capital could be channelled into productive sectors of national and regional economic activities when pooled into investment capital.

Based on these potential contributions of the digital Diaspora in creating local knowledge communities, the Information Age could make 'brain drain' become an anachronistic term and could be replaced with brain enrichment, or brain gain.

A major challenge for the development community that has been the subject on many development-oriented Listservs has been how to determine the information needs of rural communities of the developing world. This presents another opportunity for the digital Diaspora to define the local knowledge needs of their homes of origin to the development institutions of their host nations. The external development community could consider the digital Diaspora as the foundation to establish reliable development information brokerages, since these brokerages would desire to understand and appreciate both indigenous and modern knowledge. The potential role of the Diaspora community in the security of their adopted homes came into the fore in the immediate aftermath of the September 11 attacks against the U.S.: the nation's intelligence community frantically sought citizens who were fluent in the local Afghan languages.

Many developing country intellectuals who reside abroad obtained their basic education in their villages; families and communities have seen their children through rural schools, and many continued on the educational ladder in urban centres, and overseas. The major problem, however, has been the disjunction between the knowledge proffered by modern institutions (such as schools, clinics, research, and industry) and the knowledge system that actually serves the majority. Most modern institutions in the developing economies today continue to reflect the period of colonial knowledge domination over the knowledge of the local communities. Consequently, both modern and indigenous knowledge institutions have weak capacities in these countries.

The knowledge needs of rural communities, and the development of human capital to meet those needs, could realize the potential contribution that progenies of rural communities, who may be residing in advanced economies, where they may constitute the labour force of some reputable institutions; they could serve as guides, linking modern and indigenous knowledge systems. Another shortcoming of development practice could be the substitution of the local intellectual or the Diaspora with the notion of 'participatory research,' which insinuates anybody sitting down with rural peoples to collect their thoughts and debrief practitioners of indigenous knowledge. Indigenous know-how is passed on orally between generations, and no amount of energy expended by an outsider would provide the understanding of the local knowledge system to the depth that is necessary to generate sustainable solutions; comprehension of the full dimension of indigenous knowledge is almost of a birthright issue. Building partnerships toward knowledge for development presents opportunities for the stakeholders to focus on development aspects in which they have the greatest expertise and capacity, but trust is a principal requirement for the outcomes of such strategies.

IT therefore could annul the general and overstated assumption that poor nations lacked expertise; the large pool of their intellectuals outside their regions could now be networked to partner with institutions in both their original and adopted homes for positive impacts in local development.

Local experts could also lend to enhancing development outcomes, but they would have to consider themselves as resourceful and capable of contributing to understanding of local development themes. The full participation of the local intellectual in conceptualizing the knowledge needs of local communities could reveal the real challenges in the operational domain and increase the cultural relevance of technology. The competitive and partnership advantages of the local and Diaspora experts, conferred by their cultural inclinations and understandings about what constitutes the local community's perspectives of development, could be developed into a major industry as brokers of information for the global development community regarding efforts toward local prosperity and security.

Scholars from developing countries may be considered brilliant in the fictional section of book publishing and have been internationally recognized as such. Many writers of political satire who faced persecution by despotic leaders in their countries of origin and spent their prime years in exile continued to publish; on the other hand, the politically innocuous thematic areas such as science and technology have rather been silent. That is, developing country intellectuals of technical disciplines have been inconspicuous in coming up with protocols that would add value to indigenous technical practices. These intellectuals could constitute themselves into knowledge cells and begin to assert themselves in the global development community and contribute to the decisions that would affect the communities that nurtured them. They could reflect on the cultural relevance of modern technologies for holistic applications in resolving issues of rural insecurity. They have read the same books and have been taught by the same professors that trained some of their foreign compatriots who strive to solve the problems of the developing world.

The provision of communications access to developing country intellectuals is necessary to enable brain convergence and facilitate the participation of the group in the virtual discussions that are increasingly becoming the source of knowledge input into the activities of the global development community. Many intellectuals from developing nations currently are unable to participate in these exercises to any appreciable level while their input would have provided the perspectives of the most knowledgeable about the local culture of the impact zones; they speak the indigenous languages, require no interpreters, and could be literate in at least one of the major languages of the world: Spanish, English, French, Chinese, Japanese, and Russian, among others. The role of these intellectuals could be to define the basis of indigenous existence and communication systems in order for technology, culture, and education to be brought into synchrony for an effective IT-led development model.

Intellectuals with indigenous backgrounds should express their full potential and let their minds be nourished by the wisdom of their heritage, and in return, reformulate new and relevant knowledge for their indigenous communities, with some of the ingredients of modern knowledge. The idea is to let the process loop back like an auto-feedback mechanism.

The State of Israel perhaps exemplifies features that are effective in harnessing the brainpower and resources of Diaspora groups in the contemporary world; Israel has a cabinet portfolio for the Diaspora; furthermore, the Internet has impacted the methods that are used to mobilize investment capital for this nation, as State of Israel Bonds are advertised in suburbs of Toronto, Canada, in neighbourhoods where significant members of the Israeli Diaspora reside, with a Web address for additional information to the potential investor.

The inclusion of the Diaspora in the local human resource pool of the country or region concerned would minimize the ingenuity gaps that may exist within developing country institutions.

While local groups should make a significant contribution to development programming concerning their communities, it is evident that they may not have all the necessary information to make the right choices. Communities that are not conversant with modern telecommunications cannot make effective decisions regarding the tools. They may also be unable to derive the most utility or understanding of the wide-ranging impact of the technology, hence the devotion of significant development funds to training policymakers regarding the relevance of IT. Therefore, building the Information Society in some of these nations and regions has been top-heavy in funding opportunities. The expectation is that when senior officials and policymakers comprehend and appreciate the potentials of IT, they would create the favourable environment for others to gain access to IT. This assumption may be unfounded, considering that some officials become more detached from the average situation after gaining additional advantages. A classic evidence against the assumption is that of the introduction of schools in rural communities and the resulting outflow of talents from the rural communities to institutions in urban areas, and their failure to return improved tools and processes to their rural communities while depleting the rural labour reserve.

Therefore, the training of decision makers in such economies should have realistic methods by which the knowledge acquired would result in measurable outputs of the trainees.

Understandably, there could be an imagination gap regarding modern technologies and development opportunities among communities that have traditionally been excluded from global innovations in science and technology. This gap is determined to some extent by the tools and other resources available to a group to perform defined services.

The modern Information Age did not originate from the developing world. In that regard, the imagination of local groups in some developing countries about the deployment of modern communications to network their citizens and provide institutional interfaces may be limited by their experiences with previous mass media tools. However, the capabilities of developing country institutions could be supplemented with the experiences of their Diaspora groups which currently reside in the industrialized economies. The Diaspora have experienced both worlds, and have witnessed and participated in the revolution of IT. Their experience is significant enough for them to contemplate the future of IT and the relevance to their communities of origin. In Africa, these Diaspora groups are responsible to a large extent for the fledgling information networks in their countries, for example Ghana's Network Computer Systems (NCS), and Africa Online. NCS for example was a pioneer in the use of Internet Protocols over satellite media in the West Africa sub-region. The Nairobi-based Africa Online, which has 450 employees, operates in eight countries (Ghana, Cote d'Ivoire, Kenya, Namibia, Swaziland, Tanzania, Uganda, and Zimbabwe); the company began in 1994 as an initiative of fellow Kenyans—Ayisi Makatiani (an electrical engineering student at the Massachusetts Institute of Technology or MIT), Karanja Gakio (another graduate of MIT who was operating an E-mail service for his friends and family members in Kenya, out of his apartment), and Amolo Ng'weno (who holds an MBA from Harvard, and daughter of Hillary Ng'weno, an influential publisher and owner of media assets in Kenya) (Marsh, 2001). The company was bought in 2000 by African Lakes, a U.K. trading company, providing extra cash infusion for the company's plans to extend its operations to Zambia, Nigeria, and the more competitive markets of South Africa and Egypt.

However, developing the mechanisms to harness the potentials of the digital Diaspora would also require policy frameworks that relate to creating a harmonious interaction among external experts, the local institutions, and local labour force, so that synergism could be achieved.

Globalization, Cultural Blocs, and Brain Gain

The presence of descendants of many identifiable groups of developing countries in elite institutions around the world could be conducive to building constituencies of these nations within the corridors of global power and influence. These Diaspora groups could partner with civil society organizations in the industrialized economies that champion the cause of developing nations on global policy and development issues. *Africa*, for example, is a biological, philosophical, and cultural home to more people than those who currently are located on the continent of Africa. Similar relationships exist among other visible groups, such as Indians, Chinese, and Latino groups. IT could increase the efficiency with which Africa, for example, re-establishes links with the African-Brazilian, African-American, African-European, and African-Caribbean/Latin-American communities to be connected to communities on the continent of Africa to evolve their shared African heritage, learn from each other, and enable the external African populations to electronically tour their land of ancestry. These external communities of Africans are natural extensions of the African heritage.

The independence of African countries was not an achievement by continental Africans alone; African intellectuals in the Diaspora, civil rights leaders in America, and activists around the world were essential in that liberation philosophy and activities. The experiences of Africans in the U.S. and the Caribbean, in their own emancipation and struggles for rights and freedoms, influenced the spirit of continental Africans to orchestrate their freedoms from colonial rules. The relationship between the groups on both sides of the Atlantic Ocean may have waned in tandem with the decline of civil rights activities following the assassinations of civil rights leaders in the U.S., and as a result of the military takeovers of African administrations and the intellectual void that ensued.

The African-American population and Africa have resumed developing interactions among the various African communities. The caption of a report in the *New African* on the fifth African African-American Summit held in Accra, Ghana, in 1999, that read: "Cheer up Africa, Uncle Sam is here" (Afrani, 1999:13), revealed how local groups perceive the role of advanced economies in local development and technical cooperation in general. The caption was similar to Arch-Bishop Desmond Tutu's joy in "Hey people, freedom is coming," on news that Nelson Mandela was to be freed from his long incarceration by the apartheid regime; therefore the euphoria in announcing the African African-American Summit was just the national joy in the African. An African African-American summit is a necessary step in the logical process of establishing mutually beneficial relations within which Africans everywhere could coalesce to participate and benefit in global advances. However, the notion that Uncle Sam or someone else would *bring* development into a local community belongs to the era of failed development programming. The relationship between a local community and its Diaspora population could be viewed from an umbilical cord perspective, and U.S.-Africa relations are essential to the economic emancipation of Africa. The Information Age is perhaps the most conducive period for Africans everywhere to re-establish their umbilical cords to their land of ancestry for a common developmental process, and similarly for other cultures around the world. The Information Age provides an opportunity to build digital bridges among all African communities to identify salient features of the African civilization for resolving their common predicaments-- features that have ensured the survival of its peoples in the face of adversities spanning several centuries. The benefits should be mutual, and continental Africa should be viewed as a possible contributor to the well being of its descendants who were removed under dubious conditions.

The relationship between the continent of Africa and the African Diaspora is used to elucidate some of the features of the partnership arrangements that may be of mutual benefit in cultural blocs.

There is an increasing awareness among Africans and the African Diaspora groups that both are afflicted with social, economic, political, and psychological plagues. Human indignity in Africa is visible through human development indices and images of viciousness, hunger and starvation, deprivation, and ineptitude. The African Diaspora communities in the U.S., Brazil, the Caribbean, and Europe are also insecure: drugs, violence, murders, gang activities, crimes, and economic deprivation have weakened and dehumanized many households and communities. A large percentage of the African-American male population is incarcerated, leaving behind a multitude of cases in which a mother fends for the African-American child by herself. A report by the U.S. Justice Department, "Prisoners in 2000," revealed that, of the U.S. prisoner population of 6.5 million (the world's largest prisoner nation), black males continued to be disproportionately repre- sented in state and federal prisons, accounting for 46 percent of male inmates, compared to 36 percent for whites, and 16 percent for Hispanics (CNN, 2001, prison.population/index.html). These are serious insecurities of a race, and have also become the ridicule of the African race by others. Africans everywhere are beginning to realize that the African civilization and value systems are necessary inputs into models required by their communities to begin the process of restoration of dignity among Africans of various geographic communities.

Increased globalization demands strategic alliances; hence coalitions such as NAFTA, the European Union (EU), the Association of South-East Asian Nations (ASEAN), and Asia-Pacific Economic Cooperation (APEC) are being formed.

The African/African-American understanding is similarly inclined and the critical areas relate to group strength, focus on private capital as the engine of growth, and the requirements of responsible economic policies and 'democratic' systems of governance. However, the African revival scheme could include the establishment of a knowledge bridge for intellectualization of indigenous African value systems and practices as bases for sustainable livelihoods within African communities.

The African civilization has equipped Africans, wherever they may have (been) relocated to, with philosophical frameworks as coping mechanisms for building viable communities. Thus Africans have endured slavery, colonization, apartheid regimes, economic deprivation, and political dictatorships with direct, indirect, or passive support of some external agencies. The future of Africa and African descendants would depend on the extent to which the various geographic communities of these peoples understand the positive values of their common heritage.

As a people with distinct biological underpinnings, Africans could create the relevant industries that would meet their physiological needs. For example, advances in molecular biology are beginning to have implications in the identification of possible African 'homes' of African-Americans. Moreover, as some diseases vary in penetrance and expressivity, due to the biological blue prints that characterize ancestry, concerted studies within African groups are warranted to find the effective treatments and cures to diseases that may affect this race more than others. The descriptions of skin diseases on the Internet, for example, do not reflect the fact that the patient's skin colour could be different from the traditional template.

Since the U.S. today remains the only superpower nation and the nation most sought after in trade alliances, developing countries could rely on their descendants whose birthright includes the machinery of the U.S. and their countries of origin to develop a fair representation of their interests in the corridors of the American political economy and capital markets. The Constituency for Africa (CFA), a Washington, DC-based organization, is an example of the Diaspora groups that inform and educate Americans about African issues. The CFA has been at the centre of American efforts in addressing the HIV/AIDS plague in Africa and the developing world; this organization, in collaboration with the U.S. Congressional Black Caucus and others within the U.S. Congress, developed a platform to push for strategic AIDS funding around the world, especially in Africa, to increase public awareness, and to address the global nature of the crisis. This led to congressional approval of the Global AIDS and Tuberculosis Relief Act of 2000 (or the AIDS Marshall Plan Trust Fund Legislation) to fight AIDS and fund a new World Bank AIDS Trust (Anderson, 2000); the bill was signed by President Clinton in the summer of 2000.

Seeing the benefits of activities such as those of the Constituency for Africa, U.S. Representative Carolyn Kilpatrick (Democrat, Detroit) lamented, during a

House subcommittee hearing on Africa ("Improving the Health of Africa") in September 1999 that African governments do not have effective lobby machinery in place in Washington, DC. The same could be said of African representations in Geneva, Ottawa, London, Paris, Tokyo, Berlin, Nordic countries, and elsewhere. African nations have diplomatic missions in these cities, but they may lack the critical human resources to engage in effective representation of their knowledge opportunities to their host nation's institutions.

Contrary to Representative Carolyn Kilpatrick's observations about the absence of an effective African lobby in Washington, it has been revealed that African governments, mostly oil-producing nations and those with difficult relations with the U.S. administration, spend millions of dollars on lobbyists, with the hope of influencing U.S. policy and perceptions of their nations (Lobe, 2001). These activities were deduced from the disclosure statements that U.S. lobbyists are required to file under the Foreign Agents Registration Act (FARA). While many nations and firms engage in lobbying, Africa is relatively new to the field and is probably wasting money or getting very little returns from the amount paid to lobbyists, compared to the activities of grassroots organizations in the U.S.

Civil society groups can point at some of their achievements in lobbying their government machinery: Bread For The World (http), another Washington, DC-based NGO, as a participant in the broad and growing national networks of public and private organizations, took credit for the bi-partisan support in the U.S. Senate Foreign Relations Committee toward the 'Hunger to Harvest Resolution: A Decade of Concern for Africa' that was introduced by Senators Chuck Hagel (Republican-Nebraska) and Patrick Leahy (Democrat-Vermont) in June 2001, and the companion resolution (H. Con. Res. 102) in the House of Representatives that was introduced by Representatives Jim Leach (Republican-Iowa) and Donald Payne (Democrat-NJ) in April 2001. Bread For The World would like to see the U.S. government adequately fund and bring presidential leadership to a global effort to cut widespread hunger and poverty in sub-Saharan Africa, the only region in the world where hunger is widespread and increasing. According to the organization, of the $15.2 billion that the U.S. spends in foreign aid, only about $775 million is spent on long-term poverty-focused development programs for sub-Saharan Africa.

The African-American leadership in the Miami-Dade area, and the Foundation for Democracy in Africa, another Washington, DC-based African-centred NGO, have also been able to integrate African issues into the concerns of the Office of the Mayor of Miami-Dade. Each year since 1998, Africans, African-Americans, and other Americans converge in Miami to brainstorm on economic cooperation between the two worlds. The Port of Miami, which has been a gateway in American trade with Latin America and the Caribbean, has established a sister-port relationship with the Port of Dakar, Senegal, as a result of these interactions. However, 'Miami as Gateway to Africa,' would mean more than moving the goods and products from the U.S. to Africa. The interaction between Africa and the U.S., *via* Miami, could also ensure development of critical knowledge bridges between the two worlds for blending knowledge systems for local innovation within Africa.

Connectivity between schools in Africa and those of other African communities outside the continent could also foster a shared vision among the younger African generations, regarding knowledge about local issues, lifestyles, and cultures in each other's zone. Establishment of real information gateways with convergent media would allow each community of Africans to learn about the opportunities, challenges, social and cultural attributes of each other. The African-American Research and Cultural Center at the Broward County Library (Florida) has begun establishment of such cultural links with African and Caribbean nations (Building Bridges, 2000), which is a good beginning in cultural documentation and knowledge sharing among African groups.

Developing nations could pool resources and partner with the grassroots organizations that can champion the interests of their citizens in the policy centres to embark on effective lobbying. They could take the initiative of identifying issues about which a particular foreign nation, technology, or capital market could facilitate related activities in the identified region. This concept would also include developing the intellectual options on development that can be fed to the diplomatic missions of developing countries in advanced economies. The financial limitations experienced by diplomatic missions of developing nations abroad have restricted their capacity to function with the full spectrum of intellectuals that would have covered areas that are not political, such as science and technology. Developing country interest groups could develop and influence foreign governments' internationalism in the respective regions, through formulating guidelines for science and technology investments and other development themes that these regions would require to achieve sustainable technological sophistication in their local economies. The frameworks developed by these interest groups could be lobbied with various portfolios within the industrialized economy, for example external affairs, international trade, higher education, science and industry, agriculture, environment and fisheries, and parliamentary committees, trade and investment communities, international development agencies and international NGOs, knowledge communities such as academic and research, and public information and media houses of the host nation.

EDUCATION AND TALENT GROOMING

Western education, combined with other sectors such as technology and management economics, has been able to create the most successful civilization in many comparisons. Other regions aspire to the successes of the Western economy, for example for its economic, political, technological, and social advancements at the personal, institutional, national, and global states. Western technology has been able to restore severed limbs onto their rightful places, replace human organs, produce artificial blood, make the deaf hear, and permit leg amputees to participate in track and field events at major athletics championship meetings, apart from other technological successes that have benefited the global community. As much as the world has seen advancements in all disciplines of technology and engineering, economics, social and political administration and management, and other disciplines since Plato's time, human intelligence and innovation have not been able to create the ideal society—Atlantis (Lakeshore Technologies, 1996)—that Plato exhorted human intelligence towards. In spite of the successes of modern education, it is agreeable that no human community has reached a sustainable state. The current states of technological and economic prosperity are not able to provide for all communities or to individuals, or without endangering the environment while doing so. A major challenge still remains how best to create thinking machineries toward the ideal community.

Each succeeding state of technological innovations and economic growth is a result of the cumulative progress in understanding of nature, social organization, and ingenuity in engineering. The long history of innovation and reasoning reaches a critical state in a discipline now and then, and defines a long period in the entire human civilization, for example the *Renaissance* and the *Industrial Age.* The contribution of the present era has been described as the Digital Revolution. Therefore, the imprint of the present era on the human civilization pathway is an emphasis of digital communications technologies to enhance, with the prospect of increasing the knowledge proportion of activities and processes toward an ideal society. Modern communications have integrated large knowledge domains to create the highest power of generating solutions.

Advances in modern communications are being applied in the search for the original physical community of Atlantis that may or may not exist, but the tools could also be used to facilitate thought processes and influence the extent to which learning is able to accentuate the effects of the technological advancements in communications in creating new communities that mimic the legend of Atlantis. This demands a re-examination of the tools, methods, and processes in which knowledge is imparted in the wake of an increasing need for learning to make greater impact in personal, institutional, and societal goals.

The role of tutors, students, tools, and methods of learning need to be reprogrammed if learning is to be reformed.

While there are no standards by which the new academy could be established or operated, virtual education should not aim to clone the minds of learners, instead it should assist people in problem solving and teaching them how to learn. Virtual education could feature customized learning, and developing educational packages that would make schools relevant to local needs through adjustments in global knowledge for local impact. But as Morrison and Twigg (2001) observed, the vast majority of online courses are organized much like their on-campus equivalents; they are developed by individual faculty members with some support from the information technology staff and are offered within the timeframe of an academic semester or quarter. Many of the available online curricula follow traditional academic practices, where 'students' are given a syllabus to go and read or research, and asked to return and discuss the content. They also noted that the current versions of virtual education are evaluated by traditional student satisfaction methods, and for the most part virtual education programming is based on using information technology tools as a marginal enhancement of the *status quo*. Rossman therefore suggested that virtual education should emphasize learner-centred, not professor-centred education—learning that is tailored to each individual and community—instead of sending lectures by telecommunications, top-down, one-way (Parker Rossman, personal communication, 2000).

Open Universities and Intellectual Freedoms

The ability of universities and other knowledge domains to translate current walled classrooms and laboratories into virtual interfaces that have local, regional, and global interactions should become a core feature in the strategic perspectives of *open* universities. These institutions could create think-tanks that collect, analyse, integrate, and advance knowledge from multi-dimensional perspectives to define the position of the institution and the community it is supposed to serve. The research underlying the advances in technology, management, and social behaviour in the current state of global prosperity emanated from university campuses and research parks, mostly of the industrialized economies, but only a few universities can be credited with leadership in the key research advances in human civilization. Many universities, unfortunately, do not portray the image of knowledge hubs, where the transition between the classroom and the impact group of university research are visible as 'research parks' in significant proportions. Notably, there is a disjunction between the activities of small and medium-size enterprises and other sectors of local economies and knowledge institutions such as universities. Thus a university professor may ascend from the academic environment to a top position of a major policy institute, government, or a research outfit of a trans-national corporation (TNC). An alternative to the relocation of faculty from the university environment could be the translation of the knowledge capital of the professor into a think-tank or knowledge solutions provider in the local environment, with simultaneous deliverables to the TNC and generation of opportunities for the local community. Such 'localization' of global businesses could facilitate growth of small businesses that may complement universities as knowledge hubs; it could also reduce corporate vertical structures into horizontal formats. That is, a knowledge hub would have 'satellite' or smaller hubs that are diffused around the main hub to spur interactivity of university and other communities of knowledge-industry, research, service and trade, homes, and communities.

While this may be the case, institutional collaborations at many universities are often centred on the interests of an individual faculty, who often does not have sufficient resources to conduct all the functions of teaching, graduate student advisory, research team leadership, and outreach within and beyond the community simultaneously. What is needed is a strategic interface among individuals, institutions, industry, and communities at local and global levels, and their constitution into knowledge blocs, hence the role of facilitators and knowledge brokers.

The private sector is also increasing its presence in the education sector because they have realized that institutions could not grow without continuous learning and innovation internally. Many groups, especially TNCs, are developing their own learning environments as 'corporate universities' to develop an intelligent workforce that can drive their organizations toward the future world.

The development community could also begin to integrate their knowledge programs into open development universities as their version of the corporate university. As Stiglitz observed, the quality of human resources at the major global development institutions can be poor. Stiglitz described some of the personnel of some international development institutions as "third-rank students from first-rate universities" (Stiglitz, 2000: 3) particularly with respect to the cultural, political and economic features that characterize the various blocs of the developing world, with grave impacts on the local economies. At present, each development agency might be evolving its own knowledge programs, with minor activities in inter-agency knowledge sharing systems.

In the transition of international development agencies, including the multilateral development agencies, into knowledge institutions, institutions need to cherish and practise some of the principal features of a nourishing knowledge environment, particularly the independence of mind from institutional control or academic freedom. The current regimes of some institutions emphasize loyalty of employees to their employers and not necessarily to the impact zones of the institutions' programming.

The traditional universities guarantee the basic academic and research freedoms, which allow them to conduct research, build networks, and communicate findings without censorship by their institutions. On the other hand, some of the development institutions that are attempting to transform themselves into knowledge organizations and knowledge sharing control the dissemination of research findings by their employees. Two university professors from the same department of the same university could argue on opposite sides of major issues such as genetic engineering of food crops and issues related to agro-chemical industry giants, without the persecution of the one who espouses views that may be contrary to the department's private-sector partners. However, there are no standards to protect this academic freedom from private sector partners when university faculties participate in joint research with the private-sector or the development community. A medical researcher at a reputable Canadian medical research institution who was studying the effects of a new drug expressed concerns about the drug, disagreed with the drug maker over the benefits and risks of the drug, but the drug maker attempted to prevent the publications of her conclusions; she briefed the public about her findings, and as a result, the drug manufacturer abrogated her participation in the study. This incident led to a protracted dispute in the academic and judicial circles. The actions of the researcher were later vindicated in a report commissioned by the Canadian Association of University Teachers, which concluded that the scientist receive redress from her employers "for the unfair treatment she has received" (Cesca, 2001: A13). This and other issues led the editors of the world's leading medical journals, including the *Journal of the American Medical Association,* the *New England Journal of Medicine, Lancet* (the British medical journal), and the *Canadian Medical Association Journal* to jointly declare that they would no longer publish articles in which scientific objectivity is in question (Picard, 2001). The journals are concerned that the growing interventionist approach of pharmaceutical companies, and to some extent governments, is leaving researchers constrained and ethically compromised; they also contended that researchers, not funders, should have control over the design of studies, access to raw data, free rein to interpret findings, the choice to publish their results or not, and the protection of their intellectual integrity of the process.

Issues of similar nature abound in other research partnerships that involve universities and the private sector of other industries, such as the agro-chemical and agricultural biotechnology research industries. The development community may also be hesitant to extend the ideals of freedom of thought and expression to their staff during the transition of these institutions to knowledge institutions; according to a Washington reporter of the *Financial Times* newspaper, "the World Bank launched a disciplinary investigation into the conduct of one its most published economists, William Easterly, after an article he wrote was printed in the *Financial*

Times" (Dunne, 2001: 3) on the grounds that Easterly failed to obtain clearance to write the article. It is noteworthy that the World Bank had no objection about Easterly's book on which the article was based; indeed, the World Bank's website contains references to the book (World Bank, http). However, as the writer of the *Financial Times* noted, this might have been the case of an author who did not express the common view position in which all in a team were supposed to agree on a single voice in describing the institution's country programs.

The institutions that attempt to control the knowledge activities of their members could end up as the losers, as they would be unable to attract the best brains, retain them, or increase institutional capabilities and efficiencies; indeed, such controls may stifle the creativity inherent in their human resources. The nations that attempted to control the minds of their citizens through the banning of literature and the imprisonment of journalists, writers, and others whose views might be perceived as anti-establishment are not the beacons of hope for any civilized community and are generally considered as pariah states.

These issues reflect the need for defining the values of global knowledge sharing in development, partnerships, and participation of non-traditional schools in the search for new knowledge and the dissemination of knowledge. These issues cannot be addressed from individual institutional perspectives alone; there is a need to guarantee the publication and outreach rights of those who have some knowledge to share as the world attempts to design a system for the free-flow of information and knowledge. Partnership among different sectors in generating new knowledge also brings with it some limitations. The interests and the positions of the various partners may differ, and the ability to carve common interests would be challenging, especially to assure the simultaneous satisfaction of the multi-stakeholders, and for the partnership to have a unique form of synergy in generating new knowledge. While some members and their products and services are expected to operate under competitive market structures, which require protection of the institution's knowledge assets and products from competitors, others in the partnership may be public institutions that face the scrutiny, accountability, and responsibility of tax payers and electoral districts, and the need to justify that their activities *are* effective in insuring human security in their impact communities.

The participation of non-traditional educational units in the emerging global knowledge sharing system also requires that the new entrants understand existing frameworks that underlie the exchange of ideas, especially the access, utilization, and dissemination of ideas and services that may be protected under intellectual property agreements. The two Schumacher brothers of the Formula One Racing (Formula1.com, http) circuit in 2001 may provide some light on the intricate nature of sharing knowledge: the senior brother, Michael, drives for the Scuderia Ferrari Marlboro team, while junior brother, Ralf, drives for the BMW Williams team.

Michael is renowned as the best F1 driver the race has known, and under normal circumstances may be inclined to share the knowledge underlying his accomplishments to his younger brother, but the two racing teams they drive for are competing against each other in the construction of their equipment and race strategies. Such a situation illustrates the separation between what others could know about the research and development activities of partnership members and what may be the sole knowledge of members within a team, which may not be shared with others whether they are from the same birth parents or not. The need for knowledge protection is to enable the originators have the competitive market advantages of their investments in knowledge creation and for them to recoup the investment costs before others share in the knowledge.

The development community needs to encourage the development of such knowledge sharing standards, and instill into its members the value in giving credit to information sources and respecting the intellectual rights of researchers.

As the bilateral and multilateral development institutions attempt to train their staff in knowledge sharing ideals and methods, they would also need to develop such programs in conjunction with universities that train the traditional international development scholar so that they would have the same understandings before the student graduates. Moreover, an open development university could also be the decentralization of the United Nations University system, and bring their activities closer to the impact communities.

An open development university could coordinate and ensure that continuous education becomes entrenched in development practice, particularly as integrative thinking and problem-solving methods through access to information, data mining, analysis, application, evaluation, and research communications, so that programs can permeate the multiple sectors they were expected to impact and create a sustainable advancement in the community.

Reforming Education

Transforming formal education into continuous learning systems would recognize that there are schools in many remote areas of many developing countries, but the grammar school system may have produced a dependent educated population, most of whom expect 'government' to employ them, and often think that politics is the solution to every problem; African newspapers and magazines reflect this aberration, devoting all their writings to political events and very little to the impact of technologies in the livelihoods of the rural majority. Once the young university graduate or post-secondary college graduate is employed, there are few opportunities for further learning in any formal way, even though new technologies and management processes are developed in the global economy.

A major challenge that developing nations face in the transition of their economies into knowledge-based activities is the willingness of those in their middle and higher levels of human resources to learn new ways of doing things, as such personnel often consider themselves learned; the saddest thing is that many in this group have closed their minds to the possibility that they may not be well-equipped to develop new schemes that would effect changes in their institutional operations and deliverables. Upon all their learning in formal educational systems, they are reduced to handling papers and files as employees; as researchers and teachers, they lack modern tools. Moreover, the educational system in many regions of the developing world was based on a type of psychological warfare in which students were made to believe that the ideal path and a rise through the academic ladder through university was the only way to success. Thus the parallel fields of nation building, such as an intelligent community of technicians, teachers, nurses, marketing and general accounting, and so forth, were not popularized alongside the grammar school programs. Those who could not gain university admission accepted enrollment in the other fields as second grade, and work conditions reflected this philosophy: school teachers, extension officers, nurses, secretaries, the police, and similar services are among the lowest paid in the developing world. Second-cycle technical and vocational institutes concerning office management, accounting, tools and engineering, hotel and food industry, agriculture and health management, and extension services, however, are critical in middle-level human resource development for the private sector, government, business community, and trade sectors. The efficiency of such competent human resources in management and technologies would determine the perceived extension of developing countries into the global market.

In "Education Yesterday, Education Tomorrow" (Daedalus, 1998), a group of scholars in the U.S. considered the state of education in the U.S., reflecting on whether educational reforms were necessary, and what reform models could be evolved. Some of the observations of the panellists could impact educational reform through connectivity and knowledge flow plans for the developing world. Panel members were challenged to deliberate on why education had remained static in its attributes while other sectors of the American economy, notably communications, health care, and agriculture, had undergone tremendous innovation and rejuvenation. In response, some noted that educational reform should ensure that the products of learning and research should not remain in ivory towers but be diffused in a manner that would cause change in the learner and stimulate the desire to learn; some observed that education is not a field that anyone with minimum experience could undertake, as multiple intelligence is the goal of learning. John, for example, writing on "The Politics of Innovation" in the same volume, offered the dynamism of communications in America, which includes influence of politics, a broad mandate, and competition underlying change as a measure against which reforms in education could be weighed (John, 1998). The combination of these values with the technological innovations in the learning environment that is afforded by convergent communications could provide a rare opportunity for educational reforms.

Telecommunications are expected to make learning more flexible in time schedules (commencement, duration, and graduation), less space-based, and to be distributed in the format that is most suited to the student. Professors and students who may be separated by oceans could also be drawn into the virtual classroom *via* Web-based systems, CD-ROM, HF-radio broadcasts, video documentations, and text-based manuals to supplement the expertise and resources of the local schools in content development and course deliveries. The current learning environment in many developing economies terrorizes some pupils as it quickly discerns the 'brainy' from the 'deadhead,' but it provides no further assistance to the latter. It is not that the majority in the developing world are incapable of learning, but rather, their learning resources and teaching methods have been inadequate and inefficient. In the period of personalized learning enabled by IT, the West African Examination Council (WAEC) reported that there was a "massive show of poor knowledge on the rules of grammar" (The Independent, 1999) among Nigerian candidates in the WAEC senior high school certificate examination, while the committee of vice-chancellors in Ghana revealed that Ghanaian university teachers did not have chalk to write. Learning does not have to be that hard, and there are tools to assist learning and teaching; IT could allow customized learning for all pupils and thereby activate the learning skills of both the bright and challenged students simultaneously. The challenge lies not in the ability to design such learning systems, but the willingness of stakeholders to relearn the purpose and practice of imparting knowledge that could reward the learner and enrich society.

The goals of connectivity for education in developing nations would include interaction with communities for life-long learning systems as part of education that is relevant to people's needs, and would be to strive toward reinventing people's attitudes and institutional mechanisms, educate society about learning new methods of production and distribution, mobilize the productive capacities of villages and civil society organizations, and rebuild a society of learners and institutions of engineering of tools and processes. Community life-long learning systems could be designed so that the poor person's learning system would enable deprived communities to develop the brainpower to drive their local economies and enhance global prosperity.

Virtual education with locally relevant curriculum requires a significant re-examination of program development, student enrollment, course delivery and evaluation. School connectivity is not necessarily to target the same age groups alone, but to create an integrated and interactive knowledge flow among schools of all levels and nurturing community development, research, manufacturing, and commerce. In contemplating new learning systems, stronger emphasis should be placed on the early stages of education and not disproportionately on institutions of higher learning. Primary schools are full of young minds that have little strength without guidance, but are more adept, especially regarding IT, and can be groomed into leadership positions in the knowledge community. In creating a new culture, where information and knowledge determine the state of civilization, it is prudent to mend tender minds full of creativity; to change old minds from what they already know and stick to, however, would be an uphill task. Without a strong foundation in learning realized in the younger generation, concentrating on older minds would only bring more confusion and self-gratification.

Access to education that is relevant to peoples' needs has continued to be limited at all levels in many developing countries, with African countries experiencing the lowest literacy rates in the world (UNECA, 1998); upon all the expansion of education across the world, illiteracy has increased in the poorer countries (Soedjatmoko, 1989). The most crucial stages in human education are the early ages, as this would determine a community's ability to rejuvenate itself; unfortunately, the primary school age population is the most deprived in knowledge resources in poor nations. The United Nations Children's Fund (UNICEF) reported that about 20 percent of primary school age children in developing countries are not in school. South Asia and sub-Saharan Africa accounted for 46 million each, or about 80 percent of this number (UNICEF, 2000). The primary school age group in Africa is increasing at about 3.3 percent annually, while school enrollment for the group is rising by only 2.2 percent. To address Africa's chronic educational deficiency, the Assembly of Heads of State and Governments of the Organization of African Unity adopted the Decade for Education 1997-2006 with the objective of removing obstacles that impede progress toward 'Education for All' (UNECA, 1998). The international community as a whole has also resolved to strengthen educational systems at all levels in the 1995 Copenhagen Social Summit Plan of Action. They called for the creation of the necessary conditions for ensuring universal access to basic education and lifelong educational opportunities, and in removing economic and socio-cultural obstructions to the exercise of this right. This, they thought, was the basis of an open political and economic system, which demands that all have access to knowledge, education, and information.

Conventional teaching and learning methods have become inadequate in the wake of deepening illiteracy caused by a lack of well-trained teachers and a shrinking resource allocation toward education (d'Orville, 1996). Innovative teaching and learning schemes are therefore required in developing countries for the development of the human and institutional capacities that are necessary for the evolution of their civilizations through education in the face of globalization. In addition, facilitators and knowledge mentors may be essential in guiding the problem-solving abilities of the young, and underprivileged groups; compare, for example, the tutorial help that children may receive in the home of a low-income and poorly educated parent versus a well-educated family. Therefore, the idea of knowledge mentorship, provided by an ageless corps of facilitators, could be designed to supplement the expertise and resources of schools in these regions.

The rapid advancements in IT herald unprecedented potentials for the resolution of the education and human resources problems of developing nations. IT-led knowledge for development presumably would provide university students in developing countries with up-to-date research and academic outputs; this would impact the quality of their dissertations, and when these dissertations reflect the needs of the majority in their local communities, university learning and research could impact commercial research and development initiatives, industrial outputs, and management. However, like all other global technological advancements and innovations, the levels of development, acquisition, and utilization of IT in teaching and learning in these regions lag behind the rest of the world; about 500 students in the engineering department of Kwame Nkrumah University of Science and Technology, in Kumasi, Ghana, for example, were reported to share one computer in the year 2000 (GNA, 2000). The department comprises the mechanical, electrical, civil, geodetic, agriculture, and chemical engineering faculties, with a total of 1,500 students, and this university is the only accredited engineering university in the country of about 18 million people.

The rural-urban tension is also an important factor in reinventing schools in the Information Age. The Information Age offers the prospect that all pupils within a nation-state, including those in the rural areas, would be able to access the same high quality of course content that is currently reserved for urban elite schools. Access of rural pupils to the high quality of content is essential because regardless of where pupils obtained their basic education—rural or urban, well equipped or not—all must meet the minimum requirements in national examinations to advance on the educational ladder.

The prospects for creating the environment that would facilitate these computer-assisted distributed learning systems were buttressed by the remarks of the president of the World Bank, James Wolfensohn, to the Second Global Knowledge Conference:

> *"It is very possible and indeed likely that within the space of 5 years we will have low flying satellites capable of delivering wide band communication to villages in every part of the world. It will be possible for us to arrange for communications to poor communities ... on basis that will be free, because many of the companies have*

indicated to us that for poor communities and for education, connectivity will be free. So one could imagine in the years to come, people in villages throughout the world having access to knowledge, to experience, to advise, to guidance, in real time" (Wolfensohn, 2000, http)

However, many school connectivity programs at present focus on schools in the capital cities and other urban areas as much as the urban centres have traditionally attracted the best teachers and resources. The notion that every innovation and introduction of new technologies should begin with the urban centres has meant deprivation of rural areas although the majority of pupils are in the rural areas. Hence, education in rural areas should be the challenge and opportunity for developing countries and the telecommunications sector in order to test the possibility of reaching remote areas with high-quality education and to realise the universality in 'education for all.'

Considering these issues, the collaborative regional group of the emerging Global University System (GUS) intends "to foster youngsters around the world for the 'Virtual State' of the Twenty-First Century, with competition for excellence through affordable and accessible broadband Internet. GUS aims to prepare children, through education, for the transformation of the world, from the industrial age where obedience predominated, into the knowledge age, where creativity and competence predominate" (Utsumi, 1999: 1). The tenets of the African component of GUS pay special attention to basic schools with the intent of beginning the process of leveraging human development, because it aims to reinvent from the roots so that the top may be nourish to flourish and blossom. If society is concerned about the widening gap between nations of the South and North, the process of leveraging could begin with the youngest generation so that several decades later, children from a wide region of the world might begin to realize equity in livelihood opportunities.

Education delivery could become more competitive as more students enroll in virtual curricula and the ability to select courses across diverse campuses within the same learning period increases. However, the purpose of education would remain an issue of the local area, as knowledge needs would vary by the philosophical, technical, and other attributes and aspirations of the community; the principles that underlie fields and disciplines of studies would however remain universal. Canada and the U.S. are among nations that recognize the localization of education and have made education an issue of provincial or state jurisdiction. However, curricula are becoming global in reach through virtuality with MIT setting the stage in announcing that all materials for nearly all MIT courses would be freely available on the Internet over the next 10 years (MIT, 2001). The availability of such online educational packages from external sources in nurturing local knowledge communities could satisfy the components of curricula that relate to universal thematic principles; the relevance of education itself would require translation of the principles into local situations, just as schoolteachers may have the same general principles textbooks, but they often make their own notes to demonstrate the principles with local applications.

The design of electronic learning environments for the developing world should establish a relationship between learning in the community to the notion of transforming hitherto information-starved communities into continuously evolving and learning societies. It should contemplate innovations within the formal and informal sectors such as the knowledge of local trade and artisan groups, and the practitioners of rural occupations such as the manufacture of farm implements, agricultural production, food processing, pottery making, and marketing.

It is essential that lifelong learning systems integrate formal curriculum with skills acquisition and upgrading. Thus the role of national library systems, faculties of education and communications, and ministries of education and information services or their variations could be revised to reflect the need for modern information gathering, processing into knowledge, and applications in actualization of individuals, communities, and institutions in the various aspects of sustainable communities.

Lifelong Learning and the Youth

Lifelong learning programs in the community should not lose sight of the young, since many people are 'done' school by their teenage years in rural communities of the poor economies. This age-group in many developing countries though is faced with serious difficulties, such as high incidences of sexually transmitted diseases (STDs), teenage pregnancy, prostitution, lost opportunities, and general hopelessness. They sing and say they are waiting for The Lord, as their only hope. A growing number are making urban streets their homes, but their civilization's future is stored in them. These insecurities among the youth are indicative of the downward spiral of the poor and their communities.

A lack of opportunities in the rural areas forces unprepared young people to urban areas without an adequate education or skills-of-life to enter and function successfully an urban set-up. The pyramidal education structure does not have safety nets for the large masses that drop out, and programs for assisting the weak in learning are almost non-existent.

If developing countries pay attention to their youth, their communities will be vibrant, else they could devour their community resources. The youth are many; in some rural areas, about 43 percent of the population is younger than 15 years of age and could become desperate if situations continue to deteriorate. The young in the developing world should not be told to simply 'go and farm' or to 'go back to the village,' but the farming tools are primitive, and the rains might fail. This large percentage of energetic but idle, disenchanted, and poorly educated populations of developing countries have serious implications for sustainable development in these regions. However, the momentum of these groups could be channelled into productive labour if proper schemes in education, skill acquisition, and tools are designed and distributed around strategic national issues. The dangers posed to environmental security with such demographics in light of food inadequacy include declaration of rage on the environment in search of livelihoods whereby strong and able-bodied young males have converted large portions of land into bare ground by extracting trees for charcoal production to feed urban consumption. This means to income generation also destroys watersheds and arable land in the process.

The lack of opportunities for the young in the developing world is highlighted in the desperate efforts they make to enter the industrialized nations regardless of the inherent dangers in doing so. The story of two young boys from Guinea, Yaguine Koita and Fode Tounkara, 14 and 15 years old, respectively, made the headline news across the world in the summer of 1999 but perhaps has already been forgotten: they sneaked into the landing gear area of a Sabena airliner in a desperate attempt to reach Europe. Although they were frozen to death (Gras, 1999) by the cold high-altitude temperatures in their unpressurized space, they carried with them a letter to the world. Their message was: "Help us. We suffer a lot in Africa. We have no rights as children. We have no food. We have war and illness. We have schools but lack education. We want to study so we can be like you, in Africa" (Samara, 1999, http).

The group of youths, the 'deadheads,' whom the grammar schools did not make room for, and who were consequently denied opportunities of higher education, constitute the skilled labour force for many developing countries—tool makers, masons, carpenters, fitter-mechanics, chauffeurs, and woodcarvers, among others. They are also a significant group in the arts and crafts industry, including the producers of the *Kente* fabric, which has an international appeal. This group is perhaps the largest dispossessed group who are left to fodder for themselves in the urban sprawls or villages and who have been sentenced to a state of 'survival of the fittest.' Commercial vehicle operators, fitter mechanics, and those who chauffeur the rich in developing countries have only basic education at best, and to them vehicle ownership or its operation still represents achievement of higher status that is defined as possession of a technological device that mystifies the ordinary, hence an over exuberance in its use; they drive with brute force and not with their minds. Some of the greatest risks on the roads in developing countries are therefore due to poor maintenance and the misbehaviour of vehicle operators. News from the developing world is often about disasters, including ferry accidents in Asia, and road accidents in Africa that kill or injure so many.

Substantive connectivity schemes could enhance business opportunities for the youth, who constitute more than 50 percent of the population in some developing countries, and could provide them with the tools and skills of life; this would help them to avoid the temptation of falling into the hands of militia groups that parade villages and maim the innocent in the struggle to have access to the small pie.

The militia groups that were involved in the vicious civil war in Sierra Leone included about 10,000 children, some of who participated in some of the heinous crimes against humanity, such as the amputation of about 3,750 innocent civilians including other children; about 656 of this number have had both arms or both legs hacked off (IRN, 2001). The issue of war amputees in developing nations is tragic in many ways of which economic deprivation ranks very high, considering that manual labour is the principal productive tool and livelihood means.

The ability to operationalize IT to empower the youth to function as an intelligent human resource capital would be a testament to the ingenuity in connectivity for knowledge sharing programs. If the young are not provided with the mechanisms for self-actualization through skill development and channels to access global capital to build functional workshops and market their products globally, they would continue to become fodder for militia groups. Given the proper training and resources, developing country economies would benefit tremendously from this large reserve of labour.

Creating digital opportunities for the young should be treated differently from when they were left on their own to fend for themselves either in school or in apprenticeships and thereafter. Concerted efforts are required for capital acquisition, skill development, product standardization and certification, trademark protection, and provision of trade points to empower youth groups and their occupational outputs to capture a significant share of the global market.

FOOD OR IT? : CONVERGENT COMMUNICATIONS AND RURAL AGRICULTURE

A central issue in information and communication technologies in rural poverty alleviation in developing countries has been which choice to make: *Food or IT?* Some point out that the poor need food, and wonder how the 'computer hen' could lay edible eggs. But the proponents of IT-led knowledge for development have the understanding that connectivity could convey pertinent information that would enable the small-scale poultry farmer to learn and employ improved poultry management techniques from global sources with an adjustment for the local environment to manage the local poultry industry more efficiently and to produce sufficient birds and eggs for the local market in the least. This could be done in a manner that does not imply the indulgence in the high-input production systems of the advanced nations that are coming under scrutiny due to farm-related public health and ethical concerns.

In reality, the issue is not a choice between food and IT, but how the two affect each other. Telecommunication applications such as GIS are being used to map the resources of rural agriculture, for example the vegetation, soil nutrient status, and other physical properties, so that interventions can be more closely targeted to the community's agricultural assets. Food and IT could involve development of 'virtual extension officer' toolkits that would integrate agricultural extension into the global research and information community so that extension personnel are not intellectually isolated in the communities they serve. The two aspects of the food crises of poor communities—quantity and quality—result from a lack of improved farm inputs and processing methods, and both could be addressed in knowledge sharing systems that are facilitated by IT. Connectivity in agriculture could increase the knowledge for management of farm inputs such as land, nutrients, animal feed, weather and rainfall, tools, the genetic component of crop and animal stocks for production and processing, storage, and distribution methods.

The amount of learning that a small-scale rural farmer in poor communities has to undergo to reconcile indigenous and un-intellectualized practices with sustainable production challenges and environmental security requires that knowledge from a multitude of sources converged with the farmer as easily digestible farmer-centred agricultural research and information system. Pooling such information and discussing the farmer's needs and opportunities with the most knowledgeable groups could be accomplished in an IT environment that is customized to the knowledge-absorptive capacity of the indigenous system and the provision of interactive problem-solving workspaces.

Putting farmers at the centre of agricultural research and extension as part of the farmer responsive mechanisms for extension and research, which some development agencies would like to undertake in their food security programming for communities in need, could be achieved through putting farmers' assets and needs—knowledge, tools, processing, capital, commerce, and research themes and outputs—into national agricultural programming of schools, research, trade, and industry, through innovative communications linkages.

The philosophy of the rural farmer in the developing world, which is rooted in an indigenous knowledge system, is also crucial in the adoption of new methods. Agricultural information and communications in this regard could profile the farm household through a targeted analysis of the family's agricultural knowledge and capital assets and opportunities. This could lead to the design of direct interventions that would ensure a transition from small-scale culture to self-sufficiency and above-poverty income levels for the farm household.

The outcome of the farm household profile could become a central input in micro-credit programs; the combination of such schemes with other inputs requirements such as labour, knowledge, tools, value-addition, capital, and market dynamics would enable customized interventions through financial and production management and planning for each farm household. Would labour, for instance, be the determined requirement for optimal productivity by the particular farmer, sources for the required labour input would be seen to include the indigenous social capital systems of group labour mobilization. Similarly, for financial assistance, the community could be grouped along social capital systems that may exist within the community. Credit and loan guarantees could be provided by the development partners based on the need assessment.

Each farm household that is included in pilot programs could be trained to record major daily activities, challenges, and opportunities. In the case of households that are illiterate in the major languages of the Internet, village schoolteachers or personnel of the bureau of (indigenous) languages could act as information liaison officers. Each farm household could be assigned a code, preferably an E-mail account whether or not connectivity is accessible, to enable maintenance of the same identification code at all levels of communication regarding the individual households, and for long-term programming. Local Area Networks or Intranets could enable community broadcasts from where the participant can retrieve and enter personal information. These access points could be printed bulletins or local news groups, based on geographic location, occupation, and linguistic characteristics.

The daily or weekly journals created by households regarding occupations and methods or the means by which they practise agricultural activities might include the features of major milestones in the cultivation process, such as the type and amount of farm inputs, information on pests and disease build-up, and weather broadcasts, among others that could be obtained through formal programs. Other journal entries may include how land was obtained, when and how cropping fields were prepared, the size and location of farms, days of rainfall, sources of planting material, activities during various phases of crop development, the tools employed, any visible pest and disease occurrences and how controlled, and the general farming system including other crops inter-planted and when, harvest dates and harvest procedure, storage, marketing, proportion of produce that is consumed and the amount that is traded, and the revenue that they generate from farm-based activities.

The farmer's thoughts and queries could be collected on schedule with allowance for rapid interventions where necessary, through information guides provided to the liaison officers and extension officers from district and national agricultural offices. Agricultural extension personnel could indicate the periods they visited farmers, the subject and outcomes of their discussions with farmers, and provide technical data, such as weather forecasts and knowledge about other physical elements—soil type in the area, weekly rainfall and temperature, any known pest and disease outbreaks, and inputs supplied from regional offices.

The entries by farm households and extension officers are relevant in the identification of the farming pattern and the efficiency of services, for example whether or not government and donor programs reach the farmer, suitability of the farm location for the type of crop and how to improve soil and other physical properties, when disease and pest outbreaks are most likely and significant, and the interventions that may be required to increase the productivity of agriculture as a business.

National agricultural information hubs could integrate the support and services of all the related agricultural agencies and research centres. This would include the specialized divisions of the scientific and industrial research systems that are present in many developing countries; research units dedicated to crops, animals, soils, water, banking and commerce, and so forth exist in developing nations, but a major limitation remains the integration of the various task groups and their convergence with farmers' domains.

For each unit in the network, a liaison officer could be responsible for information flow. The network liaison could undertake activities such as updates of research output, flow of research requests from the extension personnel in the field and tracking of such requests, as well as dissemination of research findings back to a Virtual Extension Officer. An overall network officer at the regional hub would ensure communicating research requests that are unanswered at the local level to the appropriate global knowledge domain, and communicating the results back to local extension workers. This presumes that local extension personnel do not have direct communication access with such external bodies; however, proliferation of connectivity access points should eventually permit the local extension personnel to communicate directly with any knowledge hub.

The agricultural information system could involve information and knowledge repositories, which would constitute the Virtual Extension Officer as a guidebook for farmers, extension personnel, and agricultural researchers. All the observations made by agricultural extension personnel could be recorded in a district-reporting database for cross-referencing by other extension officers; it could also indicate the diagnostic abilities of the extension personnel to their supervisors and provide a basis for the career advancements of such workers.

Mass communication is desirable, but the input of farmers, the environment, and other productive attributes in farming are not universal; diseases do not invade all farms equally at the same time and space, and not all lands have the same productive capacity. Therefore, targeted information related to the assets, needs, and the micro-environment of the farmer would be ideal, and IT affords the opportunity to engage in this exercise.

E-BUSINESS CULTURE

Developing countries could take advantage of connectivity programs to develop a strong local business culture as a necessary process in contemplating their competitive position in the global economy. The strategic vision of a knowledge economy would seek to propagate the tendencies and attributes of innovation and realization of new opportunities to inspire its members to reach the heights that others have reached. It is essential that efforts in connectivity are not supplanted by e-commerce themes alone; moreover, computer-mediated business transactions could emphasize local distribution of goods, inter-regional trade, methods of product standardization, and access to start-up funds.

Private business is not new to developing countries; private business models drive the economies of rural communities in many of these economies. Families and clans may own the title to the land that members cultivate in rural communities, but individual households are required to make their own use of the land. While a community may employ the concept of group labour in agriculture, this scheme is only to enable the household to meet labour requirements. Furthermore, the social capital system returns the contribution made by other members within the social group; the currency may be different, but the principles of private ownership and responsibility are enshrined.

The concept of private business is quite pervasive in many developing nations and could be seen in roadside vendors whose items include confectionery, fruits, and water; traders who travel to agricultural areas to haul foodstuffs to markets; and others who cross national boundaries ferrying goods forth and back. Privately owned small and medium-size enterprises in tool manufacture, motor vehicle garages, mini-markets, export-import businesses, manufacturing, and about culture (the art, music, and craft industry) are major components of the business sector of these economies. The issues that hinder these businesses and their activities are similar to what the other sectors encounter—a lack of knowledge and capital resources to increase the value of deliverables, poor production capacity, and the ability of the market to support innovation and new product development. The input costs to many of these small-scale businesses are also high due to the high proportion of external knowledge or capital behind their product. For example the cost of importing machinery and parts for local repair of automobiles and the cost of fuel to operate transportation businesses while the revenue derived within the community with a low-purchasing power reduce the profit margin and the capital that could be re-invested in the growth of businesses. Some of these businesses might also have been founded on whimsies, without market survey prior to launch.

But the spirit of private business has been a part of many communities in developing nations, and these economies could capitalize on the existing enthusiasm of self-business to provide imaginative uses of electronic media that would increase the capacity of this sector.

Many of the poor economies are hoping that they can become major players in global trade if they are able to set up virtual shops to market their products. The export sector is an important component of all economies, but the type of activities and products would decide the value of the sector to the local economy and the share of global trade that the local economy occupies. A characteristic of the export commodities of developing nations is the lack of significant value addition, consequently these crude products have very little global market values. The evolution of the knowledge economies in the developing world similarly could have an export component, but the activities and products of the knowledge economy would be different from the failed theories of export promotion in which knowledge from the export sector did not create the widespread effect on other components of the local economy and social development. As a result, the issue of developing nations serving as offshore venues or locales for outsourcing activities for foreign knowledge economy needs alone should be critically examined. U.S. businesses were reported to have spent $5.5 billion in 2000 on outsourced products and services from countries such as India and Ireland, in very diverse fields—clerical workers, computer programmers, scientists and doctors—and the value of this business is expected to reach $17.6 billion by 2005. African countries are also beginning to enter the outsourcing business; American health insurance claims are likely to be processed in Ghana, through a business outsourcing in which Affiliated Computer Services of Dallas sends digital images of the information from Lexington (Kentucky) to Accra (Ghana) (Bray, 2001). The key in business outsourcing of this nature is the presence of low-wage workers; but the costs of energy, machinery, connectivity, and other equipment are not cheaper in poorer countries compared to the industrialized nations.

Local capacity building is often cited as a possible impact area of these outsourcing opportunities, but the experiences of these economies do not lend evidence to these assumptions. For these outsourcing activities to have a significant impact in the local economies, efforts are required to translate the foreign relationship into local economic activities that could utilize the knowledge that is acquired in the process to service local needs as well.

Outsourcing could benefit service providers in the developing world, but that should not be the emphasis of these economies when the world import demand for IT equipment and components is expected to exceed $1 trillion by 2005 (ITC, 2001); developing nations should consider the overall IT market including the manufacture of equipment as a niche that they could participate in and begin to develop their strategic roles. However, a survey of 50 'connected' small and medium enterprises in Southeast Asia, North Africa, the Middle East, and eastern Europe conducted by the International Trade Centre (U.N. Conference on Trade and Development / WTO) showed that few of the program managers considered Web strategy as integral to overall business activity, and many did not envision IT as a basic element in the long-term strategy of their businesses. A common reason for this apathy toward Web strategy among the respondents was the perception of the difficulties associated with introducing online financing and payments, among others. However, as virtual trading communities evolve, they develop their unique currencies. PayPal for example, which claims to have 16 million members world-wide, has created a real-time payment solution for communities around the world by building on the existing financial infrastructure of bank accounts and credit cards to enable businesses or consumers who have an E-mail address to "securely, conveniently, and cost-effectively send and receive payments online" (PayPal, 2002, http). Moreover, e-business competency does not pertain to electronic sales or payments alone; potential business partners and customers could glean information about the business specializations, products, location, philosophy, and other attributes; Web strategies are also important, considering that the Internet has become the business front office to an extent that it could challenge the shopping mall in the future.

Ghana, for instance, proposes to become the trade and investment hub of the West African sub-region as part of the country's Vision 2020 program. This program seeks to transform the country into a middle-income country by the year 2020. The program recognizes that the realization of this vision requires basic economic infrastructure that the government could not undertake alone; consequently, projects have been identified under various sectors, and the Ghana Investment Promotion Centre (GIPC, http) has been charged with promoting these projects and to attract the necessary capital investments. Despite the spread of Internet-based activities in the country, only two of the 79 projects that are listed on the Web page of the Ghana Investment Promotion Centre have E-mail addresses, and none of these businesses has a website of its own.

Business registration in developing countries could be combined with provision of E-mail addresses, designation of URLs, and a guide to businesses that may host portals for the business. Precedence has been established in designation of domain names, whereby businesses have been able to retrieve their names from *cybersquatters*. This could imply that all businesses are assigned a domain name by virtue of the entity's name. Additionally, for the developing nations in which public-sector activities are weak and lag behind the private sector in adopting innovation, it may be important for the public sector organizations of such economies to partner with the private sector. However, such nations employ several means to block some activities of the private sector as a way to guarantee the market of the public-sector business; for example African countries initially prevented the deployment of voice-over-Internet protocols (VoIP) as a way to protect the public telecommunications monopolies that are usually laggards in modern technologies. IT applications on the other hand are integrating the traditional telephone into the capabilities of the Internet and PC. The North American consumer was intrigued by such a campaign in which a mother had taken away the telephone privileges of her teenage daughter, but the joke was on her mother who was not aware that her daughter could still have a voice conversation with her friends *via* a PC and actually make fun of the 'punishment' meted out to her.

The practice in which each vendor hopes to set up a virtual shop and others would come and buy has spread to all economies, including one of the few remaining bastions of communism. The Cuban government is also cashing in on the e-commerce wave as its state-owned multi-purpose tourism corporation (Cubanacan) administers an Internet site by proxy, through a Canada-based enterprise that retails Cuban goods virtually (Newman, 2001). This arrangement, with all purchases processed in Canada, enables the patrons, mostly Cuban-Americans, to circumvent the U.S. economic embargo against Cuba.

E-commerce should be viewed as an aspect of a viable business culture and not as an end in itself; although e-commerce transactions may be on the ascent in some industrialized nations, businesses devoted to this application have been among those hardest hit by the downturn in the profitability of the telecommunications sector. In the U.S., about half of the adult population had made some purchase online by the end of the first quarter of 2001, mostly on travel tickets, clothing, and apparel. These e-commerce transactions amounted to about $3.5 billion in March 2001, and represented an increase of 36 percent over the previous year (NetRatings, 2001). However, e-commerce companies accounted for 109 of the 210 dot-com companies that closed in 2000 in the U.S. (Evans, 2001). This high incidence of business failure is an obvious indication of the need for imaginative e-business environments.

There is an obvious role for integrating production, commerce, distribution, and banking. Currently, local art and craft vendors in the developing world continue to push their ware at tourists and foreigners in the real world. In addition, traders, mostly women, who are invited to some of the numerous developing nations-centred conferences convening in the U.S., ferry their indigenous crafts and clothing to these venues only to transport them back to their home countries. Selling in the virtual state, however, does not require the producer and trader to be present at the final point of sale, but the structures for virtual trade—trust, payment and delivery guarantees, and delivery on schedule—are yet to be developed in many developing country economies. The outcomes of e-commerce models in developing countries could include facilitating the electronic business environment that would enable local vendors at the Grand *marché* in Bamako, Mali, to sell in the *Le plus grand marché* or global market.

Computerization can also facilitate services in other sectors such as the hotel industry, where local hotels could be backlogged with check-in and check-out of their guests during major international conferences in some developing countries, due to drawn out procedures of manually entering transactions in huge logbooks. These real effects of IT in nurturing business opportunities in developing countries should be carefully considered by governments and their development partners, instead of operationalizing e-business as purely buy-sell oriented.

Perhaps the narrow definition and emphasis of the Information Society as an electronic version of shopping malls, or as final sales point with customers swiping credit cards to order goods and services online, partially explains the majority of failed dot.com start-ups being e-commerce-related. The aspect of potential customers being informed about the multitude of comparable products so that they can make product comparisons online should be considered as a part of e-trade; the final purchase or 'closing the deal' could however occur in a real shop in the customer's geographic community. A customer may not purchase a book at an Internet 'bookstore' but could read excerpts of the book and book reviews online and may visit a local bookstore in reality to make the final purchase. Thus isolation of the electronic influence on commerce would require new models of analysing consumer activities; basing the impact of communications on direct online purchases alone would be a distortion of the true value of the Internet in 'consumer confidence' measurements.

This emphasis of shopping, as the power of the Internet, flies in the face of claims by technology firms and industry that they lack intelligent human resources.

In spite of the high rate of dot.com business failures, there has been a mad rush to replicate Northern-type e-commerce formats in developing countries, where a few are setting new trends in copious consumerism, consuming more than could be generated locally. This level of consumerism has led to a rapid depreciation and crushing of local currencies and deprivation that is felt most severely by the poor majority, while depravity runs amok in high places.

In addition, e-commerce programs that do not take domestic markets into account also need to be rethought.

In November 1998, an open pick-up truck arrived at the outskirts of Accra, in Ghana; the truck was loaded with maize and palm nuts, staple foods in the country. There is hardly anyone in that city who would not have a meal made of maize or palm nuts in a day—corn dough for preparing meals such as *banku* and *kenkey*, and soup and cooking oil from palm nuts. On top of the cargo sat a young woman and a young man, the former was very likely the 'market woman,' and the latter likely the 'driver's mate' or helper. The truck stopped at a red traffic signal and its occupants were faced directly with a huge billboard with the words *Digital, Better, ... Mobile Phone Network*; undeniably, mobile phone networks have spread rapidly in the developing world, including the Africa region where there were 100 mobile networks in 2001, up from 33 in 1995, and the market is expected to reach 100 million users by 2005 (Utsumi, 2001). The functions of these mobile units are invariably voice operations, which may be a perpetuation of the oral culture instead of building a digital culture. Marketing in rural communities of many developing countries is not synonymous with commodity exchanges, as it is known in the West. For e-commerce to effect changes in food crop marketing and distribution in these regions, the challenges of domestic distribution of goods need to be understood; mere billboards heralding the sale of modern gadgets to the minority, which is about 20 percent of the population in the case of Africa, would not resolve the wastage that is associated with harvests being unable to reach markets and the resulting high price of foodstuffs in urban centres.

The role of communication devices in providing knowledge for development or in 'attacking poverty' demands something more concerted, more imaginative, more customized, and even more forceful and sustaining than simply replicating external models in local situations.

Marketing in developing countries is more than just the producer, the vendor, and the consumer; several traditional events and interactions are scheduled to coincide with 'market days,' and IT could be used in planning community health outreach programs, such as HIV/AIDS campaigns. Hence, Holland (2000) says that the wisdom of Ancient civilizations is needed to shape the electronic age, especially among the global youth, to inform people about commonalities and to develop a healing trade, not only in material goods but also in spiritual values.

Marketing involves critical timing of harvest, availability of transportation, and choice of marketplaces. The role of IT in providing fast and efficient communication among food crop producers, retailers, and transport operators could reduce the percentage of produce that is lost through delay in transporting harvests to markets. Rural teleconnectivity that enables farmers to interact with market women and transportation owners would ensure precise timing of harvests and arrival of traders on site to transport produce to the market.

Therefore, provision of electronic trade points to interest groups is an essential requirement. However, trade gateways without the empowering business culture, financial backbones or investment capital, and financial managers would not be gateways into the global market at all.

The development of computer literate middle-level management personnel would also be a vital requirement for developing nations to enter the global market. The importance of this profession in utilizing modern telecommunications to create universal visibility and universal standards such as designing Web pages, managing data, and other digital processes is implicit. Such programs may entail the digitization of business forms and expenditure flows, and other transactions; they could also facilitate the ability to organize data using programs such as spreadsheets to facilitate statistical information gathering regarding the performance of businesses or institutions for evaluation and decision-making.

E-commerce projects in developing nations that are modelled on the traditional notion of export and which place more emphasis on international business relations without a nurturing of the domestic business environment would perpetuate the tradition of poor nations producing goods and services for the external market, often primary goods whose value the developing world has been unable to determine or influence.

WOMEN AND DEVELOPMENT COMMUNICATION

All over the world, but especially in the developing world, women have handled communications on behalf of their bosses who are usually male. It is imperative that advancements in the communications sector similarly benefit this group and empower their career development. The impact of modern communications on this profession could reflect the multiple applications that modern communications afford to those who were secretaries and telephone switchboard operators in the 'old economy' so that they could be imagined to evolve into knowledge facilitating roles in the knowledge economy. School connectivity programs, which relate to secretarial and business management that attract high female applicants, could aim to develop a cadre of *Internet literate* middle-level business information management personnel. This could translate into new levels of personnel within bureaucracies and businesses, with accompanying enhancements in the professional outlooks, including remuneration. This would particularly benefit young women and single women, and provide them with the independence that would engender their own aspirations, without the thought of depending on a richer man as a husband as is often the notion in developing economies; this concept of women's independence would be ideal.

Poverty alleviation programs that target women groups, when based on substantive, systematic, and innovative diagnoses of the state of women, family, and development, could lead to finding appropriate digital opportunities for the group. Rural women and many women in the urban areas in the developing world are among some of the world's most vulnerable and dispossessed groups and probably those who are affected the most by the poor technological state of developing countries; rural women and children undertake the domestic chores such as fetching water from streams, carrying farm produce on the head to road junctions and markets, grinding vegetables and cracking kernels on rocks, and using inefficient cooking environments that produce health hazards, apart from the prolonged durations of undertaking household chores due to inefficient domestic and kitchen tools. The so-called liberation of men in Western cultures is not more than the ease with which chores could be undertaken as a result of technological advancements in domestic tools and kitchen appliances—laundry appliances, dishwashers, powerful vacuum cleaners and sterilizers for carpets and floors, and self-cleaning refrigerators and ovens. Similarly, the liberated Western woman can operate a tractor or push a button to mow the lawn or plough snow. Living has been simplified to the level that little physical strength is expended in undertaking domestic chores, at least for those who can afford these tools. On the other hand, the majority of rural women in the developing world are predisposed to health hazards in their domestic duties, formal jobs, and biological states, such as reproductive health; these situations arise from dependence on non-intellectualized indigenous knowledge and lack of access to modern knowledge and practices. The tradition of occupational divisions of labour in developing countries derive from the perceived energy that may be exerted in performing tasks; for example, while there are claims that rural women in developing nations perform the bulk of duties, including farming, rural people in these economies are aware of the types of duties that are traditionally in the domain of women or men. Women in many rural African communities, where both sexes are engaged in agriculture, may be assigned the role of vegetable cultivation but rarely as yam producers, due to the physical labour required in yam cultivation with primitive tools.

Education is another important area in which women are disadvantaged in developing countries. Access to lower levels of the educational structure—basic and secondary schools—might be gender neutral in some developing countries, but female pupils and students could still face intrinsic biases compared to their male colleagues in career drives. The female student is disadvantaged in the time that is available to prepare for competitive national examinations; domestic duties detain girls at home and render them fatigued at the end of the day or even at the beginning of the school day. The practices in 'keeping up appearances,' such as braiding hair, further diminish the time available for girls and young women to study; it could take about six hours in one session of braiding the hair of an African female student. The social norm of a young woman being married off early or eventually to a successful man also preys on the ability of girls and young women to pursue focused academic and far-reaching career drives. Careers that draw a large number of women, such as secretarial, nursing, and teaching, are also associated with low remuneration. To be concerned about gender and development communications would also imply that there is no career limited to any gender group; all are equal. To this, educational systems that highlight gender inclusion in IT-led opportunities could be developed, and female role models could be related to the girl child.

Effective campaigns on the education and career development schemes of young women could be transferred into integrated perspectives in national education curricula and programs. Developing country universities could establish concerted and interdisciplinary gender-focussed programs at all levels of education and research in all sectors of national economic planning that pertain to women and their economic and social inclusion. Such programs could feature identification of the knowledge systems that relate to women and their being, their position in the family, society, occupation, biology, health, and the economy.

HEALTH SECURITY AND CONNECTIVITY

The visibility of rural communities in developing nations to global centres of health knowledge could provide early health warning systems and effect containment of strange diseases in their early and innocuous stages. Programs are emerging in which patients and medical and health specialists are connected virtually for diagnosis of conditions, which is ideal. These programs could determine the causes of symptoms, but the patient may not be able to access the drugs prescribed by the virtual doctor if the connectivity efforts are not linked to the development of local pharmaceutical industries. The danger that faces poor communities is that their needs are not viewed with the urgency that may be required to immunize a local community until the rest of the world is threatened by these insecurities. The generation and sharing of data about local situations, and access of local health care institutions to global health knowledge and resources, can facilitate pattern identification, predicting danger, and activation of emergency response and preventive strategies. The late recognition and deployment of resources to address some of these insecurities implies that only the particular outbreak is considered in the interventions.

An effective telehealth campaign however requires that the broad aspects of health, from healthy lifestyles for prevention to diagnoses and care provisions, be tackled. If the health indicators of local communities were fully visible to the global health industry, and assuming that the mechanisms to recognize the causes and spread of communicable and contagious diseases were available with rapid response teams, the world could have responded sooner to many of such insecurities, and many million lives would have been saved with minimal effort compared to the high cost of treatment that these nations could not afford; the budget to undertake such control measures against HIV/AIDS for example would have been much less than the nine or ten billion that the U.N. now says is needed for comprehensive control and care programs in HIV/AIDS alone.

Utsumi observed that teleconnectivity for health might provide the best opportunity for developing countries to acquire the most effective communications infrastructure. An effective application of telecommunications in health management would require flexible and varied media formats, including broadband telecomunications for two-way audio, full-motion video-conferencing, television-quality netcasting, and high-resolution image transfer protocols. The transmission of health images and participation of expert medical teams in diagnoses, surgery, and treatment regimes could not be achieved through rudimentary connectivity systems. Utsumi's model is for developing countries to aggregate the humanitarian services components of satellites in orbit to access broadband Internet *via* international satellite and fibre-optic cables, with the objective of increasing the quality of audio and video delivery, high interactivity, and system throughput as a global objective of closing the digital divide for improving e-learning and telehealth services (Utsumi, T., 2001). The social and humanitarian components of satellite operations could enable availability of information channels for health education to reach into rural areas of poor nations, and the availability of such connectivity could be used for other connectivity purposes, such as community access for agriculture.

Poor communities are currently a cue for diseases, plagues, hunger and famine, high rates of illiteracy, infant mortality, dangers of childbirth and related issues of peri-natal health, among others--ie., issues that do not affect other civilizations to the same extent. These insecurities could not be resolved by the provision of rudimentary communications for emergency situations alone. Provision of walkie-talkies to traditional birth attendants to communicate with health centres during protracted childbirth could reduce the incidence of maternal mortality during childbirth; however, safe motherhood is not an event but a process that spans the stages of preconception, pregnancy, post-natal periods, and early childhood.

A recent *Ebola* scare in Canada occurred when an African woman who had arrived in the country only a few days earlier was displaying severe symptoms of fever (CBC, 2001). The public being alerted, the patient was quarantined, and tissue samples were rushed to the Centers for Disease Control and Prevention in Atlanta. It was another sign of the health insecurities of poor communities while demonstrating the alertness of a functional health research, treatment, public monitoring, and information systems that are required in an increasingly globalizing world in which health insecurities are truly *sans frontières* or without borders.

Nurturing knowledge communities in developing countries could not ignore the HIV/AIDS epidemics either, hence this plague is used to discuss teleconnectivity, knowledge flows, and health herein. The epidemic is a hard lesson to developing country institutions, their intellectuals, and international development agencies on their lapses; that the world could be overtaken by a plague so devastating, at the highest point of global biomedical and pharmacological sciences, is a demonstration of lack of equity in health knowledge sharing. Since HIV was identified in 1980 as the causal agent of AIDS, the developed economies instituted public awareness campaigns to curb the spread in their own regions, but they were unable to impress upon their partners in the developing world to create effective programs that addressed the situation. Following the devastation of several economies in Africa, and the spread of the disease in other regions such as India, China, and the Caribbean, the world has begun to make concerted efforts to address the situation.

The HIV/AIDS statistics are familiar: HIV/AIDS is nowhere more threatening than on the African continent, where 25 million of the 36.1 million HIV/AIDS cases have occurred (UNAIDS, 2000); African children are affected by the disease in two principal ways: while breast-feeding confers enormous benefits such as preventing malnutrition, illness, saving lives and money, it is also one way for an HIV-positive mother to transmit the virus to her infant, and a child stands the greatest risk, about 20 percent, of vertical or mother-to-child transmission during the time of late pregnancy and childbirth. There is an additional 14 percent risk that an infant will become infected through breast milk. UNAIDS has estimated that eight million children have been orphaned by this epidemic. In addition, the AIDS incidence in Africa is likely to diminish life expectancy by 20 years, decrease work productivity, and increase infant mortality rate, among others.

Speakers at the U.N. Special Session on HIV/AIDS in 2001 to mobilize global resources to control the disease (U.N., 2001), including the British secretary for international development, Clare Short, and the U.S. secretary of state, Colin Powell, noted that the global response to the HIV/AIDS crisis came too late. Admittedly, there have been several regional, national, and local efforts including the establishment of UNAIDS as an inter-agency program, and providing access to drugs for those who are living with the disease prior to the U.N. Special Session on HIV/AIDS to contain the disease, but most of these initiatives lacked the resources required to make a meaningful impact.

The lengthy processes that global institutions must undergo to internalize new ideas and develop policy strategies on matters of immediate attention were expressed by the fictional character of *Sir Richard Appleby* (played by Sir Nigel Hawthorne in real life) of the British comedy *Yes, (Prime) Minister*:

"They will react, with some caution, to your rather novel proposal.
They will give it the most serious and urgent consideration, and insist

on a thorough and rigorous examination of all proposals in line with detail feasibility study and budget analysis before producing a consultative document for consideration by all interested bodies, and seeking comments and recommendations to be included in a brief for a series of working parties, who will produce individual studies, which will produce the background for a more wide-ranging document, considering whether or not the proposal should be taken forward to the next stage." (Camiel, 1997, http)

Global institutions have been unable to respond in a rapid manner in a number of situations that require rapid deployment of health resources and funds; the Rwandan massacre, the wars that divided the former Yugoslav Republic into miniature states, and the amputation of civilians in Sierra Leone are some of the examples of the inability of global institutions to foresee, forestall, or rapidly resolve crises. An early-warning system in health operationalized in rural communities and integrated into the teaching hospitals at the national level, and the connectivity of the national system to global health knowledge domains could enable local health practitioners to identify any emerging health trends, the threats that could ensue, and the possible mitigation factors.

The HIV/AIDS situation might be the clarion for developing country intellectuals to respond to their generational role, as a group, having been provided with the same education as others in the industrialized economies. These intellectuals, some of whom are in the medical research programs of major global institutions and industries, could serve as virtual doctors to monitor the health and environment of poor communities by alerting their counterparts in these communities about health care discoveries and the threat of new diseases. Such monitoring regimes of the local and global health environments would allow the global health community to foresee what may lie beyond the immediate horizon instead of responding to the aftermath of crises. Developing country intellectuals should resolve that never again would their people be caught so unprepared, like the people of a village in Achebe's *Things Fall Apart,* in which the principal actor, *Okonkwo,* surmised that the community members were 'fools' for they did not arm themselves while at the village market; that negligence resulted in their capture by the colonial authorities, who were seeking to expand territorial influence over Nigerian indigenous communities (Achebe, 1958).

A worthwhile program is the effort of the World Health Organization to develop a partnership with the leading scientific publishers in the biomedical sciences to provide the health sector of developing countries with access to advances in health research (WHO, 2001). In addition to access to journals, Kouba and the WHO have developed an interactive computer package that could be used in animal disease control (Kouba, http). These are positive developments in bridging the health knowledge gap that exists between the poor and rich communities.

The culture of silence has been blamed for the manner in which HIV/AIDS was able to gain so much ground in Africa, and now in the rest of the developing world. In tackling the subject from this perspective, HIV/AIDS and other health insecurities of these communities would be a function of information flow, opportunities, knowledge and education, peace, and technological sophistication. As the former Zambian President, Kenneth Kaunda, expressed with the zeal of the African independence leaders: "In this age of information technology, we are used to seeing the three letters www; let www be our driving force, our inspiration in this war [against] AIDS—www—we will win!" (Kaunda, 2000: 2). Developing nations could capitalize on the opportunity provided by the current global focus on HIV/AIDS to contemplate on substantive and quantifiable measures to design healthy communities. If the culture of silence was responsible for the rapid spread of HIV/AIDS and other diseases, then the environment of convergent communications should provide the ingredients for building the firewalls that would contain the spread of emerging diseases, including HIV.

However, major HIV/AIDS conferences that have attracted global media followings and proceedings could make imaginative uses of connectivity in developing nations. These conferences should not be organized in the traditional formats, where traditional media are used in the dissemination of conference declarations to the majority of the community members. On the other hand, simultaneous Web castings through the fledgling telecommunications sector to increase the size of participants from grassroots organizations that are unable to attend these meetings. In this era of giant screens being mounted at public places for reception of live entertainment events, only those who are able to enroll in conferences are able to follow events live; there are no *telescreens* mounted in urban centres of developing nations to engage the general public in the live events of these conferences. The people about whom these conferences are convened could only follow whatever slants of the proceedings that the traditional press decided, often the promises of the political leadership, which are often unfulfilled. Moreover, grassroots organizations including indigenous health practitioners who participate in these conferences do not have access to the tools that would include them in global health knowledge flows on a continuous basis.

That no group has taken responsibility for this epidemic in developing countries reflects the general situation that the poor are in a state of survival of the fittest. In Japan, France, and Canada, where contaminated blood resulted in the spread of some diseases, there have been public apologies, prosecutions, and compensations. But the spread of the disease in Africa has been attributed largely to heterosexual activities, which places the burden on the individual to be 'responsible,' yet there are few penetrating and effective sex education campaigns in schools and communities.

It is important to tackle the issue of treatment and care provision to those who have contracted HIV/AIDS and other emerging diseases, yet it is also important to 'immunize' those who have escaped their direct infection so far. Information and knowledge flows and utilization can lend to building firewalls to contain the spread of epidemics. There should be the possibility to 'immunize' all children who are able to 'logon' to a computer against HIV/AIDS for instance: electronic bulletins could be created and carried by major Internet Service Providers on their gateways to inform and educate anybody who is able to access the Internet or an intranet. These bulletins could inform people about the nature, transmission, prevention, and care associated with the virus and the disease. Currently, in poor communities, where the people's needs are different, an Internet subscriber who may be going through the Web to access E-mail may automatically read the major headline news around the world, but it will not be specific to the subscriber's local environment. The cues on a typical Internet-based E-mail access in Africa are 'Cool click says: So you are in love,' 'People and Chat,' and 'Shopping.' Telehealth for sustainable health requires that every opportunity be seized to deliver relevant information. Internet providers in developing countries could volunteer to carry health warnings, especially regarding HIV/AIDS, on their systems to reach all schools that are connected to their services, because it is a race against the destruction of humanity in their communities; it is possible that convergent communications could be used to broadcast safe sex programs to save lives.

Poverty in an urban environment can induce aberrant values, and wars in the countryside have put women and children in the paths of ravaging men. The nature of some global businesses, for example the mining industry in southern Africa, which require migrant workers to leave their families and work in communities that are several hundred kilometres removed from their spouses, are also partially culpable for the spread of STDs and HIV/AIDS. Therefore, as businesses contemplate the lifelong learning systems for their employees, they could also study the ways in which their business practices impact other aspects of the health of the entire community.

The sophistication of converting indigenous knowledge in health and medicine—the twigs, barks, roots, and leaves that are the first lines of defence in treatment in rural communities—into functional states could also be impacted by connectivity for health initiatives. The other aspects of human health such as food and nutrition, and clean water also matter. Therefore other core activities such as those related to agricultural information, tools, and processes are required for building healthy communities. If peace triumphed over anarchy in some of these poor communities there would be no soldier boys roaming the countryside in the name of 'revolution,' raping young and old women while claiming immunity from

HIV/AIDS. If the poor were able to eat well and had proper education that would inform their life choices, the extent of morbidity and predisposition to illnesses would be reduced, and their immunity or ability to naturally fend off pathogens could be enhanced. Developing a healthy community through knowledge flows would also involve designs of sustainable interactions with the environment, and the development of land replenishment systems that did not push rural farmers to cultivate previously uncultivated lands, where plagues lie dormant in their habitats and are not awakened. Moreover, improvements in human living conditions, especially in urban slums, are necessary so that they do not serve as disease reservoirs. Health and economy are intricately entwined, hence facilitating opportunities for the young and vulnerable groups, particularly young women, should impact their health security as well. Considering moral practices that influence the spread of HIV/AIDS in Africa, the values that are inculcated by the strong family orientations of many indigenous communities may break down once the supervision of the family is lost in rural-to-urban migrations. It is therefore important for young women to be provided with the means of achievement and hope in life through skill acquisition and career paths. Such opportunities and skills would enable young women to function independently and securely in urban centres.

These goals are achievable through a penetrating communications and information flow, provided that knowledge for preventive health and the ability to make diagnosis virtually are linked to the manufacture of drugs in the local economies.

LEADERSHIP AND GOVERNANCE IN THE INFORMATION AGE

Developing countries have begun to respond to internal and external demands for the establishment of 'good governance' mechanisms as a precursor to local prosperity and security. The emergence of Southeast Asia as a viable economic region was made possible by availability of Western capital and technology, and a rich source of human resources in the local communities, but only the nations that demonstrated astute political leadership were able to provide the enabling environment for synergism among the elements of local prosperity. Good and effective governance, apart from civic relations, would include access to information and knowledge that would enable businesses, individuals, and communities to benefit from the activities of governance structures and their institutional regimes, for example the departments of agriculture and food, health, education, business, among others. While political democracy is vital to providing a peaceful operational domain for knowledge sharing to take hold, concentration on political aspirations alone would not meet basic requirements. Good governance could ensure that the tools and processes of livelihoods and income-generating activities are available, in addition to promotion of political structures. Governance is more than political dimensions alone; good governance has several institutions that are dedicated to the well being of citizens who need access to the machinery and services of these institutions. The development of relevant curricula in science and technology, a focus on research and development, and institutional capacity building are also necessary elements of good governance.

Governments in the industrialized nations have interactive spaces for the public to access their elected officials and other public services; the Web sites of parliaments, government institutions, and civil society groups do not just provide a listing of elected officials, but they provide the community with the means to communicate with elected officials and public institutions. However, members of the public in many developing nations cannot reach their elected representatives through similar sites in their countries. Good governance within a knowledge society would require frameworks to procure communication technologies for innovative deployment around strategic goals in nation building, including as information channels within the constituency to create the necessary transparency and account-ability of governance institutions in the networked economy. This transparency would ensure a responsive oversight of the larger community regarding strategic national goals. These networks into the constituency would benefit the elected representatives as well, as they would be able to inform their electorate about the activities of their representatives on their behalf.

Decentralization is a strong element of governance in the industrialized world, and the assertion of local authorities over the quality of life of the members of their local communities has become a trend, a phenomenon described as the reverse flow of sovereignty (Eger, 1997). For example, while the U.S. federal government was not a signatory to the Kyoto Protocol on the environment (CNN, 2001, kyoto.talks.1824/index.html), the city of Seattle in Washington State, U.S., has committed itself to net-zero emissions of greenhouse gases and related models of environmental security.

Seattle like many other cities in the industrialized world compete with each other for global resources, including as location of businesses, institutional head-quarters, tourism, and global summits; the choice of a community as the destination or location of these resources is a factor of the quality of life and the international reputation of the community. Seattle in this case would compete against other communities that are also known for their environmental and sustainable develop-ment programs, for example the German city of Freiburg, a community of about 200,000 inhabitants in the Black Forest, which is considered a pacesetter for 'green' living in German, a country that is among the leaders in sustainable environment.

Seattle mayor, Paul Schell, and the city administration are of the opinion that clean energy, environmental protection, and economic prosperity go hand-in-hand. The city considered its history of long-term investment in energy conservation and renewable resources to have paid off as the cheapest, cleanest, most reliable power in the U.S. (Schell, 2001). This strategy, the city believed, stood in stark contrast to the new energy priorities of the U.S. administration of President George W. Bush proposed by the task force chaired by his vice-president, Cheney. That proposal emphasized expansion of fossil fuel production and nuclear power supply, which some experts contend could both accelerate global warming and add to the stockpile of dangerous nuclear waste. The wealth and quality of life in Seattle, however, derives from the quantity, timing, and distribution of water, through a well-regulated natural cycle that delivers water in winter and stores much of it as snow for year-round use. The water cycle drives the productivity of the forests, inexpensive and pollution-free hydroelectric systems, agriculture, salmon runs, and tourism. Seattle is obviously concerned about scientific studies, which predict that global warming could disrupt their water cycle. Therefore the city considers global climate change as a profound local issue, and developed programs and policies to address the issue. The municipality's utility (City Light) for example is committed to meet all of Seattle's growth in electrical power needs with zero net emissions of greenhouse pollutants. In addition to the traditional reliance of the city on hydroelectric power, the city is making investments in other renewable energy sources such as geothermal and wind systems, and would use fossil fuels as sparingly as possible. Other components in the city's energy and environmental programs include reducing traffic, protecting water supplies, and saving salmon.

Decentralization of governance and its deliverables also feature in current development programming that impact the poor regions of the world. These decentralization programs ideally would consider the notion of sovereignty from the local perspectives, and empower the institutions that serve such communities. Good governance modeling could learn from what has nurtured local civilizations in the developing world for centuries, even in the present chaos that some of these communities now find themselves. To many who are not very conversant with leadership in these communities and their indigenous institutions, indigenous governance may be defunct. In reality, however, human mobilization in rural communities is under the jurisdiction of indigenous leaders, who are considered as a part of the informal administration by the modern political administrative structures.

Community leaders are involved in several aspects of civic, health, and economic attributes of indigenous and rural communities in Africa for instance. The establishment and maintenance of public places of convenience, protecting rivers and streams, clearing of farm roads, dispute settlements, and enacting and supervision of laws and taboos in rural communities are among the deliverables of indigenous governance regimes. In Ghana, for example, where there are at least 32,000 chiefs (Ayittey, 1990), there are no village mayors, police posts, post offices, or health clinics in many rural communities. The indigenous governance system, a representative body whose membership is drawn from the various clans of the village, shares the task of policymaking, security, and communal health. The various families are duly represented in this governance arrangement and money does not buy inclusion. Similar indigenous administrations exist in urban Africa; the king of the Ashanti ethnic group is in the city of Kumasi, and the paramount chief of the Ga ethnic group is in Accra; a chief can be removed from the throne on evidence of misconduct, similar to impeachment of a leader in the Western democracies.

Some of the colonial powers in Africa recognized the authority of indigenous governance and exploited this system in their colonial administrations, for example in the British policy of Indirect Rule of West Africa, although for different reasons than what the subject here entails.

Several reasons might be offered for marginalization of the indigenous system of representation when descendants of indigenous communities, now local elites, assumed leadership of their own nations, among which could be that chiefs were perceived by independence movements as puppets of the colonial powers. Such line of reasoning, however, ignores historical evidence of the strong opposition mounted by prominent indigenous governments against invasions by external forces; the Ashanti Empire fought the British imperialist in the First Ashante War (1823-24) in which British troops under Sir Charles MacCarthy were heavily defeated (Orwin, http). In another case, a woman, Queen Mother of Edwiso, Nanahemaa Yaa Asantewaa, led the men of the powerful Ashanti Empire to battle against the British colonial authorities in the 'Yaa Asantewaa War' (Glantz, 2001). Many influential chiefs and kings who opposed the occupation of Africa by European empires were punished, brutalized, banished, or exiled to remote islands to sever their influence and relationship with their people (Discovery Theater, http; Prempeh College, http). Today, Ghanaians still carry their indigenous leaders in palanquins, not by coercion but to honour the chiefs for their role in governing the community. This honour is reserved for only those to whom rural people hold allegiance; hence, no leader of a political party or national government is accorded this honour. On the other hand, rural dwellers escaped to the farms when district council officials descended upon villages to arrest those who might have defaulted in the payment of poll tax; this situation was opposite to volunteering at communal duties where songs and drums could be heard during clearing bush paths to the farms, cleaning primary schools, cemeteries, streams, and church compounds; or making a new community pit latrine. These communal duties were by the people for themselves. Moreover, the formal leadership or its representatives in Ghana would not address a local durbar in any community without first paying tribute to the indigenous leaders—*Togbuiwo, Mamawo*, or *Nananum*.

All the achievements of indigenous mobilization are via the infamous *gong-gong* beater or *town crier*, the purveyor of information, good and bad. These institutions have therefore demonstrated their appreciation for communications and their skills in interactivity; they have excelled in employing communications to strengthen the deliverables of their institutions in their communities. Integration of modern telecommunications into these domains could foster these indigenous governance regimes and their deliverables by permitting them to tap into global knowledge domains. It is therefore vital that the location, ownership, operation, maintenance, and the administrative issues concerning modern telecommunications be entrusted into the community's indigenous fibre-network for penetrating community-oriented communications. This is especially urgent in view of the manner in which other forms of communications such as the radio, television, and print media have been owned, managed, and operated by state machinery in developing countries. These media systems have often been used as instruments of oppression and subjugation of subjects while the *gong-gong* that is operated by indigenous leaders has communicated interactively with citizens, even to assemble members of these communities to listen to national government memoranda.

The assumption that IT would bring peaceful coexistence among various ethnic groups has to be examined from the perspective of regional integration and economic, social, and political prosperity. The theme of African Unity has been the rallying point, or departure, for the Organization of African Unity (now African Union) since the wave of independence across that continent; however, African unity has proven illusive through the formal structures of governance, while indigenous leaders have built bridges across their 'national' boundaries by inviting leaders from related ethnic groups that may be located outside their national boundaries to indigenous festivals, without regard to the artificial borders that four decades of post-independence administrations have not dismantled. Furthermore, modern African leadership could not escape blame in some of the political tensions and upheavals including ethnic wars within and beyond their national boundaries, which are often erroneously blamed on tribal wrangling induced by indigenous leaders. The crises of Rwanda, Burundi, Angola, Sierra Leone, Liberia, Sudan, and Somalia, to name a few, were not initiated by indigenous leaders or their peoples. Those crises and others are manifestations of irresponsibility and lack of credibility of modern national administration, and resulted from disregard of the inherent values in the indigenous governance system.

The positive attributes of indigenous administrations could be enhanced to serve as agents of decentralization of political machinery, and IT could assist their communication potentials toward the realization of the new system of inclusive governance. Indigenous leaders in Ghana and editorial comments in the Ghanaian media have made similar observations: Nana Addo Dankwa II, Okuapemhene, for example, at a workshop organized by the National House of Chiefs and the National Commission on Civic Education, expressed the need for harmony between traditional values and the people's wish for good governance and democracy, and suggested that there should be a way to match the two for the benefit of society (Daily Graphic, 1998; Ghanaian Times, 1998). Chiefs in Ghana are prohibited from political activities, but they could be chief executives of national institutions, as if local governance and the national political process were independent within national development frameworks. The solutions to perceived interference of chiefs in national security when they are politically active could have been more ingenious than the exclusion of the wisdom of the institution of indigenous from the mainstream governance regime.

Building a secure nation or region should not be seen from military perspectives alone, because no amount of ammunitions and troops would bring lasting peace. A true high command would be the decentralization of local administrative authority to empower local communities so that a group of political adventurers, armed with a few rounds of ammunition, could not 'take over' a broadcasting house and constitute itself into 'government' in these nations.

REFERENCES

Achebe, C. (1958). *Things Fall Apart*. London: Heineman Educational Publishers.

Afrani, M. (1999). Cheer up Africa, Uncle Sam is here. *New African*, (July/August), 13.

Anderson, S. (2000). Ronald Dellums: A 'loudmouth' leaves retirement for the global war on AIDS. *Los Angeles Times*, (Aug. 20), M3.

Ayittey, G. (1990). Guns, idiots, screams. *The New Internationalist*, (June), 8-9.

Baser, H. (2001, June 26). Change—Absorptive capacity and brain drain. *Reforming Technical Cooperation for Capacity Development*. [Online]. United Nations Development Program / Capacity.org. <http://www.capacity.org/undp-forum/detail_forum.phtml?act_id=130&username=guest@capacity.org&password=9999>[2001, June 26]; citing Antoine Reverchon (2001). Nord-Sud: la guerre des cervaux s'amplifie. *Le monde,* (Mar. 6).

BBC. (2001, June 4, byford.shtml). Changes in receiving BBC World Service in English. *British Broadcasting Corporation News* [Online]. <http://www.bbc.co.uk/worldservice/schedules/010518_byford.shtml>[2001, June 10].

Bray, H. (2001, July 24). The wiring of a continent—Africa goes online. *The Boston Globe* [Online]. <http://www.boston.com/dailyglobe2/205/nation/Africa_goes_online+.shtml> [2001, July 26].

Bread for the World. (2001, July 12). Foreign relations panel approves bill calling on bush, congress to boost aid to Africa.. [Online]. Bread for the World. <http://www.bread.org/media/index.html>[2001, July 13].

Building Bridges. (2000, Sep.). Construction begins. *Building Bridges* [Online]. 5(2). The African-American Research Library and Cultural Center, Broward County, Florida. <http://www.co.broward.fl.us/lii07200.htm>[2001, Nov. 1].

Camiel, C. (1997). The national education service. Minutes of "Yes Prime Minister," Season 2 episodes, YPM 2.7; first aired on BBC: January 21, 1998. [Online]. <http://www.yes-minister.com>[2001, Aug 13].

CBC. (2001, Feb. 7). Ebola ruled out. *Canadian Broadcasting Corporation Newsworld* [Online]. <http://cbc.ca/cgi_bin/templates/view.cgi?/news/2001/02/07/noebola_010207>and<http://cbc.ca/programs/sites/viewer.cgi?FILE=HM20010207.html&TEMPLATE=healthmatters.ssi&SC=HM> [2001, Feb. 7]: "A sense of relief today from a medical team working in Hamilton, Ontario. Health Canada now says a Congolese patient being treated there is NOT carrying the Ebola virus. Now the question is, what DOES she have?"

Cesca, S. (2001). Drug tests need rules, report says. *The Globe and Mail, Toronto*, (Oct. 27), A13.

Clinton, Hillary Rodham. (1996). *It Takes a Village.* New York: Simon and Schuster.

CNN. (2001, Jan. 23, marconi.01/index.html). [Online]. <http://www.cnn.com/2001/TECH/computing/01/23/marconi.01/index.html>: "January 23 marked a very special milestone in the development of long-distance communication. Exactly a hundred years ago, at 4:30 p.m. local time, Italian-born radio pioneer Guglielmo Marconi sent the first ever long-distance wireless transmission from the Isle of Wight to Cornwall on the British mainland. The January 23 transmission was the furthest wireless transmission ever made (299 kilometres or 186 miles). It also proved that radio waves could be transmitted across the horizon, something the majority of the scientific establishment had insisted was not possible."

CNN. (2001, July 23, kyoto.talks.1824/index.html). Deal reached at climate talks. *Cable News Network* [Online]. <http://www.cnn.com/2001/WORLD/europe/07/23/kyoto.talks.1824/index.html>[2001, July 25]: "Delegates to the United Nations Climate Change Conference in Bonn, Germany, agreed on how to enforce the international treaty covering nearly 180 nations on greenhouse gases, and how to impose penalties for violations. The 1997 Kyoto treaty aims to reduce global carbon dioxide emissions by 5.2 percent of 1990 levels by 2012. The deal leaves the U.S.—the planet's biggest polluter—as the only world power not to accept the Kyoto accord. President George W. Bush rejected the Kyoto framework in March, on grounds that it would harm the U.S. economy."

CNN. (2001, Aug. 12, prison.population/index.html). Prison population growth slows in 2000. *Cable News Network* [Online]. <http://www.cnn.com/2001/US/08/12/prison.population/index.html>[2001, Aug. 26,].

Daedalus. (1998). Educational yesterday, education tomorrow. *Daedalus: Journal of the American Academy of Arts and Sciences,* 127(4), [Online]. <http://www.daedalus.amacad.org/issues/fa98rel.html>[2001, Aug. 25].

Daily Graphic, The. (1998, July 24). Ashante Congress and unity. *The Daily Graphic*, Accra, Ghana, p. 8.

Discovery Theater. (2001). King Prempeh I. [Online]. Discovery Theater, The Smithsonian Institute. <http://discoverytheater.si.edu/prempeh/kp03.htm> [2001, Aug. 5]: "Prempeh I was enstooled as king of the Asante in 1888 ... The old Asante confederation in what is today central Ghana had clashed repeatedly with the British on the coast. Prempeh was driven by the belief that the Asante should remain a sovereign power independent of British control. On January 20, 1896, citing a debt incurred twenty years earlier, British authorities entered Kumase and arrested Prempeh and Asantehemaa Yaa Akayaa as well as Prempeh's father. Fifty-two chiefs, women, children, and attendants were also taken captive. Prempeh and the other captives were detained at Elmina Fort until they were moved to Freetown, Sierra Leone, in 1897. Even at such a distance, Prempeh exerted great influence, a fact that perplexed the British authorities. In 1900 he and the others were taken to Mahe, the largest of the Seychelles, in the Indian Ocean off the east coast of Africa. [While in exile, Prempeh] worked to promote the health, welfare, and happiness of all in the camp, making sure that peace and order reigned. By the early 1920s, a number of civil organizations began pressuring the British for Prempeh's release; his mother, father, brother, and all but a few of the chiefs from the original group of captives had died. Perceiving less threat in Prempeh's return to Ghana than in resisting international pressure, British authorities released Prempeh and fifty-four others. They left the Seychelles on

September 12, 1924. When they entered Kumase on the morning of November 12, thousands of Asante were on hand to greet their king."

d'Orville, H. (1996). Tackling information poverty. In d'Orville, H., (Ed.), *Beyond Freedom: Letters to Olusegun Obasanjo*, p. 483-494.

Dunne, N. (2001). World Bank to probe conduct of economist after critical article. *Financial Times*, London, (Sep. 8), 3.

Eger, J.M. (1997, Oct. 26). Smart communities concept, cyberspace and cyberplace: Building the smart communities of tomorrow. [Online]. The World Foundation for Smart Communities. <http://www.smartcommunities.org/pub_cyberplace.htm>[2001, March 30].

Evans, J. (2001, Jan. 3). Study: 210 dot-com companies closed in 2000. *IDG News Service* (Boston Bureau) [Online]. <http://www.idg.net/go.cgi?id=390478>[2001, Jan. 5].

Everett-Green, R. (2001). Most still surf the waves, not the Web. *The Globe and Mail*, Toronto, (Apr. 21), R4.

Formula1.com. [Online]. <http://jsp.formula1.com/f1archives/index.jsp>[2002, May 17].

Ghanaian Times, The. (1998). Towards cultural death [2]. *The Ghanaian Times*, Accra, Ghana (Editorial), (Aug. 25).

GIPC. Joint venture partnership search. [Online]. Ghana Investment Promotion Centre. <http://www.gipc.org.gh/opportunity/venture/index.html>[2001, July 12].

Glantz, L. (2001). Yaa Asantewaa—Warrior queen. Birmingham Online Theatre (Preview). *British Broadcasting Corporation* [Online]. <http://www.bbc.co.uk/birmingham/entertainment/previews/yaa_preview.shtml>[2001, Sep. 20]: "Yaa Asantewaa—Warrior queen is the true story of a heroic female freedom fighter that stood against Britain's efforts to steal the golden stool, the sacred Asante symbol of unity. She led an army of thousands to battle against the British but was outgunned and captured. Yaa Asantewa was then exiled to the Seychelles where she died in 1921."

GNA. (2000, Oct. 24). Kwame Nkrumah University of Science and Technology (KNUST) computers: 500 students to one computer at KNUST. *Ghana News Agency* [Online]. <http://www.gna.com.gh/>[2000, Oct. 26].

Goldman, S. (2000). WAP in Asia: Fact and future. [Online]. Internet World Asia Opening Keynote Address, November. Wireless Application Protocol Forum Ltd. <http://www.wapforum.org/new/20001107InternetWorldAsia.ppt> [2001, Aug. 7]. See also: WAP 2.0 technical white paper. [Online]. (2001, Aug.). [Online]. Wireless Application Protocol Forum Ltd. <http://www.wapforum.org/what/

WAPWhite_Paper1.pdf> [2001, Aug. 7].

Gras. (1999, Oct.). List of 1622 documented refugee deaths through fortress Europe. [Online]. Gras. <http://www.gras.at/schengen/s0.html> [2001, Oct. 30].

Hall of Fame. Inventor profile: Alexander Graham Bell. <http://www.invent.org/hall_of_fame/11.html> The National Inventors Hall of Fame. [2001, March 17]: "On April 6, 1875, Bell was granted the patent for the multiple telegraph, which sent two signals at the same time. In September 1875 he began to write the specifications for the telephone. On March 7, 1876, the U.S. Patent Office granted him Patent Number 174,465 covering, the method of, and apparatus for, transmitting vocal or other sounds telegraphically...by causing electrical undulations, similar in form to the vibrations of the air accompanying the said vocal or other sounds. After inventing the telephone, Bell continued his experiments in communication, which culminated in the invention of the photophone-transmission of sound on a beam of light—a precursor of today's optical fiber systems."

Holland, E. (2000, May 17). The future of African development in the electronic era. AFRICANDO 2000 conference, Miami, Florida, U.S.A., May 2000. The Foundation for Democracy in Africa. [Online]. <http://www.democracy-africa.org>

IAAF. (2001, Aug.). The world's (Les mondiaux): The world's biggest track meet. [Online]. The 8th International Amateur Athletic Federation (IAAF) World Championships in Athletics. August 3-12, Edmonton, Alberta, Canada. <http://www.2001.edmonton.com/?l=en&p=100>, <http://www.2001.edmonton.com/splash.asp>, <http://www.iaaf.org/wch01/index.html> [2001, Aug. 8]: "The IAAF World Championships in Athletics is the world's biggest track meet—track and field, and third in scope only to World Cup Soccer and the Summer Olympic Games. The 8th IAAF World Championships brought together more than 1,800 elite athletes from 200 countries to compete in 46 athletic events. An estimated half a million spectators were in Edmonton for the period; another four billion tuned in worldwide. The medal count, after six days of competition was: Russia, 13 (2, 7, and 4, for gold, silver, bronze, respectively); U.S., 8 (3, 3, 2); and Ethiopia, 6 (2, 2, 2).

Independent, The. (1999, Nov. 2). The West African Examination Council (WAEC) identifies weaknesses in candidates. *AllAfrica.com* [Online]. <http://allafrica.com/stories/19991102_feat11.html> [1999, Nov.3]. See also: Funding tertiary education—VC speaks (1999, Nov. 2). *AllAfrica.com* [Online]. <http://www.africanews.org/west/ghana/stories/19991102_feat6.html> [1999, Nov.3].

IRN. (2001, March 5). Sierra Leone: German NGO to train child amputees. *Integrated Regional Information Networks* [Online]. United Nations Office for the Coordination of Humanitarian Affairs. <http://www.reliefweb.int/IRIN/wa/countrystories/sierraleone/20010305.phtml> [2001, July 21].

ITC. (2001). Executive Forum 2000. Export development in the digital economy. [Online]. International Trade Centre, UNCTAD/WTO, Geneva. <http://intracen.org/execforum> [2001, Nov. 1].

John, R. R. (1998). The politics of innovation. *Daedalus: Journal of the American Academy of Arts and Sciences,* 127(4), 187-214.

Kaunda, K. (2000, Dec.). Towards a more effective leadership response to the HIV/AIDS pandemic. [Online]. Keynote speech at the Africa Development Forum 2000, Addis Ababa, Ethiopia, December 3-7, 2000. United Nations Economic Commission for Africa. <http://www.uneca.org/adf2000/daily_updates/index.htm> [2001, Jan. 15]: "What, then, must we do to move towards a more effective response to the HIV/AIDS pandemic? Madame chairperson, I have already referred to AIDS taking more African lives than all the wars of the 20th century. Let us strike back, then, by declaring war, total war, on HIV/AIDS—not a national war that appears only in speeches at conferences and meetings, but a war that becomes part and parcel of the life of this continent, of every nation, every community and family, of every individual. This is a just war. All the right is on our side. There is no right, none whatsoever, on the HIV/AIDS side. In this war, we must win. In this war, if we are all committed and dedicated, we will win. WE WILL WIN. In this age of information technology, we are used to seeing the three letters WWW. Madame chairperson, distinguished ladies and gentlemen, let WWW be our driving force, our inspiration in this war with AIDS—WWW—WE WILL WIN!"

Kouba, V. EPIZOO: A computer software package to be used in veterinary public health and animal disease control. [Online]. Communicable Disease Surveillance and Response, The World Health Organization. <http://www.who.int/emc/diseases/zoo/epizoo.html> [2001, May 15]: The software was developed by professor Kouba of the Czech Republic for the analysis of information on animal health and diseases, including those that are transmissible to humans.

Lakeshore Technologies. (1996). The lost continent of Atlantis. [Online]. Lakeshore Technologies, Inc. <http://www.laketech.com/AD_LC.HTML> [2001, July 19]. The article was adapted from Luce, J. V. (1969). *The End of Atlantis: New Light on an Old Legend.* Thames and Hudson (reprinted 1993 by Efstathiades Group): "Plato's writings embodied the now lost words of Solon, a Greek ruler who visited Egypt circa 590 BC. Plato's account of Atlantis was thus a retelling of the story of Solon, who in turn told the stories that he had heard during his trip to Egypt. In Egypt, Solon heard of the ancient land of Keftiu, an island-nation named for holding one of the four pillars that supported the Egyptian sky. Keftiu was, according to the Egyptians, an advanced civilization that was the gateway to and ruler of all of the lands to the far west of Egypt. Keftiu traded in ivory, copper, and cloth. Keftiu supported hosts of ships and controlled commerce far beyond the Egyptians domain. By Egyptian record, Keftiu was destroyed by the seas in an apocalypse. Solon carried this story to Greece, and passed it to his son and grandson. Plato preserved enough detail about the land of Atlantis he recorded from Solon's grandson Critias the younger."

Lobe, J. (2001, May 20). African governments spend millions on U.S. lobbying. *Inter Press Service* [Online]. <http://ips.link.no/IPS/eng/serv/AF.html> [2001, May 20].

Markoff, J. (2001, June 12). Microsoft is ready to supply a phone in every computer. *New York Times* [Online]. <http://www.nytimes.com/2001/06/12/technology/12SOFT.html?searchpv=day02&pagewanted=print> [2001, June 14].

Marsh, A. (2001, Feb. 26). Mapping a pan-African market. *Red Herring* [Online]. <http://www.redherring.com/story_redirect.asp?layout=story_generic&doc_id=RH180018018> [2001, Aug. 29].

Mijumbi, R.M. (2001). ICTs as an empowerment tool in the 21st century: Women in enterprise development. ITU Telecom Africa 2001, Johannesburg, November 12–18. [Online]. International Telecommunication Union. <http://www.itu.int/TELECOM/aft2001/cfp/auth/4856/pap_4856.pdf> [2002, May 12].

MIT. (2001, Apr. 4). MIT to make nearly all course materials available free on the World Wide Web. [Online]. Massachusetts Institute of Technology. <http://web.mit.edu/newsoffice/nr/2001/ocw.html> [2001, Apr. 6].

Morrison, J. L., & Twigg, C. (2001). The Pew Learning and Technology Program initiative in using technology to enhance education: An interview with Carol Twigg. *Technology Source* (May/June) [Online]. The Michigan Virtual University. <http://horizon.unc.edu/TS/default.asp?show=article&id=859> [2001, June 30].

MTC. Telecommunications policy for an accelerated development programme 1994-2000. [Online]. Ministry of Transport and Communications, Ghana. <http://www.communication.gov.gh/> [1998, July 24].

Newman, L. (2001, July 27). E-commerce debuts in Cuba. *Cable News Network* [Online]. <http://www.cnn.com/2001/WORLD/americas/07/27/cuba.e.commerce/index.html> [2001, July 28].

NetRatings. (2001, Apr. 24). Nearly half of all Americans buy online. *Nielsen// NetRatings and Harris Interactive* [Online]. NetRatings Inc. <http://www.nielsen-netratings.com/news.jsp?thetype=date&theyear=2001&themonth=3> [2001, Apr. 26].

Noronha, F. (2001, July 18). Simple computer that reads your e-mail for you. *Indo-Asian News Service* [Online]. <http://in.news.yahoo.com/010718/43/11fgk.html> [2001, July 18].

NPS. Mount Rushmore. [Online]. U.S. National Park Service. <http://www.nps.gov/moru> [2001, Aug. 5]: "Gutzon Borglum and 400 workers, between 1927 and 1941, sculpted the 60-foot busts of Presidents George Washington, Thomas Jefferson, Theodore Roosevelt, and Abraham Lincoln to memorialize the first 150 years of American history—the birth, growth, preservation, and development of the United States of America." See also: The Lincoln Memorial. [Online]. U.S. National Park Service. <http://www.nps.gov/linc> [2001, Aug. 5]: "The Lincoln Memorial pays tribute to President Abraham Lincoln and the nation he fought to preserve during the Civil War (1861-1865). The Gettysburg Address is inscribed on the south wall of the monument;" George Washington's Mount Vernon Estate and Gardens. [Online]. <http://www.mountvernon.org> [2001, Aug. 5]: Mount Vernon is the preserved home of George Washington, the first President of the U.S.A.

NTT. (2001). FOMA on a fully commercialized basis began operation on October 1. [Online]. NTT DoCoMo, Tokyo, Japan. <http://foma.nttdocomo.co.jp/english/whats/index.html> [2001, Oct. 19].

Orwin, R. History of Ghana. *Worldwrite* [Online]. <http://www.worldwrite.org.uk/site/ghana/pack2.html> [2002, May 18].

PayPal (2002). The way to send and receive money online. [Online]. PayPal. <http://www.paypal.com> [2002, May 18].

Picard, A. (2001). Public health. *The Globe and Mail*, Toronto, (Sep. 10), A1.

Prempeh College. Photo gallery. Homepage. [Online]. Prempeh College, Ghana (unofficial Website). <http://prempeh.org/photos/royalgal.html> [2000, Mar. 10]. See photographs of King Prempeh and entourage en route to Seychelles therein.

Ribeiro, J. (2000, June 22). 'Simputer' aims at the developing world. *IDG News Service* (Bangalore Bureau) [Online]. <http://windows.idg.net/english/crd_internet_192403.html> [2001, July 1].

Rosecrance, R. (1999). *The Rise of the Virtual State: Wealth and Power in the Coming Century.* New York: Basic Books.

Samara, N. (1999, Oct. 25). Speech by Mr. Noah Samara, chairman and CEO, World Space Corporation. [Online]. Africa Development Forum, United Nations Economic Commission for Africa, Addis Ababa, Ethiopia. <http://www.un.org/Depts/eca/newweb/html/1025address_noah_samara.htm> [1999, Nov. 25].

Schell, P. (2001, July 12). Global climate change starts at home. *Seattle Daily Journal of Commerce* [Online]. <http://www.djc.com/news/enviro/11123679.html> [2001, July 29]. See also: Seattle Mayor Paul Schell critical of Bush administration energy plan. (2001, June 19). [Online]. Press release, City of Seattle. <http://www.ci.seattle.wa.us/news/detail.asp?ID=1790> [2001, July 29].

Simputer, The. [Online]. The Simputer Trust. <http://www.simputer.org> [2001, June 4].

Soedjatmoko. (1989). Education relevant to people's needs. *Daedalus: Journal of the American Academy of Arts and Sciences*, p. 211-219.

Stellin, S. (2001, Apr. 11). Bandwidth constraints begin to worry schools. *New York Times* [Online]. <http://www.nytimes.com/2001/04/11/technology/11EDUCATION.html> [2001, Apr. 30].

Stiglitz, J. (2000, Apr. 17). What I learned at the world economic crisis—The insider. *The New Republic* [Online]. <http://www.thenewrepublic.com/041700/stiglitz041700.html> [2001, Oct. 30]. "IMF experts believe they are brighter, more educated, and less politically motivated than the economists in the countries they visit. In fact, the economic leaders from those countries are pretty good—in many cases brighter or better-educated than the IMF staff, which frequently consists of third-rank students from first-rate universities. (Trust me: I've taught at Oxford University, MIT, Stanford University, Yale University, and Princeton University, and the IMF almost never succeeded in recruiting any of the best students.)"

U.N. (2001, June 27). Declaration of commitment on HIV/AIDS: Global crisis—global action. [Online]. U.N. Special Session on HIV/AIDS, New York, NY, June 25-27 2001. The United Nations. <http://www.un.org/ga/aids/conference.html> [2001, July 13].

UNAIDS. (2000). *Epidemic Update.* [Online]. United Nations Joint Programme on HIV/AIDS (UNAIDS). <http://www.unaids.org/epidemic_update/index.html> [2001, Jan. 6]. UNAIDS comprises HIV/AIDS programming of the United Nations International Children's Emergency Fund (UNICEF), United Nations Development Program (UNDP), United Nations Population Fund (UNFPA), United Nations Office for Drug Control and Crime Prevention (UNDCP), United Nations Educational, Scientific and Cultural Organization (UNESCO), the International Labour Organization (ILO), the World

Health Organization (WHO), and the World Bank.

UNECA. (1998, July 24). *African Economic Report–1998*. [Online]. United Nations Economic Commission for Africa, Economic and Social Policy Division, Addis Ababa, Ethiopia. <http://www.un.org/Depts/eca/divis/espd/aer98.htm#i> [1999, March 20].

UNICEF. (2000, Dec. 12). *The State of the World's Children 2001*. [Online]. United Nations International Children's Emergency Fund (UNICEF). <http://www.unicef.org/sowc01/> [2000, Dec. 20]: "The most critical stage of a child's development is the early years, and it provides the best opportunity for investing in human beings. In the first 36 months of a child's life, brain connections multiply and the motor that will fire the child's thinking and behaviour patterns for the rest of his or her life is formed. As children learn to speak, sense, walk, and reason, the value system against which they will judge good and bad, fair and unfair is also formed. This is the most vulnerable period in a person's life and one that demands the most care from society. This is the central theme of 'The State of the World's Children 2001.' It argues that ensuring a child's rights is a process that must begin very early, even before the child is born, because investing early in a child's health, education, and nutrition is a relatively efficient and effective way of guaranteeing positive future returns through savings on health and other services."

Utsumi, T. (1999, Dec. 19). Season's Greetings from GLOSAS/USA. [Online]. The Global University System. <http://www.friends-partners.org/utsumi/gul/late-1999/12-19-b.html> [1999, Dec. 20].

Utsumi, T. (2001). Quest for global peace: Personal recollections. [Online]. The Global University System. <http://www.friends-partners.org/GLOSAS/GPA-Taipei_8-15-01/Quest_for_GP.html> [2001, Aug. 12]: The paper was Utsumi's contribution to the Global Peace Assembly, which was organized by the Vice President of the Republic of China, the Federation of World Peace and Love, the Association of World Citizens, the Millennium World Peace Summit, and the Women's Federation for World Peace, in Taipei, Taiwan, August 12-19, 2001.

Utsumi, Y. (2001, Nov. 12). Africa's new voice: Exposing old myths, establishing new targets. [Online]. International Telecommunication Union, Telecom Africa Summit, Johannesburg, South Africa, November 12-16, 2001. <http://www.itu.int/TELECOM/aft2001/cfp/auth/4929/ppt_4929.ppt> [2001, Nov. 20].

Ward, A. (2001, March 28). BBC World Service hits record. *Financial Times* [Online]. <http://news.ft.com/ft/gx.cgi/ftc?pagename=View&c=Article&cid=FT3YPSPFVKC&live=true&useoverridetemplate=ZZZ99ZVV70C&tagid=ZZZPB7GUA0C&

subheading=UK-Financial%20Times> [2001, March 29].

WDR. (2000). *World Development Report: Attacking Poverty (2000-2001)*. The International Bank for Reconstruction and Development, The World Bank. Table 19: Communications, information, and science and technology, p. 310. New York: Oxford University Press, Inc.: The figures for personal computers were based on 1998 data. There are more recent data attributed to other sources for both the number of Internet hosts and the number of PCs for each nation, but the figures used here were from an equally reputable source.

Wescott, G. C. (2001, June 10). Salary supplementation. *Reforming Technical Cooperation for Capacity Development*. [Online]. United Nations Development Program / Capacity.org. <http://www.capacity.org/undp-forum/detail_forum.phtml?act_id=34&username=guest@capacity.org&password=9999> [2001, June 10].

WHO. (2001, July 9). World Health Organization and top publishers announce breakthrough on developing countries' access to leading biomedical journals. [Online]. World Health Organization. <http://www.who.int/inf-pr-2001/en/pr2001-32.html> [2001, July 15].

Wolfensohn, J. D. (2000, Mar. 7). Remarks by World Bank president via videoconference to the Global Knowledge II conference of the Global Knowledge Partnership, March 7-10, 2000, Kuala Lumpur, Malaysia. [Online] <http://www.globalknowledge.org.my/pressroom_speech_7mar00jdw.htm> [2000, Mar. 15].

World Bank. The World Bank Group. [Online]. <http://www.worldbank.org/research/growth/> [2001, Oct. 25].

Chapter VI

Globalization and Frameworks for Digital Opportunities

Globalization may have already become entrenched, and developing countries may not have the power to reverse the phenomenon. Instead, given that activities remotely could affect the majority in a local environment, including poor communities that are not even aware of global economic regimes, managers of developing countries' institutions are faced with the burden of developing effective interventions to minimize negative impacts of globalization of capital while enhancing the opportunities for their citizens.

The influence of the Information Age on a nation's wealth creation may be through its ability to create new competitive advantages in which the nation-state acts as a sink to pull global knowledge and capital flows. Development of human resources and establishment of the facilitating business environment in developing countries are therefore essential in creating the fertile environment that can attract the flow of capital and know-how toward building the Information Age in these countries. This would in turn nurture their knowledge economies and lead to sustainable economic and social progress. Developing countries need to design creative means to divert some of the global wealth and knowledge resources toward their issues. This needs to be done in a manner that could be mutually beneficial to the North and South, without being parasitic of the North or allowing themselves to be exploited by such capital and knowledge flows.

For developing country regions, 'globalization' could begin with 'localization,' working its way to 'regionalization' and perhaps successfully into global trade. Developing countries could use the opportunities of IT in enhancing links among local communities, and these local linkages could build up into a higher order of regionalization through integration of common values and creation of open channels for discussing and resolving disputes.

The inability of these nations to reflect critically about the forces that separate their peoples while they attempt to orchestrate regional and global integration frameworks perhaps explains the sources of failure of previous attempts at sub-regional and regional integrations. Moreover, images, such as the recurrent food crises in some regions, elite-induced warfare, and rebel activities are leading to donor fatigue syndromes and may make the focus on developing nations a lost case. Yet these are the elements that a concerted deployment and imaginative use of IT may resolve and avert in the future, by creating knowledge-based activities.

GLOBAL DEVELOPMENT INSTITUTIONS

The development community has championed new paradigms about development programming, which emphasize knowledge sharing *via* telecommunications. It may be important for these institutions to learn from the failure of earlier development models, for example the structural adjustment programs to develop safety nets for those who may be adversely affected during the implementation of programs that could be considered as shock therapy. The solutions prescribed by these institutions are not perfect, and a major cause of failure of the models has been the lack of understanding of the structural underpinnings of their impact zones, for example the culture, infrastructure, economic, and political arrangements. Experts have admitted that the nations of Southeast Asia that followed the dictates of the international development and donor institutions during the Asian Financial Crisis in the late 1990s were not necessarily the ones whose economies emerged strongest: Thailand, for example, which followed the IMF's prescriptions the most closely, performed worse than Malaysia and South Korea, which followed more independent courses (Stiglitz, 2000). Stiglitz's account of the differences in the philosophies of the development partners is a chilling revelation of the lack of a partnership approach in the economic rescue packages prescribed by the main agents of economic reforms in the developing and emerging economies; it also highlights the one-size-fits-all type of economic modelling for nations that are culturally, technologically, and economically different from each other, and demonstrates a poor understanding of external development agents about local situations.

In another case, a group of protesters, much less conspicuous than the WTO protests in Seattle, warned against the World Bank plans to finance a gas pipeline project in an African country, on the grounds that it would destroy the livelihoods of indigenous communities. They suggested that social development was more important than laying pipelines in a region where the oil industry has come into conflict with local cultures (RAN, 2000). The World Bank was very disappointed to learn subsequently that the first receipts of the 1,000 km pipeline project were actually not used to improve education, health, or public infrastructure, as agreed upon in approving the loan (Farah and Ottaway, 2000); ironically, even the poor nations consider sophisticated military weapons as instruments of peace and are unable to see the wisdom in the axiom that knowledge makes one person more powerful than the army of 10 rulers.

As a result of these lapses in structural adjustments and other economic rescue packages for the developing world and emerging economies, the livelihoods of rural dwellers and many in urban areas have been negatively and disproportionately impacted by macroeconomic policies that emphasized commodity export and insinuated alien policies without regard to the social realities in the impact areas. Connectivity for knowledge flow should be mindful of such failures and include the design of social support systems so that the calamities that often drag down nations as they attempt to emerge, such as the economic crises that were recently visited upon some of the emerging economic zones in Southeast Asia, Latin America, and Eastern European nations, would be less frequent and less severe. The financial crises that rocked Southeast Asia and other transition economies were reminders of what can ensue when capitalism is operationalized in communities that do not have sound regulatory structures of markets and financial systems to protect investors, businesses, and the general public. In Indonesia, for example, children were withdrawn from schools and further depriving their brain of scholastic nourishment and career development. Depravity, ineptitude, and blind replication of development models that are unadjusted for cultural, economic, and local infrastructure would compound the situation of developing countries, if 'market fundamentalism' took hold without adequate rules and appropriate structures for engagement.

On the other hand, the 'markets' are not rigid or divine; often their features are overruled in times of local or global constraints: as it was becoming apparent that the September 11, 2001, terrorist attacks against New York City, The Pentagon, and Pennsylvania could tip the economies of industrialized nations toward recession, central banks in the U.S., Europe, Japan, and Canada injected more than 100 billion dollars into the international payment system in a coordinated effort to keep money flowing, as some of the major financial markets remained closed for a relatively long period immediately following the attacks (Ebner, 2001; McKenna and Wills, 2001; Stinson, 2001); the U.S. Federal Reserve Board trimmed interest rates by one-half of a percentage just before the resumption of trading at the New York Stock Exchange; and investors were also wooed by pundits to demonstrate patriotism, so that a stock market meltdown might be avoided. The U.S. Federal Reserve and stock market regulators took extraordinary measures to shore up the financial sector; regulators lowered the bar for companies to buy back their own shares. Without these measures, the Dow Jones Industrial Average, the most widely followed market index, could have performed worse than the near-record weekly decline of 14.3 percent it recorded that week; the highest decline of the index was 15.5 percent in July 1933, during the Depression.

Participation of the majority and the poor in the globalization of people, trade, and services needs to be carefully orchestrated to lead to socially just designs of economic growth that would permit the majority, including the poor, to participate in the benefits of global innovations. The knowledge needs of these economies demand market adjustments that would facilitate actualization of digital opportunities; for example, the research industries of the industrialized economies could be induced to contribute to knowledge generation about poor societies through tax incentives for spreading innovation.

Policymakers in some developing countries are also realizing that the institutions that prescribed remedies for their economic woes did not have the necessary elements in their models. For example, Ishmael Yamson, the chair of Unilever Ghana, made a scathing indictment of the development community in the period leading up to the 2000 presidential and parliamentary elections in that country. He noted that the development options that were emphasized to the country by the architects among the development partners did not help to restructure the nation's economy away from traditional commodity export dependency; they promoted the expansion of the mining sector, cocoa ,and non-traditional commodity exports to the exclusion of sectors with the capacity to sustain growth. Yamson thought that the development options should have included a clear strategy to restructure the economy to seed value-added manufacturing, services, telecommunications, and other sectors of the evolving new economy that have the potential to create sustainable growth and development (Mensah, 2000). The extent to which these remarks were genuine, or heeded by the nation would be determined by the post-electioneering activities of the national administration and citizens. Moreover, the ability of the public, especially the local media, to act as effective oversight organs will determine the extent to which these issues are thoroughly discussed and integrated into future development programming.

Some programs within the donor community that are supposed to assist developing countries fulfill their knowledge needs are yet to develop clear strategies to enable the local communities to access global information; many are also doubtful of the relevance of knowledge networks in sustainable development. Some of the organizations that currently have knowledge for development programs are yet to re-align their internal programs or educate their personnel sufficiently about these strategies; in some cases their personnel doubt the relevance of communications to the poor or the possibility that the knowledge of the poor is necessary in the schemes at all. In some cases, the generals may have sound plans, but some in the command chain and the foot soldiers may not have understood the battle plans.

Therefore, upon 50 years of development practice, the chorus is still sung that rural people hunt for mushrooms from the wild, crack palm kernels on rocks, sharpen machetes on rocks, grate vegetables on rocks; women give birth anywhere, and humans and domestic animals drink and bathe in the same creeks and ponds.

It is now recognized that there are various actors in sustainable development, and that building a viable information culture is both a local and global responsibility. The donor and development communities may not have the knowledge to develop effective local networks directly, but they could contribute in other ways. Development of local points to ground digital bridges for knowledge flows toward poverty alleviation should be undertaken by the groups that have the closest contact with the impact community. Grassroots organizations and small businesses that have the capacity and competitive advantages in local communities may be the ideal anchors of global knowledge inputs into local knowledge systems and construction of digital bridges. On the other hand, development institutions may often be too remotely conversant of the micro-environments that constitute the domains of grassroots organizations, or what Brodman has termed *micro-knowledge* (Janice Brodman, Education Development Center, Inc., personal communication, August 18, 2001). Much of the data that are the inputs into development models that emanate from multi-lateral programming relate to wide areas, and this does not lend to high accuracy and efficiency in remote programming for local communities by their development partners. The development community may also be subject to the political manipulations of local elites, who are often segregated from the ground. However, the networked economy could evolve new partnership arrangements that are inclusive of grassroots communities. These local groups could be engaged in the identification of issues that should be factored into programming about themselves, and as means to stimulate creativity locally in the operationalization of development frameworks.

The bilateral and multilateral institutions may not be able to spread into remote communities with the efficiency that local groups exhibit or be successful in program implementation without the cooperation of the local groups. However, they could assist in the development of nurturing environments in the local communities by deploying their fiscal power and knowledge networks to enhance the capacities of local information and knowledge brokerages. That way, the Information Society in the developing world would begin to realize one of the expectations of the IT revolution, which is to create new employment and opportunities in the impact communities.

Many local groups have questioned the intrusion of global institutions into areas that they consider as under local control and local initiatives. Some civil society groups oppose the tenets of some of the new programs within overseas development agencies and multilateral institutions, which emphasize portals about development knowledge; they fear that these programs could centralize Internet coverage of development issues, and their establishment was seen as a bid to sift and control the flow of ideas, instead of encouraging existing initiatives (Kabissa, 2001). The grassroots organizations view these initiatives as top-down programs that have not been sincere in the inclusion of local groups as significant stakeholders in programs that are designed to impact them. Local and global civil society organizations are allowed to participate in electronic and face-to-face dialogues leading to the creation of some of these frameworks, but their contributions are either ignored, or are incorporated without reward to the contributors. This would suggest that the ideas gathered from the public have little or no value, or that there is no mechanism to reward talent, and this could deprive the global development community of a rich source of ideas for development programming. Therefore, while the internal programs of the development agencies are highly capitalized, the grassroots programs are undercapitalized. Under such a scenario, the new theory of global development that presupposes equity in access to resources would be an illusion.

The multilateral and bilateral institutions could concentrate on other areas that would make their policies work best for their clients instead of competing in the domain of the grassroots organizations. For example, these institutions could deconstruct the walls that compartmentalize their internal units as discrete functions; this deconstruction could foster lateral thinking among their various units, offices, and personnel, and stimulate more frequent participation in inter-agency programming. These institutions could facilitate the construction of digital bridges by redeploying their vast human resources and financial backbones to help local groups to build their capacities in knowledge-based activities and make meaningful inputs into development programs.

The donor institutions and external development organizations could also assist local groups that have already identified local information and knowledge needs, and groups that have developed approaches to serving them, by providing these groups with the resources that would enable their ideas to be translated into tangible products. They could help local groups to mobilize funds, assemble the technology community regarding satellite availability and other tools, act as guarantors for venture capitalists, develop new tools to assess connectivity programs, develop guidelines to draw investment capital into poor regions without disturbing fragile economies, and suggest how TNCs could reinvest profit within the region of operation. They could also help to set realistic goals to close the information gap, by developing new methods to monitor and evaluate the evolution of local telecommunications applications, and negotiate on behalf of these communities for access to these tools and other knowledge inputs.

Other areas in which donor institutions could be effective are in ensuring that communications content includes indigenous knowledge *and* application to modern challenges, providing information that would change attitudes so that the ancestral knowledge, the basis of livelihoods of the majority, is not looked upon scornfully by personnel and programs within their institutions. This includes their country offices and personnel from developing countries who may have been educated *out* of indigenous knowledge; a major activity within these institutions would be the education of their own staff to fully comprehend indigenous knowledge and its role in sustainable development.

Multi-stakeholder partnerships, including local communities, businesses, national governments, NGOs, TNCs, and multilateral and bilateral organizations that are being established to develop information societies around the world should not lose sight of the principal elements of successful economic ventures—variability and competition. Partnership for knowledge sharing should be based on exchange of ideas that would support the visions identified by the various members, but partnership should not necessarily imply uniform outputs or cloned products. Development assistance should seek to equip the impact community with the mechanisms to identify ideas that are worthwhile, and for product variability in the local markets so that quality of knowledge services can be enhanced continuously. Such thoughts are in line with the products from the private sector: The Coca-Cola Company has local operations in nearly 200 countries, where the company's non-alcoholic beverage concentrates and syrups are used to produce more than 230 beverage brands, including Coca-Cola, Sprite, Fanta, Dasani, and Powerade, while the Pepsi Company produces Pepsi, 7-UP, Mirinda, Lipton's Iced Tea, Aquafina, Mountain Dew, among others; similarly, water is bottled by Perrier, Evian, Aquafina, Poland Spring, Crystal Geyser, among others. Product variability as part of the free market system, if it is a desirable economic attribute, should not be limited to the private sector or developing country governments alone.

The donor community has been making compelling arguments for developing nations to deregulate their markets and allow market structures to take hold. This deregulation should include the programs of donor and development communities as well. The deliverables of the various divisions and units within the donor and development communities should also be compared to the performance of their counterparts in the private sector of the industrialized economy where the development organization may be located and evaluated as such. This would increase the relevance of their programs to actual development outcomes, as they would compete with the private-sector units for the market share.

Competition, the basis of the world order that has triumphed over other philosophies of organization, is not only between business organizations in one market. Competition exists among nations and regions as well as between the rich and the poor; the rich economies of today are aware that kingdoms and empires have a lifespan, and a great empire of today could disappear when major paradigms shift. Developing nations could not expect that others would provide them with the plans that would enable them to compete against those who 'assist' them. This basic instinct that underlies human and institutional interactions may not be obvious to the actors, however development programming entails a passion and the desire to help the helpless; the helpless do not achieve equity with their saviours. That more than half of the overseas development assistance of many donors returns to the donor nation in the form of employment and business opportunities for their own citizens and institutions is indicative of this human nature. The benefits of the information society under such assistance could only be in trickle amounts to those who are helpless, and leapfrogging of the poorer communities would remain hypothetical but not actualized.

Thus development programming also needs some structural changes and internal transformations within the donor institutions, as much as developing nations have to rethink local development inputs and outputs.

GLOBALIZATION AND ACTIVISM

Global development policy should understand local concerns so that such policy frameworks could work toward peace. Issues concerning the development of social safety nets to mitigate the negative impacts of globalization have been the causes of some violent clashes between institutions fostering globalization and civil society groups, notably, the Seattle convention of the WTO. President Clinton was tactful in welcoming the presence of the protesters:

> *"And we are called upon here to meet against a background of a lot of people coming here to protest. I condemn the small number who were violent. ... But I'm glad the others showed up, because they represent millions of people who are now asking questions about whether this enterprise in fact will take us all where we want to go. And we ought to welcome their questions, and be prepared to give an answer, because if we cannot create an interconnected global economy that is increasing prosperity and genuine opportunity for people everywhere, then all of our political initiatives are going to be less successful." (PBS, 1999, news)*

However, these remarks have not dispelled the mistrust between civil society groups and the institutions of globalization, in fact, the protests against the WTO conference became a trendsetter. The confrontations between civil society groups and global summits stem from the yawning gap between the policy positions of global political and economic institutions and civil society groups. Civil society groups perceive these institutions and their perspectives on global issues to unduly reward private capital at the expense of social development, policies that are 'anti-people.'

The result of this tension is that world leaders and their economic teams have not been able to meet without the protection of heavily armed police units and barbed wire fences since the Seattle convention of the WTO. Global economic and political leaders become fenced-in, further isolated from the general public that their deliberations are expected to impact. The World Bank and IMF for example ended their 2000 annual meeting in Prague early, due to violence. The South African Finance Minister, Trevor Manuel, who was chair of the meeting, delivered his concluding remarks to an almost empty hall and remarked that: "It is a pity that it has descended into violence" (BBC, 2000, 944341.stm). The Summit of the Americas in Quebec City was convened to discuss fundamental issues regarding the formation of a hemispheric trade bloc of the Americas, but the participants were physically and philosophically detached from the people whom they were seeking to integrate. As a storm of protests against the summit by civil society organizations was brewing, the police outlined how they had fortified Quebec City with a six-kilometre security fence including a 3.8-kilometre concrete wall that was topped by a chain link fence around the meeting venues--a security perimeter that protesters referred to as 'the wall of shame.' Residents and workers in the city needed passes to move around; 6,000 extra police officers were drafted, extra guards and nurses were on hand to deal with any cuts or bruises, and a local jail transferred inmates elsewhere to create room for protesters that would be arrested (CBC, 2001, security.html; CBC, 2001, summit_prep010406). The apprehension of the Canadian security forces stemmed from the Seattle protests and an earlier encounter during the November 1997 meeting of the Asia-Pacific Economic Cooperation leaders in Vancouver (CBC, 2000, apec97.html).

Other manifestations of the suspicion with which some civil society groups and activists view the activities of global institutions were at the European Council meeting of the heads of state and government of the EU in Göteborg, and at the July 2001 meeting of the leaders of the G8 nations in Genoa, Italy. And the confrontations have been getting more violent and war-like: in response to the 100,000 anti-globalization and debt relief activists that were expected at the Genoa meeting, the Italian government deployed about 20,000 police and soldiers to patrol the city and waters off the port; the security forces had the full range of ammunitions at their disposal for crowd control, including surface-to-air missiles, fighter jets, naval ships, and minesweepers (CNN, 2001, genoa.protests/index.html). These tense environments are not conducive to brainstorming on complex issues.

The donor institutions and development community have programs to address equity in trade, reduce poverty, increase knowledge flows between economic spheres, and provide access for the world's majority to the deliverables of global capital including new drugs, and communications. Perhaps, the refinement and implementation of these policy frameworks have been mismanaged or lack sufficient knowledge capital, after all these institutions are not immune from the effects of a global ingenuity gap. Stiglitz (2000), for example, noted that the solutions provided by some global financing and development institutions to some of the ills of the developing world would have deserved failing grades, had these scenarios been student examinations at a university.

Civil society groups on the other hand constitute the impact communities and the groups that operate within the communities that are most negatively affected by global capital mismanagement, political adventurism, economic fluctuations, and environmental recklessness. These acts may not have been foreseen or intended; on average, humanity exists within all persons, and the development community is made up of people, most of who have the interests of humanity at heart. Also many demonstrated passion in their voluntary services to assist poor communities in their development efforts through programs such as the Peace Corp, prior to their substantive careers in development. Therefore, the negative impacts of globalization may be due to the global ingenuity gap and not to an intentional act to dispossess some; the failure of development programming since the end of World War II and the political independence of many nations that constitute the developing world is due to multiple failures by actors in both the donor and recipient nations.

A major test for global institutions, therefore, is how to engage civil society to develop mutually agreed positions and development alternatives.

The activism of grassroots organizations has been generating some support from governments of the industrialized economies toward the cause of weaker economies. In a victory for anti-globalization pressure groups, France became the first major industrialized country to support proposals for a tax on international financial transactions, a policy position of groups such as the French pressure group, Attac, and others; the anti-globalization movement has a strong base in France, among farmers and intellectuals. The French Prime Minister, Lionel Jospin, agreed with the views of these pressure groups and announced that his government would put forward a proposal for the so-called 'Tobin tax' at a subsequent meeting of European finance ministers. The Tobin tax, named after Professor James Tobin, the Yale professor of economics and Nobel-prize winner, seeks to impose a tax of one percent on all international currency trades. With global trade on the foreign exchange markets alone running at about $1.5 billion every day, theoretically, the tax could raise many billions, and some predict it could more than double aid flows from rich to poor countries (Schifferes, 2001). The idea would be to reduce speculation against certain currencies, and to raise money that could be used for development in less economically developed regions. The UK campaign group, War on Want, has called for Britain to follow the French lead.

Information and telecommunications could enhance dialogue between the opposing sides on common themes to generate synergies; civil society groups have already proven their ability to mobilize their sympathizers. Ironically, civil society groups have been able to use one of the principal tools and features of globalization—connectivity—to mobilize themselves around other tenets of globalization.

The various civil society groups that forge temporary unions to oppose global leaders do not have common positions on all issues. Their ability to unite around the broad areas that are common to them is a demonstration of how groups could forge partnerships to achieve common goals. The creativity of these grassroots organizations in human mobilization, compared to more resourceful organizations that cannot communicate their intentions effectively, further demonstrates that large organizations are not necessarily the most efficient or the most knowledgeable about local issues. Furthermore, many of the civil society groups that are increasingly becoming the public's conscience are made up of young people who would inherit the policies of current institutions, hence the need to solicit their input.

UNDERSTANDING LOCAL ISSUES
AT THE GLOBAL LEVEL

The inability of local communities to inform the global community about their values causes major misunderstandings at the global level. For example, many leading nations and institutions of the world did not foresee the wisdom in convening a Truth and Reconciliation Commission similar to the South African process to begin the process of building and managing global peace. The South African government and peoples, on the other hand, understood that the conflict during the evil apartheid era resulted in violence and human rights abuses from all sides, hence the commission was established to document the confessions and allegations of rights abuses or violence undertaken by any member or group of society. The World Conference Against Racism, Racial Discrimination, Xenophobia and Related Intolerance that was convened under the auspices of the United Nations High Commission for Human Rights and hosted by the Government of South Africa in the summer of 2001 could have been such an opportunity for the various communities of the global village to document their perceptions of pain and abuse due to other communities. That conference, in the least, could have initiated a process to deliberate on the allegations and possibly lead to global justice that could broker a long-term peace, for the visions of global equity to take hold. Instead, in light of the boycott of the conference by some communities, the downgrading of representation to junior levels of authority by others, protests, and the 'blasphemy' of one group by the other, the failure of the convention was echoed in the closing remarks of the High Commissioner, Mary Robinson: "It has been an exhausting nine days for all of us, but I believe it has been worth it. … I do not claim that this Conference has solved the problems of racism, racial discrimination, xenophobia, and related intolerance. The issues have been addressed, not answered" (WCAR, 2001, http). In an unrelated case, only two days after this conference ended, the world would be shocked by the terrorist attacks against the U.S. in New York, Washington, and Pennsylvania on September 11, 2001.

The need to appreciate local issues by the global development community could become a major exercise in building global security. The interests of the poor are also subject to manipulation by local elites and the plight of those affected locally may be exacerbated by the uninformed actions of external communities that would have been intended to rescue those affected. The events leading up to the 2002 presidential elections in Zimbabwe revealed major misunderstandings between the local and global levels.

The value of land may have been diminished in the knowledge economy of the industrialized economies, but land remains the most prized possession in the existence of poor communities. It is often a tragedy when such needs of the poor become mired in international politics and the manipulation of local elites. The violence associated with the Zimbabwean land crises, and the perception of an abuse of the democratic process by those in power in that country are giving the wrong signals about the need of the majority to possess a piece of land in their own countries, especially land that they considered as their heritage. But it is naïve to see the land crises in Zimbabwe as anything new; land ownership has been a potent issue in major battles in human civilization. In spite of the general perceptions of an evil plot by the Zimbabwean authorities to cling on to power by exciting the people through the land issue, African nations continued to support the Zimbabwean actions, while condemning the violence that has been associated with the encroachment on white-owned farms by Zimbabwean blacks (see BBC, 2001, 1429431.stm and related links; Chitiyo, 2000; Electronic Mail and Guardian, 1997). Africans agree that there should be more peaceful ways to resolve the land crises in southern Africa and elsewhere, but they are also conversant of the role of land in the existence of rural African communities.

The 'home' of an African is where the ancestral land is located—your village, your hometown—and this is the only land that they have free and equal access to --the source of food, material for shelter construction, and the place of birth and burial. Therefore a meeting of African foreign ministers in July 2001, ahead of the annual summit of the Organisation of African Unity, rallied behind Zimbabwe over its land reform program, proposing to establish a committee to support Zimbabwe in future talks with the EU and other parties. African governments continued to adopt a cautious approach to the Zimbabwean crisis in the fall of 2001 in spite of the worsening human rights and political situations in the country that could affect the presidential elections in Zimbabwe in early 2002. A delegation of southern African ministers who travelled to the Zimbabwean capital, Harare, just one week after the U.S. House of Representatives had endorsed a bill calling for sanctions against the Mugabe government, were opposed to the idea of sanctions against Zimbabwe; the ministers said that they had gone to Zimbabwe as friends of that nation, and that addressing the crises required a careful and mature approach (Phillips, 2001).

African leaders and others familiar with the underlying causes of the Zimbabwean crisis are perhaps acutely aware that the issue can arise in South Africa, and Namibia as well, as all these nations share similar histories of the causes of the land dispute—apartheid; Namibia and South Africa are also grappling with the potentially explosive issue of land redistribution and reforms. South Africa and Namibia could therefore learn from the continuing violence in Zimbabwe and take measures to address the issue and not hope that it would just disappear, for fear that discussing the issue would scare investors.

The primary causes of these land crises and potential conflicts relate to the allocation and utilization of land, demography, race, poverty, and wars. Long before Zimbabwe became independent, many communities that the blacks considered their ancestral homelands had been confiscated one way or the other. Zimbabwe's black population who are alive today remember that this land grab was still a policy of the apartheid Rhodesian government as recently as the beginning of the 1970s. That regime declared the lands of many blacks as 'European areas' and the original landowners were forcefully relocated to marginal lands. Some of the victims of this policy recalled that each of the affected black family was allowed to take only three head of cattle, regardless of the size they owned, and the rest was sold to white farmers at a fixed price of three dollars; the new lands where the blacks were relocated to had less rain, the soil was poor, and families were crowded together with just six acres to a family. These are the victims of the colonial land grab, who are determined to return to the grave area of their ancestors that they were forced to leave behind.

White minority rule ended in Zimbabwe in 1980. Twenty years later, according to government figures published before Zimbabwe's War Veterans led an occupation of white-owned farms in 2000, white farmers still owned a disproportionate share of the country's prime agricultural land: Some 4,400 whites owned 32 percent or 10 million hectares of the agricultural land (in some areas, this could be as high as 60 percent) while about one million black small-scale families farmed 16 million hectares or 38 percent. Moreover, much of the white-owned land is in more fertile areas with better rainfall regimes, while the black farming areas are often in drought-prone regions.

The external community and media dwelt on the plight of the black farm-workers on the white-owned tobacco plantations in discussing the land crisis in Zimbabwe, but these workers were already among the poorest of the poor; most of the 350,000 farm-workers earned about US$30 a month or two 50 kg-bag of maize flour (*mealie meal*), the staple diet.

Zimbabweans of all races realize that this is a situation that must be rectified, but there is little common ground on the process. The EU and the U.K. argue that previous land reform programs were tainted with corruption, and that a genuine land reform should be part of a transparent, integrated, and consultative process that increases production and alleviates poverty. The Zimbabwean authorities, on the other hand, contend that only 19 percent of the land acquired for distribution was prime land, the rest was either mediocre or unsuitable for agriculture or grazing, and the number of candidates for resettlement was higher than originally projected after the war of independence. As most of the forced removals were done much earlier in the century, and those who may have been directly involved in carrying out the policy may have died by now, a typical response from white farmers has been why they should be punished for the sins of their ancestors. The mainly black Indigenous Business Development Centre in Harare however noted that it is only when Zimbabwe's blacks challenge the economic *status quo* that there is a row about unconstitutional behaviour.

There are economic implications for the forced reacquisition of land from white farmers; much of the land is used in the cultivation of tobacco, which accounts for 30 percent of Zimbabwe's foreign exchange earnings as the world's third biggest exporter of tobacco, hence the fears that taking highly mechanized, profitable tobacco farms, dividing them up, and giving small plots to subsistence farmers would spell economic disaster. On the other hand, others argue that smallholders can be as efficient as the huge estates if they are given the right infrastructure; they point to the fact that 70 percent of Zimbabwe's maize and cotton has been grown by small-scale black farmers who could diversify into cash crops such as flowers and tobacco, as their counterparts in Kenya and Malawi.

Others are sceptical about the position that the West took regarding the Mugabe regime's electioneering, pointing to similar occurrences elsewhere in Africa that are not equally condemned: very few people around the world may have been aware that presidential elections were held in another African nation at about the time of the 2002 elections in Zimbabwe; the presidential election in Congo-Brazzaville at about the same time as Zimbabwe's was characterized as a "one-man race" (BBC, 2002, 1865069.stm), following the withdrawal of other candidates on grounds that the contest was flawed from the beginning; European observers however declared that the election was held in an acceptable fashion and passed off without major incident.

The violence associated with the resistance by political, business, media, and civil society groups to the issues of democracy and accountability in the administration of the Mugabe regime in Zimbabwe, and the violence leading up to the 2002 Presidential elections in that country are rather shameful and should be condemned by those in the free world. Moreover, on the day the EU was demanding clarifications about the status of international elections observers, monitors, and opposition groups, with the threat of economic sanctions against the Zimbabwean government, "several hundred supporters of the Uganda People's Congress (UPC) who marched through the streets after the authorities banned a rally at Constitutional Square" (BBC, 2002, 1756724.stm) were being fired upon by police in the Ugandan capital, Kampala; they were calling for the same political environment of multi-party democracy as their Zimbabwean opposition colleagues, after 12 years of Museveni's single-party brand of governance. Miton Obote, two-time ex-President of Uganda, and current leader of the Uganda People's Congress, does not have a good record of his own, but both the Museveni government in Uganda and Mugabe's Zimbabwe have been involved in the war in the Democratic Republic of the Congo that is threatening to destabilize central, eastern, and southern Africa, and for whose cessation Nelson Mandela has devoted tireless energy even in his declining health.

The inability of the global community to apply equal measures in addressing insecurities in the region provides grounds for dictators to argue that they are being unfairly treated; Zimbabwe for example offered the explanation of British resentment arising from the issue of land redistribution and the effect on white farmers as the cause of the EU threats of sanctions, perhaps knowing that there were other nations in the Africa region that did not allow political activity; indeed, when the meeting of Commonwealth foreign ministers in London five weeks prior to the Zimbabwean presidential elections failed to endorse the push by the U.K. to expel Zimbabwe from the organization, the official Zimbabwe media saw it as "a humiliating defeat for the mighty British empire" (BBC, 2002, 1793444.stm), echoing a return to the rhetoric of the battle for independence; Mugabe also pointed to the disputed Florida results of the 2000 presidential elections in the U.S. to suggest that the West did not have a fair electioneering either. Moreover the meeting of the disciplinary Commonwealth Ministerial Action Group in which the eight-member council was split along racial lines in their opinions about the events in Zimbabwe is revealing that the suspicions that existed between the colonies and colonizers might still be simmering, with the "old white Commonwealth represented by Britain, Australia, and Canada, urging Zimbabwe's suspension while the new Commonwealth of African and Asian countries preferred words of condemnation" (BBC, 2002, 1792746.stm).

Not long after the Zimbabwean crises, the South African security forces under the government of the African National Congress destroyed 1,200 shacks that were built near Johannesburg airport by squatters (CNN, 2001, safrica.land/ index.html). Prior to South African independence, about 80 percent of the land was designated for white occupation, while the black majority had limited rights in about 20 percent of the country, usually in the most remote, undeveloped areas; three million black people were forcibly displaced in this abuse between 1960 and 1983. The African National Congress (ANC) government made land reform one of its priorities after independence in 1994 to rectify this imbalance, while the Pan Africanist Congress supports the squatters, because they find the pace of the government's efforts to restore land to those dispossessed under apartheid, and plans to transform the ownership of land to be too slow. The ANC government however won a court eviction order on the grounds that the safety of the squatters was at risk, as the land they had encamped on contained electric pylons and an underground oil pipeline. Similarly, 10 years after independence, up to 80 percent of Namibia's arable land remains in the hands of around 5,000 commercial farmers, most of them white-owned, while vast tracts of communal land have been denuded by years of mismanagement and are overgrazing.

There are other contentious issues that reveal differences in perception by the impact group and the global community: the issue of reparations to the victims of the Trans-Atlantic Slave Trade was one of the contentious aspects of the World Conference Against Racism, Racial Discrimination, Xenophobia and Related Intolerance organized by the United Nations High Commission for Human Rights. The subject was featured on the American ABC Television program *This Week* on September 2, 2001; one of the pundits appearing on the program remarked that an African living in a remote community on that continent might end up being obliged to make reparations to a middle-class in the U.S., apparently because the villager's ancestors sold people as slaves, who ended up being taken to the cotton fields in the U.S. Obviously, not everyone reads from the same page of history, and opposing sides record different interpretations of events, as Africans contend that the slave castles that line the West African coastline, and the human transport systems and sales points that were designed to facilitate the human trade were not evolved by Africans; Africans were not aware of what happened at the other end of the trade route. Still worse, not every culture has the same medium to document important periods in their civilization, and oral cultures from which the slaves were taken even today remain the least resourceful in presenting their evidence. However, each individual of this day ought to ponder the circumstances under which he or she could sell their children into bondage. Slavery has been shown to continue in some parts of Africa today, but mostly in war zones, such as Sudan. Considering that colonial powers took anything in their occupied lands that they perceived worthwhile for their own use, and labour was needed in the emerging production systems in the period following the discovery of new lands, the mechanisms by which such labour was obtained by the more powerful authorities would have been more dubiously orchestrated by the community that needed the labour than in distant communities that did not know where the labourers were needed or the size required.

Perhaps, those who have not experienced the concerns raised by a community should not be the ones to decide how painful an act was on its victims. Those who were the primary impact groups of policies or acts usually understand the issue from a different perspective than those who may only be casually aware. For example, Africans on the continent of Africa, or recent African migrants in North America and Europe, should not be the ones who make decisions on the issue of affirmative action in the U.S. This is not to imply that African nations were not directly impacted by the Slave Trade; the continent lost its productive human resources, and this would have caused severe economic and social distortions in the local communities. However, those who are the descendants of people who endured the trans-Atlantic crossing and who were put to work under the most heinous conditions should be the ones who decide what course of action they wish to follow; continental Africa could support the African Diaspora communities in their actions, but Africa should not be the more opinionated on such issues.

Similarly on affirmative action, African intellectuals who obtained their early education in Africa prior to migrating to North America and Europe would have had different experiences and purpose in life, compared to the circumstances in which the original African Diaspora groups in these communities would have experienced. For example, many Africans from Africa and the Caribbean, who migrated to Europe and North America after the Second World War, went to these regions in search of jobs, and some already had significant education in their countries of origin. These people therefore may not fully comprehend the social, political, and economic exclusions that the local black populations would have endured. It is important that the homeland and the Diaspora groups have a mutual understanding of the roles of each group.

These and other issues are more understood by local groups than any global development expert from outside could comprehend. Therefore, globalization that could be a shared value ought to begin from the local communities, building up into common national frameworks and regional blocs.

REFERENCES

BBC. (2000, Sep. 27, 944341.stm). Prague IMF summit ends early; Banks and global corporations were attacked overnight. *British Broadcasting Corporation* [Online]. <http://news.bbc.co.uk/hi/english/world/europe/newsid_944000/944341.stm> [2000, Dec. 20].

BBC. (2001, July 8, 1429431.stm). African ministers back Mugabe reforms. *British Broadcasting Corporation* [Online]. <http://news.bbc.co.uk/hi/english/world/africa/newsid_1429000/1429431.stm> [2001, July 9].

Other relevant *British Broadcasting Corporation* [Online] reports include: Who owns the land? (2000, Apr. 26). <http://news.bbc.co.uk/hi/english/world/africa/newsid_594000/594522.stm> [2001, Jan. 201]; Mugabe warns of land reform 'anarchy.' (1998, Sep. 9). <http://news.bbc.co.uk/hi/english/world/africa/newsid_167000/167825.stm> [2001, July 9]; Up for grabs. (2000, July-Sep.). *Focus on Africa Magazine.* <http://www.bbc.co.uk/worldservice/africa/features/focus_magazine/archive/zimbabwe/land.shtml> [2001, Sep. 1]; A flash of anger. (1998, Jan.-Mar). *Focus on Africa Magazine* <http://www.bbc.co.uk/worldservice/africa/features/focus_magazine/archive/zimbabwe/farms.shtml> [2001, Sep. 1]; Land for the landless. (2001, Jan.-Mar.). *Focus on Africa Magazine* <http://www.bbc.co.uk/worldservice/africa/features/focus_magazine/archive/namibia/namibialand.shtml> [2001, Sep. 1].

BBC. (2002, Jan. 12, 1756724.stm). Uganda police shoot at demonstrators. *British Broadcasting Corporation News* [Online]. <http://news.bbc.co.uk/hi/english/world/africa/newsid_1756000/1756724.stm> [2002, Jan. 16].

BBC. (2002, Jan. 30, 1792746.stm). Zimbabwe splits Commonwealth. *British Broadcasting Corporation News* [Online]. <http://news.bbc.co.uk/hi/english/world/africa/newsid_1792000/1792746.stm> [2002, Jan. 31].

BBC. (2002, Jan. 31, 1793444.stm). Zimbabwe declares 'diplomatic victory'. *British Broadcasting Corporation News* [Online]. <http://news.bbc.co.uk/hi/english/world/africa/newsid_1793000/1793444.stm> [2002, Jan. 31].

BBC. (2002, Mar. 10; 1865069.stm). One-man race in Congo poll. *British Broadcasting Corporation News* [Online]. <http://news.bbc.co.uk/hi/english/world/africa/newsid_1865000/1865069.stm> [2002, Mar. 18].

CBC. (2000, Mar., apec97.html). After APEC. *Canadian Broadcasting Corporation* [Online]. <http://cbc.ca/news/indepth/apec/apec97.html> [2001, Dec. 15]: "In November 1997 very few Canadians had ever heard of an organization called APEC. Today they may not know what the initials represent, but they certainly are more familiar with the organization than ever before. That familiarity comes from the constant media coverage of an incident that had caused Prime Minister Jean Chretien and his government more grief than anyone would have expected. There was the resignation of the Solicitor General, ... and many irate words spoken in the House of Commons. It's all the result of the November 1997 Asia-Pacific Economic Cooperation summit in Vancouver. At the time the economic situation in the region was glum. The Asian economic crisis was dominating headlines. The [Canadian] government went to great lengths to make sure the meetings were a success, and "success" was at least partially defined by who showed up [and] wanted the list to include Indonesia's President Suharto, many young Canadians didn't. They [the young Canadians] were extremely angry about his [Suharto's] human rights record. They planned a series of demonstrations to get their point across. The [Royal Canadian Mounted Police] RCMP used a heavy hand against those protesters. In order to clear a path, the police made several dozen arrests and used pepper spray on dozens more."

CBC. (2001, Apr. 6, summit_prep010406). Quebec City prepares for summit violence. *Canadian Broadcasting Corporation* [Online] <http://cbc.ca/cgi-bin/templates/view.cgi?/news/2001/04/06/summit_prep010406> [2001, Apr. 6].

CBC. (2001, Apr. 20, security.html). Summit of the Americas. *Canadian Broadcasting Corporation* [Online] <http://cbc.ca/news/indepth/summit/security.html> [2001, Apr. 21].

Chitiyo, T. K. (2000). Land, violence and compensation: Reconceptualising Zimbabwe's land and war veterans' debate. *Track Two,* 9(1), [Online]. <http://ccrweb.ccr.uct.ac.za/two/9_1/zimbabwe.html> [2001, July 9].

CNN. (2001, July 13, safrica.land/index.html). More S. African shacks demolished. *Cable News Network* [Online]. <http://www.cnn.com/2001/WORLD/africa/07/13/safrica.land/index.html> [2001, July 14].

CNN. (2001, July 20, genoa.protests/index.html). Protester dies in G8 summit clash. *Cable News Network* [Online]. <http://www.cnn.com/2001/WORLD/europe/07/20/genoa.protests/index.html> [2001, July 20].

Ebner, D. (2001). This market is suffering. *The Globe and Mail,* Toronto, (Sep. 15), B1.

Electronic Mail and Guardian. (1997, Dec. 8). The case for redistributing Zimbabwe's land. *Electronic Mail and Guardian,* Johannesburg, South Africa [Online]. <http://www.mg.co.za./mg/news/97dec1/8dec-zim_land.html> [2001, July 24];

Farah, D., & Ottaway, D. B. (2000). Chad misuse of oil funds for arms jolts World Bank. *The International Herald Tribune,* (Dec. 6), 7: In June, when the World Bank agreed to back a controversial oil pipeline from this impoverished desert nation to the Atlantic coast, it declared that it had found a way to prevent corrupt officials from stealing the country's wealth. ... World Bank officials said that their 'Chadian model' would prove that they could overcome the nation's endemic corruption and that it might be applied to other corruption-prone oil-producing lands. So when [the recipient nation] had used $4.5 million of the first oil revenues to buy weapons instead of social programs, [it] sent a jolt through the bank, ... World Bank director for Chad and several other ... countries [in the region], said he was sobered and disappointed."

Kabissa. (2001, July 10). A declaration from concerned knowledge workers: Bank's Development Gateway. *Kabissa-Fahamu Newsletter*, No. 29 [Online]. <http://www.kabissa.org> [2001, July 10].

McKenna, B., & Wills, A. (2001). Regulators move to prevent panic selloff. *The Globe and Mail*, Toronto, (Sep. 15), B1.

Mensah, M. (2000, Oct. 30). World Bank, IMF to blame for nation's economic woes, declares Yamson. *The Daily Graphic*, Accra, Ghana [Online]. <http://www.graphic.com.gh/> [2000, Nov. 1].

PBS. (1999, Dec. 1). Clinton addresses the WTO. *The Newshour*, MacNeil/Lehrer Productions. Public Broadcasting Service. [Online]. <http://www.pbs.org/newshour/bb/international/wto/clinton_wto_12_1.html> [1999, Dec. 2].

Phillips, B. (2001, Dec. 10). Zimbabwe sanctions opposed. *British Broadcasting Corporation News* [Online]. <http://news.bbc.co.uk/hi/english/world/africa/newsid_1702000/1702583.stm> [2001, Dec. 11].

RAN. (2000, June 6). The Chad-Cameroon rainforest oil pipeline. [Online]. Rainforest Action Newtork. <http://www.ran.org/ran/info_center/press_release/000606.html> [2000, Nov. 15]. "Under the constant threat of brutal government repression, it is highly unlikely that the citizens ... will reap any benefits from the World Bank's proposed oil pipeline if it goes forward now and, clearly, they stand to be harmed if they try to voice their concerns," said a spokeswoman for ... Association for the Defense and Promotion of Human Rights prior to the World Bank's vote. In addition to concerns about corruption and human rights abuses, critics point out that the project will require the forced relocation of people living along the pipeline route, and will affect thousands of indigenous ... people (commonly referred to as Pygmies) that live in the region. Many groups have also expressed grave concerns about environmental repercussions from the pipeline, which will run through rainforest areas inhabited by endangered chimpanzees, gorillas, and forest elephants, and open up forest interiors to poachers and illegal logging. The project's oil fields are located in the heart of ... food production, where oil spills could have potentially disastrous consequences.

Schifferes, S. (2001, Aug. 29). France backs Tobin tax. *British Broadcasting*

Corporation News [Online]. <http://news.bbc.co.uk/hi/english/business/ newsid_1514000/1514647.stm> [2001, Aug. 29].

Stiglitz, J. (2000, Apr. 17). What I learned at the world economic crisis—The insider. *The New Republic* [Online]. <http://www.thenewrepublic.com/ 041700/stiglitz041700.html> [2001, Oct. 30].

Stinson, M. (2001). Fed injects record cash into system. *The Globe and Mail*, Toronto, (Sep. 15), B3.

WCAR. (2001, Sep. 8). The World Conference Against Racism, Racial Discrimination, Xenophobia and Related Intolerance, Durban, South Africa, August 31—September 7, 2001. [Online]. Office of the United Nations High Commissioner for Human Rights. <http://www.unhchr.ch/html/racism> [2001, Nov. 1]: The High Commissioner's closing remarks on September 8, 2001: "True measure of work at Durban will be difference it makes in lives of victims, High Commissioner for Human Rights tells closing of Anti-racism Conference." *United Nations High Commissioner for Human Rights News* [Online]. <http://www.unhchr.ch/huricane/huricane.nsf/view01/ 5FAF026AB0A6D50041256AC1005D2A6B?opendocument> [2001, Sep. 19].

Chapter VII

Capitalizing the Knowledge Economy of Developing Nations

Teleconnectivity and knowledge for development philosophy needs a companion—a knowledge trust fund—that would secure the necessary technical, financial, and human resources to facilitate the identification of ideas and their translation into the desirable outputs. Such a knowledge fund could aim to amalgamate fund and knowledge sources to maximize knowledge gain, enable crosscutting research, effect cost sharing, and reduce budgets while engaging in holistic research for sustainable development in the wake of inadequate development funds.

The present development model of information and communications as the principal means to facilitate knowledge flows parallels the establishment of schools in the developing world at the time of independence of these nations. Many nations embarked upon major efforts to educate their citizens; schools were built as partnerships involving national governments, local communities, religious organizations, overseas development agencies, and international volunteer groups such as the American Peace Corp, and mirror groups in Europe, Japan, and Canada, all working together to provide learning environments (tools, and human resources) to the new nations; the various religions continue to provide education to a large percentage of communities at the basic and secondary school stages today. Many developing nations, understandably, do not have their own financial resources to build their communications infrastructure for knowledge flows, and the same partnerships that were involved in constructing schools earlier would be required to contribute to the construction of digital bridges with these communities. This is a reflection of the failure of the earlier educational system to engender sustainable development or to wean these nations from dependency on external aid for any major initiatives in their local economies.

Global efforts however abound to assist poor nations to develop such capacities, as described earlier. These initiatives have dramatically increased the ability of many communities in the developing world to participate in knowledge sharing activities, but the oral cultures, archaic methods and practices, and inefficient institutions are yet to be transformed into viable communities. A major limiting factor in creating a vibrant information culture and seeding innovation in the impact communities could be a lack of capitalization of ideas and networks that emanate from the local communities themselves. This weakness is most felt among NGOs, small and medium-size enterprises, grassroots initiatives, civil society programs, and others of similar profiles that are community-focused and knowledgeable about the local values and aspirations, and which could help make the bold leaps that are required for a vibrant information culture. For example, Bissio observed that while $100 billion are needed to provide basic IT access to two billion people in the developing world, the G7 countries have pledged $1 billion (Bissio, 2001). The infoDev program of the World Bank is a major source of funding for telecommunications and development in the developing world. In November 2001, 12 potential recipients of *info*Dev funding were announced, out of 145 applicants; there was no grassroots organization of African origin among the potential recipients in that round of funding. The potential recipients globally were four U.S.-based proponents, three in Brazil, and one each in France, South Africa, Russia, India, and Spain. Of these, five focused on Latin America and the Caribbean, four targeted Africa, and one each for South Asia, East Asia, and Europe & Central Asia. Of the African impact groups, the Washington, DC-based Volunteers in Technical Assistance (VITA), WorldSpace Foundation, the South African Council for Scientific and Industrial Research, and the Unified System of Business Laws (UNIDA, France) were the selected recipients. UNIDA, for example, brings together the African Development Bank, the West African Development Bank, Accor, Bollore, Comilog, Nestle, Texaco, BNP Paribas, Agip, Belgolaise Bank, Societe Generale, Heineken, Gras et Savoye, AGF, Total-Elf-Fina, Credit Lyonnais, Air France, and Ernst & Young.

In light of the limiting funding opportunities for smaller groups and community-focused organizations participating in constructing digital bridges, innovative methods of disbursement could be devised. A drawback of current funding regimes for unsolicited proposals from the affected communities is that of 'accept' or 'reject,' especially when proposals are declined more because of inadequate funds than the substance of the proposal. As McCarthy noted, most of these proposals compete against each other (Steve McCarthy, World Association for Online Education, personal communication, April 6, 2001). Competition is desirable in identifying the programs, which could generate the best outcomes for the impact communities as well as optimizing development funds, but fair competition requires availability of a fair resource environment. In addition to 'accept' or 'reject,' a third option that could 'combine' ideas that are similar and targeting the same geographic or thematic area could be evolved.

New methods of evaluating proposals concerning knowledge for develop- ment using IT are required as proposals for research into knowledge economy activities are currently evaluated with old assumptions. Often, many reviewers and other experts who determine the relevance of project proposals lag behind proven ideas, operating without regard to the changes that the Information Society has unleashed. Recognition of civil society, indigenous knowledge, and NGOs should be without hesitation. For example, while knowledge has been recognized as impacting all activities, some reviewers do not see the value in academic pursuits regarding teleconnectivity and indigenous domains. Reviewers of proposals also need not be physically close to the funding institutions; this would increase the pool from which experts are drawn to review proposals and provide a rich corps of evaluators, who understand the multiple factors that affect knowledge network activities. Some reviewers, in the year 2000, did not have room for knowledge networks, indigenous knowledge, or the possibility to blend knowledge. More- over, reviewers and their processes could be made transparent; currently, they are shielded from the proponents while students know whom their professors are even if they are given failure grades, and accused persons know the judges and jurors who may incarcerate them.

In many cases, the nature of the funding regime is not different from securing private capital, at least considering the requirement that the proponent should first have significant 'matching' funds prior to accessing the global development fund; in other instances, 'government approval' may be requested, and inclusion of national institutions may not be readily seen as sufficient government involvement. This requirement for government involvement as a precondition for access to global development fund is contrary to the emerging trend of local governments assuming an increasing responsibility for the well-being of their residents.

Many funding regimes concentrate on governmental-level funding, although it has been shown in other models that private and small-scale initiatives make strong contributions to the wealth of nations. Many grassroots and small-scale connectivity programs currently compete unfavourable and fruitlessly with major organizations for the same funding opportunities. The notion that large institutions or government agencies have the most ideas about development knowledge or connectivity may not be supported in some economies where the national leadership and its institutions have not been able to translate their capacities and market structures into strategies that enhanced the livelihoods of the majority of citizens; in some cases, these institutions actually impede the activities of the private sector and civil society organizations. The outcomes of programming by these institutions would not suddenly become efficient because of modern communications. In such cases, partnerships for development communications need to undergo internal reforms, and identify the activities that would best be accomplished by other groups.

The donor community has been exhorting developing nations to establish 'good governance' and free-market structures as preconditions for continued financial assistance. However, good governance would not come from the national leadership to the subjects. The overthrow of some notable dictatorships have been led or instigated by the public, which is the legitimate oversight of good governance. Good governance is therefore the outcome of several stakeholders, including civil society groups, the intellectuals, businesses, and youth groups, among others that act as oversights of governance institutions and principles. Good governance in the developing world requires a stronger participation of civil society, including indigenous institutions. The empowerment of these groups would require direct access to development funds for establishment of independent information access points, and civil society groups and other stakeholders should not need the blessing of governments to contemplate the application of knowledge networks in the sustainable development of local communities.

The global knowledge for development community could explore in-depth how the donor and overseas development agencies, communications manufacturers and innovators, and impact communities could interact effectively to maximize the returns on the investments in IT infrastructure. The donor community could ensure that there are guidelines for individuals, institutions, and groups that receive assistance from public sources in building their IT capacity to provide training to other groups or devote a certain percentage of resources to public good.

These observations suggest that greater efforts should be dedicated to providing unambiguous evaluation criteria and resources concerning proposals about knowledge networks that originate from the impact groups so that they can meet eligibility criteria.

PRIVATE SECTOR AND FOUNDATIONS AS FUNDING SOURCES

It is in the interest of the global telecommunications industry to assist in the development of the Information Society in the developing world to avoid market saturation of their products. As Dumelie observed, the G8 countries have a vested interest in the future development of knowledge economies because the subject area represents large commercial interests that are tied to increasing the power base of G8 countries and their economies (Roger Dumelie, Canadian International Development Agency, Ottawa, personal communication, April 16, 2001). If the developing nations become part of the global Information Society, there would be a larger market for the telecommunications industry as well. However, a sustained capacity of developing countries to purchase the products and services of the telecommunications industry would depend on the relevance of the outputs and services to the economic, social, and physical needs of the local community. An irresponsible government could expend national funds on a few rounds of purchases of these tools before determining what to use the tools for, as is common in trade with despotic and corrupt regimes. However, technology companies hopefully seek to develop long-lived trade relations with these nations. Therefore, it is in the interest of the telecommunication hardware manufacturers and applications developers to support content creation in knowledge for sustainable development globally, including developing nations.

At present, some of the most endowed foundations, including those that may have derived their seed grants from the telecommunications sector, do not see any wisdom in connecting developing countries to the global information grid; they would rather support vaccination programs and similar traditional aid programs. Immunization of children in developing countries would contribute tremendously toward human security globally, but there are no vaccines to many of the ills that plague these communities, apart from developing their knowledge infrastructure. Moreover, development challenges are more than clinical; they include a lack of information and modern knowledge, economic, psychological, and technological challenges. Establishment of local knowledge networks that include developing country institutions could create the critical research capabilities of the communities in need so that they would learn how to develop vaccines and other security measures by themselves.

Private-sector companies other than the telecommunications sector have been increasing their contribution to development of talents through partnership programs with schools and colleges in the industrialized nations; the beverage industry has been very conspicuous on some campuses in the industrialized economies. These companies could extend the same help to developing nations: soda drinks have displaced the indigenous beverages among the middle class in developing nations, and rural dwellers pant for these soda beverages like the deer pants for water. The Coca-Cola company revealed its global influence: "From our heritage to our mission to the people who bring our products to thirsty consumers, The Coca-Cola Company is a part of lives everywhere" (Coca-Cola Co., http). The movie, *The Gods Must Be Crazy*, demonstrated, perhaps inadvertently, how Coca-Cola was introduced into indigenous cultures (Virtual Shopping Mall, http); the movie characterized a South African bushman encountering 'civilization' for the first time with great puzzlement. The business and advertisement successes of bottling foreign beverages have not been transferred to the local beverage industries while 'technology transfer,' 'appropriate technology,' and other terms were emphasized in some of the models that sought to bridge the technology gap between the haves and have-nots. On the other hand, the marketing success of the soda industry could impact the promotion of an information culture by involvement in IT campaigns for schools and youth connectivity schemes, although this is not an endorsement of the market activities of these businesses or their products.

LOCAL FUNDING SOURCES

As the Information Age is so crucial to the development status of a nation, developing countries need to make all efforts to contribute significantly from their own meagre resources toward building their local communications infrastructure. The managers of funds on behalf of knowledge for development schemes should be selfless in their activities; they could develop critical project evaluation and analytical methods for funded projects to entail visionary outlooks, implementation, and longevity. Very often a foot soldier on the side of the poor in the frontline trenches of the battle against rural poverty soon learns that children of the poor are sometimes enemies of their own parents and communities; often, some of the these children at the armoury refuse the cry for weapons, preferring instead to honour requests from more innocuous frontlines in order to build their personal defence perimeters or little fortresses. On the other hand, they could use their offices to serve their impact zones, which are also their homes of origin.

Developing nations could also conceptualize national security to be broader than in military terms alone; knowledge—more than guns—would determine the relative peace that a nation enjoys. Reference has often been made of the lopsidedness of the defence budgets of some developing nations, compared to social development. Indeed, a redefinition of national security to emphasize human security could free up budget portions devoted to the purchase of military weapons for the 'protection of the state' that often connotes protecting a head of state. A qualified head of state needs fewer military weapons for 'protection;' after all, no amount of weaponry in a nation's arsenal has protected any world leader, including presidents of superpower nations, and leaders of major religious bodies from the line of fire of those who intend to misuse weapons. As wisdom makes one wise person more powerful than 10 rulers in a city, national security should emphasize a search for wisdom. Wisdom, however, is achieved through accumulation of knowledge (experiences), which in turn is acquired by access to pertinent information.

The international sporting events for instance, in which developing countries participate, could be another inherent opportunity for these nations to capitalize their knowledge economies. The developing nations and transition economies have been major contributors to the entertainment and business of sporting events such as the Olympic Games, and soccer's World Cup, but these economies have not been viewed as capable hosts and are consequently denied the widespread economic and social benefits that host nations may derive. The host nations of these global sporting events generate revenues, such as from broadcasting rights, and the infrastructure and sporting spirit that become the heritage of the host community. The idea in declaring the hosts of these events several years ahead is to enable the host community to develop the required facilities, often by borrowing money from the global financial markets and solicitation of TNCs for investments in return for product endorsements. As suggestions are emerging that developing nations could host global gatherings of economic and political leaders in the wake of the recent riots at such meetings in the industrialized nations, organizers of other types of global gatherings should begin to consider how best to equitably share in the wealth of their collective activities. These events could be re-organized to contribute to the developing world as much as the richer nations, perhaps through revenue-sharing arrangements.

The Diaspora and Local Investment Capital

The establishment of local venture capital markets by developing countries could also be viewed as a priority issue in capitalizing local knowledge economy activities. Programs that insinuate traditional development assistance and lack mechanisms to develop viable local capital markets might not generate the long-lasting effects of programs in local economies. An unrecognized source of investment capital for many developing countries has been the large number of their Diaspora populations in the industrialized economies; not only the intellectuals but also the taxi drivers, factory workers, and those employed in the hospitality industries in Europe, North America, Southeast Asia, and other regions. But the mechanisms to mobilize capital from the Diaspora toward investment in critical sectors of national and regional economies need to be carefully thought out. Governments of developing countries could work together to lobby the industrialized economies, where significant Diaspora communities exist, for recognition of the extended indigenous family values. For example, citizens of developing countries that reside abroad make significant financial remittances to their families and relatives. The average monthly per capita remittances of this group could be higher than the $25 contributions to 'sponsor' a child through aid agencies by citizens of the industrialized world. While such sponsorships are tax-deductible, the larger remittances by the Diaspora to their families are not official so far as income tax declarations are concerned, therefore the tax burden on the Diaspora groups becomes punitive; it is executed as if the income earner had spent all the income on his or her nucleus family that resides in the industrialized economy. Developing nations could lobby for tax concessions to the contributor, and mechanisms to recognize such contributions as public goods. This could result in a significant increase in the amount of foreign currency contributions by the Diaspora to the economies of their countries of origin.

The Diaspora groups could also take advantage of the business partnerships that are features of their adopted industrialized nations to make more imaginative use of their investments in their homes of origin. The streets of Accra in Ghana in the last decade have been lined with vehicles 'for sale.' The vehicles are usually imported by individuals, most of who are working abroad, with each individual making his or her own investment decisions. In a country where owning a vehicle is a status many would only dream of, Ghanaians abroad send vehicles home to be sold as 'business' activities. Often the vehicles do not meet government stipulations, such as vehicle age, and are confiscated and destroyed. Many of the vehicles remain unsold for long periods; thus the 'investment' capital generates no positive returns for an extended period, and remains unavailable as venture capital to develop critical sectors of the local economy.

The features of African economies, and some of the countries in Latin America, Asia, and the Caribbean and other islands are not those of manufacturing, as in the category of Rosecrance's *body nations* of the emerging economies of Southeast Asia (Rosecrance, 1999). These countries, especially in Africa, are about consuming manufactured goods produced in other regions and may therefore be classified as *mouth nations*. This has resulted in the plummeting of their local currencies against international currencies, and with a low purchasing power, only a few in Africa are able to consume the tangibles of the body nations, leaving about 80 percent of Africans to derive all their possessions from the land.

Citizens of developing nations who reside in the industrialized economies are partly to blame for the rapid and continuous depreciation of local currencies in their homes of origin. This group, with more available foreign currency compared to those in their original countries, indulge in the consumption patterns of the West; the local elites soon copy their ways of life, for example in the rapid expansion of real estate formats that require more construction inputs, such as cement and roofing materials, from factories with low productivity; this creates an artificial demand and drives up the cost of housing. Therefore, these Diaspora groups should be part of the solution to local economic problems, and a major contribution would be in pooling their financial resources into investment capital for access by small-scale businesses in the local economies.

National commissions on investment in developing countries could contemplate the investment policy guides that would build confidence among their citizens residing abroad in order to pool their savings into available capital for development; they could develop mechanisms for guaranteed returns on investment to attract the capital assets of their Diaspora groups.

REFERENCES

Bissio, R. (2001). Universal access: Can the digital divide be bridged? In Thurnheer, K. (2001). *Knowledge—A Core Resource for Development*. Helvetas Documentation on the Swiss meeting on global knowledge sharing and information and communication technologies, Berne, Switzerland, (2001, Mar. 20); <http://www.helvetas.ch/km/workshop/papers.html>, or <http://www.helvetas.ch/km/workshop/docs/bissio.pdf> [2001, Mar. 30].

Coca-Cola Company, the. [Online]. <http://www.thecoca_colacompany.com/tccc/index.html> [2001, Mar. 7].

Rosecrance, R. (1999). *The Rise of the Virtual State: Wealth and Power in the Coming Century*. New York: Basic Books.

Virtual Shopping Mall. The Gods Must Be Crazy (1981). [Online]. Virtual Shopping Mall. <http://www.virtuallyshopping.com> [2001, Mar. 1]: Starring Marius Weyers, Sandra Prinsloo; Director: Jamie Uys. Synopsis: South African bushman encounters 'civilization' with great puzzlement. Runtime: 109 minutes; Genre: Comedy.

Chapter VIII

Preservation of Cultural Identity and Preventing Piracy of Indigenous Intellectual Properties

While the benefits of modern communications in sustainable development could herald new opportunities, there are dangers associated with the introduction of such tools and programs, including cable television, from external environments into communities that have different technological status and cultural values if foreign contents are not managed to interact in harmony with local values. Violent clashes of cultures and possibly dilution of locally held values could result if education about the philosophical bases of the foreign culture is not provided in parallel. Therefore, frameworks such as the United Nations Television Forum should ensure that introduction of new media and programming into new cultural terrains are not wholesale endorsements of the external values depicted. No democratic society should legislate what its citizens could watch on television, however, each cultural domain could saturate its own airwaves with the programs that are deemed as culturally appropriate and cherished by local norms. Nyamba of the Université de Ouagadou in Burkina Faso for example, in his *Aspects Sociologiques, Etude de Cas*, described cultural attributes and social interactions in Africa and wondered if introduction of online messaging would obliterate the values inherent in the indigenous salutations (Nyamba, 1999).

INTERNET LANGUAGE AND INFORMATION LIAISONS

The Information Society is not by default set to obliterate minority groups, although the manner in which IT is operationalized could cause distortions in the existing structures of local communities. Nevertheless, Internet language has been seen as one of the features of the digital divide and sometimes becomes an issue that some language groups cite as their exclusion from sharing in global knowledge. Utsumi however described the convergence of cultures and religions into the modern digital telecommunications that are based on logic: the Greek word *Logos* (meaning Soul, God, and Truth in religion) is also the origin of the English word *logic*, which was translated into *word* in the King James Version of The Bible, and word is the basis of communication and understanding; the Indian invention of the concept of *zero* and the Arab introduction of zero along with Arabic numerals to the West, combined with the Judeo-Christian monotheism of *One* and Absolute God, and the relationship of *zero* and *one* to logic, like *yin* and *yang*, are features of the current advances in telecommunications (Utsumi, 2001). Utsumi therefore saw modern telecommunications as the medium for building peace among nations and across religions. Indeed, those who are participating in building the knowledge networks of the developing world could learn from the zeal with which missionaries and followers of the various faiths converted communities to the course of the originators of the faith organization. For example, Christian communities could learn from the activities of disciples of Christ such as the Apostle Paul, who defined the bases and practices inherent in the values of the Christian faith and the spread of their messages to communities far and wide; similarly, other religions have their own examples of network building that they can draw lessons from.

With IT, groups located outside a local environment could dial into that environment and share experiences in multimedia formats. The Internet informs anyone, anywhere, and at any time, about all entries held; for example, Web entries inform the global community at the desire of the information seeker, through 'keyword search' for example, that the word *Ewe*, apart from the possibility that it pertained to the female sheep and trade in its products, is also a first language for 2.5 million people that are located in Ghana and Togo (SIL, 1996). The Internet browser, who is familiar with the Ewe territory, would recognize some of the other smaller languages that they share settlement arrangements with, for example, *Akpafu-Lolobi* (population: 16,100), *Akposo* (population: 5,400 in Ghana; 94,900 in Togo), *Nyangbo* (population: 3,900), and *Tafi* (population: 2,900), among others. Other authors, for example Ladzekpo, portray some of the cultural attributes of the Ewes (Ladzekpo, 1995).

IT presents the opportunity for any community, group, or individual to tell the world about whom they are and where they are, or learn about other cultures.

The history of colonial Ghana (Gold Coast) includes the exile of influential chiefs and leaders of ethnic groups to remote islands. That was the strategy to weaken the coherence and organizational capacities of the local communities so that colonial rule would take root. The Ashanti king, *Prempeh I*, and his council of elders were exiled to Seychelles for that matter. Such information could now be viewed by anyone anywhere, who is able to dial into the Smithsonian and navigate the links to learn about this history. Also, conducting a keyword search of *Timbuktu* (or Tombouctou) could generate options that lead to *Ministere de la Culture et du Tourisme* of Mali (1999), where a great deal of information about Timbuktu, and the people of Mali could be gleaned. The pages inform the reader of Timbuktu's history as a centre of African civilization during the reign of the old African empires, prior to the period of colonial rule in the region; therefore the people of Mali can disabuse the minds of people in other cultures who erroneously use Timbuktu to mean a far-out place. Microsoft's Encarta also contains an entry for this city on the southern edge of the Sahara, probably founded in the late 11th century AD, connected with the Niger by canals and which served as a great commercial entrepôt, a regional trade centre, and an international centre of Islamic learning; Tombouctou had a population of about 40,000 in the early 16th century (Encarta, 2000). Yet when Sadowski asked the audience at a major conference convened in Bamako, Mali, in 2000 to address the communications and knowledge needs of that country and the entire region, if America owns the Internet, there were at least a few hands in the audience for *oui* or yes (Sadowski, 2000).

The issue of ownership, or the perception of its "foreign" origin, has dogged the Internet since it became a universal information resource, but often based on linguistic properties. Developing countries need to deliberate on their language characteristics in the Information Age, and if there should be information pluralism on the Internet, the burden lies on the users and people of the various languages, including the intellectuals of the various ethnic languages to create the visibility about their peoples.

Moreover, none of the major foreign languages is capable of resolving critical knowledge needs in the developing and transition economies, if these nations are unable to develop any relationship between the major indigenous languages and the major foreign languages.

There is ample room for all cultures to be represented on the Internet. The Internet allows mobilization of intellectuals of minority cultures to generate information about their own heritage and contemplate how to use that information. What is essential is the ingenuity of local knowledge and IT champions to contemplate the unique ways in which IT could be adapted to local situations, provision of access points, learning how to use the tools, and development of pertinent content to meet local needs. Generating information about local communities is an art of storytelling, and this would be done best by those whose histories and experiences are to be narrated.

The Information Society is about knowledge-based activities, and the concern of minority cultures is often about sustainability, especially since most of these groups are in the poor regions of the world. However, if all the contents of the Internet today were translated into an indigenous language, much would be meaningless to the majority of their rural peoples, most of who are literate only in their ethnic languages. It is at the level where global data is converted into locally relevant information and are usable by rural communities and other non-intellectual communities that the language of presentation would be important. Therefore, it is in building strong intranets or local area networks--where schools are networked in curriculum delivery, where hospitals and traditional health practitioners are connected together, and where technical schools and rural engineers are interacting--that local languages would be relevant.

Access to the Internet as currently constituted may benefit only those who are literate and functional in the Internet language of English or other major languages, as contended by those who view the Internet as another means to colonization. But developing country intellectuals, who are literate in all modern languages, as a group can mine information from the Internet and input that into LAN systems for relevance to their rural communities. The bureaux of local languages in the various countries could have a new role in translating material into functional languages before dissemination to the target communities.

A notable development in this regard is the launch of the Arabic Internet Names Consortium (AINC) with the objective of coordinating efforts to develop and deploy Arabic Domain Names system and applications. The Arabic Domain Names system could facilitate the internationalization of the Internet for all Arabic-speaking people of the world, allowing them access at all levels, without linguistic barriers (Arabia Online, 2001). Some computer applications developers are reducing the time-lag between the launch of different language versions of the same product by the same company; Microsoft for example was working toward reducing the time-lag between the launch of its English and Arabic versions of the Microsoft Office XP package to zero, from previous schedules that could be delayed as much as 18 months (Siddiqui, 2001).

Furthermore, computer programmers are breaking language barriers and allowing languages to become interchangeable, including extremely difficult and problematic scripts that made it difficult to mechanize some languages, notably the Nastaleeq script. Information provided at the homepage of some software manufacturers in Asia indicated that some of the region's scripts were so difficult to mechanize, and as a result there was no typewriter that could type in the Nastaleeq style for instance. However, advances are making it possible for software designers to create several bilingual applications with packages such as 'Urdu 98' (for Windows) and 'Nastaleeq Nizami' (the first complete Urdu and Farsi typesetting software for Apple Macintosh) that are able to make Urdu documents, including database applications, Internet Web pages, presentations, and other multimedia software (PDMS, http).

Rural communities in developing countries often rely on schoolteachers to interpret government memoranda. Thus many villages desire that the local school-teachers include at least one teacher who is a native of the village to function as an information liaison. Similarly, in the Information Age, developing countries should visualize the transformation of such roles into substantive local information brokers or intermediaries between the machine and communities, especially in cases where the majority of rural dwellers are illiterate in the major Internet languages.

Ideally however, households, indigenous knowledge practitioners, and communities could be trained to generate information about their own communities and practices; they could create journals of major transitions and occurrences on a continuous basis and such information on standard templates or formats could lend to the inter-conversion of the data into digital formats. These activities may be important in creating village portals and in enhancing the security of communities. An indigenous healer could notice the number of patients who visit his or her 'clinic' each week, patients' complaints, diagnoses made, and prescriptions and follow-up regimes that may be recommended. This would be an attempt at record keeping that would be relevant for determining trends and patterns, and logical predictions of the future.

PREVENTING PIRACY OF INDIGENOUS INTELLECTUAL PROPERTIES

It may also be argued that intellectualization of indigenous knowledge would temper with the sanctity of such knowledge systems. There is a real threat that establishment of digital bridges into the developing world would encourage external agents to siphon off valuable knowledge from the poor communities, just as natural resources such as minerals and forest products, and local arts and crafts were subjected to. The products of the digital bridge might also serve the interests of external institutions and not benefit the communities of interest. A knowledge system however is more than to serve as museums, or for tourist attractions alone; peoples' livelihoods depend on knowledge. Lack of intellectualization of indigenous knowledge and lack of relationship to national development programming in formal education, research, and industry have combined to relegate the practitioners of indigenous systems to the group that has been excluded from the benefits of advances in global science and technology. Local knowledge, ideally, would be dynamic, evolving with advances in global knowledge.

It is also possible that documentation of indigenous knowledge would open up the secrets of practitioners, for example indigenous healers, who often guard the ingredients of their concoctions. Global and local groups that already have the technical resources and capital to transform active ingredients of indigenous knowledge of herbs into commercial products might predominate the commercialization and deny the originators further access to the intellectual property. New Zealand's Maori groups for example, who feel that there have been a number of situations where some of their cultural activities, such as the *haka* war dance and Maori words, have been misused, are exploring ways to prevent such misuse; they threatened legal action against the toy firm, Lego, on the grounds that the company had copyrighted Maori language and images for use in toys, which the company denies (Walton, 2001).

To counter these threats, policy regimes could stipulate the governance arrangements necessary in integrating indigenous knowledge into global knowledge pools, including that the right to commercialize any product would be the right of the local community, local industries, and their mutually agreed partners in the global development community and investment capital markets. Activities that involve indigenous knowledge practices could be treated as the intellectual property of the community from where they might have been originally collected. National institutions could act as brokers and catalyze local-global knowledge for development partnerships, so that local groups channel such opportunities to the benefit of their communities.

The concept of ownership of an idea, a practice, a product, or the terms of institutionalized definitions of intellectual property may differ between indigenous groups and global treaties that a nation may be a signatory to. The concept of ownership in the Maori culture for example is such that the rights carry on forever, possibly because indigenous knowledge about herbs, traditional birth attendance, music, and other indigenous trades are held within families and clans. The New Zealand intellectual property legislation, however, does not have the specific concepts of indigenous rights enshrined, but this is an issue that the government was reported to be taking seriously.

Finding legal protection for the culture and designs of indigenous peoples is becoming an important issue all over the world. Some intellectual property experts and indigenous groups argue for a separate protection for indigenous intellectual property so that traditional owners can be guaranteed financial returns when their cultural works are used for commercial purposes. But this requires of developing nations, and regions that have a significant wealth of indigenous knowledge, to document, digitize, and codify their local knowledge systems to fully appreciate what knowledge they have, so that they would be able to exchange the knowledge at an equitable value. Moreover, processing indigenous knowledge through value addition would enhance its features and attract more reward in exchanges.

The initial lack of local expertise to handle data mining and translation into knowledge may hinder the effectiveness of splicing information. Connectivity programs therefore often include training components. Such training efforts should include long-term strategic intellectual exchanges with international centres of advanced learning and research that would work with local institutions to enhance their capacity of utilizing IT to translate local information into knowledge products. While the local telecommunications infrastructure might not be reliable initially, such difficulties could be overcome with ingenuity of designs, training of local technical personnel to handle minor and somewhat major technical glitches, and access to input from internationally reputed individuals and groups.

REFERENCES

Arabia Online. (2001, Mar. 21). Arabic Internet Names Consortium sets founders meeting. [Online]. Arabia Online (Guernsey) Ltd. <http://www.arabia.com/egypt/business/article/english/0,5127,11337,00.html> [2001, June 12]. See also: Seminar on the Arabization of domain names in Jordan. (2001, Mar. 17). [Online]. Press Release Network. <http://www.pressreleasenetwork.com/pr-2001/march/mainpr543.htm> [2001, June 12].

Encarta. (2000). Tombouctou. Microsoft Encarta Online Encyclopedia, *Microsoft Corporation*. <http://encarta.msn.com/index/conciseindex/01/00155000.htm?z=1&pg=2&br=1> [2001, Jan. 30].

Ladzekpo, C. K. (1995). Scenes from rituals of the Ewe. Homepage. [Online]. Center for New Music and Audio Technologies, Berkeley, California, U.S.A. <http://www.cnmat.berkeley.edu/~ladzekpo/Scenes.html> [2001, Aug. 5].

Ministère de la culture et du tourisme, Mali. (1999). [Online]. Government of Mali. <http://w3.tourisme.gov.ml/galeries/tombouctou1.html>; <http://w3.tourisme.gov.ml/t2000/racinesan.html> [2001, Jan. 30].

Nyamba, A. (1999, Dec. 7). *La Parole du Telephone ou Les Significations Socials et Individuelles du Telephone Chez les Sanan du Burkina Faso*. RuralCom'99 conference, Cotonou, Benin, December 2–7, 1999. [Online proceedings at: <http://www.esmt.sn>. Ecole Superieure Multinationale des Telecommunications (ESMT), Dakar, Senegal.]

PDMS. Pakistan Data Management Services. <http://www.pakdata.com>; Information about Urdu98 is at <http://www.pakdata.com/urdu98.htm> and Nastaleeq Nizami at <http://www.pakdata.com/nn.htm> [2001, June 12].

Sadowski, G. (2000). Civil society, local authorities and ownership of ICT–Global diversity and regional integration (Panel). [Online]. Bamako2000, Bamako, Mali, February 2000. <http://www.bamako2000.org/SITES/BAM2000/rencontre/programme.html#pleniere>, <http://www.bamako2000.org/SITES/BAM2000/documents/discours/sadowski.html> [2001, July 30].

Siddiqui, N. (2001, June 1). Latest Microsoft version launched. *Dawn (Internet Edition)* [Online]. <http://www.dawn.com/2001/06/01/int3.htm> [2001, June 6].

SIL. (1996). Ghana. In Grimes, B. F., (Ed.), *Ethnologue*, 13th Edition. SIL International (formerly the Summer Institute of Linguistic). [Online]. <http://www.sil.org/ethnologue/countries/Ghan.html> [2001, Aug. 5].

Utsumi, T. (2001). Quest for global peace: Personal recollections. [Online]. The Global University System. <http://www.friends-partners.org/GLOSAS/GPA-Taipei_8-15-01/Quest_for_GP.html> [2001, Aug. 12].

Walton, D. (2001, Aug. 9). Maori push for legal protection to control use of their cultural heritage. *British Broadcasting Corporation News* [Online]. <http://www.bbc.co.uk/worldservice/business/highlights/010809_maori.shtml> [2001, Aug. 9].

Chapter IX

Postlude

The Information Age is relevant to the prosperity and security of developing nations and their indigenous, local, or rural communities. The relevance of telecommunications to these communities includes the ability to use information tools to create interacting spaces for knowledge sources to converge with the user-community and generate solutions for the challenges in their livelihood attainments. The establishment of such area networks in communities whose communication methods are predominantly oral, and which have poor telecommunications infrastructure, demands imagination among planners, businesses, and impact communities to translate the telecommunications and digital exclusion into digital opportunities. The digital opportunities could be deduced from the information and knowledge needs of these economies, such as the need for better access to telecommunication infrastructure, tools, knowledge networks and communities of practice, expertise, and opportunities to build on local knowledge. Communications-centred knowledge for development programming, as a matter of necessity and to serve as effective knowledge gateways, should function as information and knowledge brokerages related to the collection, processing, packaging, and marketing of relevant content in knowledge for development, and not as a conglomeration of gadgets alone. Connectivity should enable people to learn, solve problems, produce more efficiently, preserve natural systems, and foster peace among communities and nations. Ideally, connectivity could be a viewing point of knowledge systems into other knowledge systems, including individuals and institutions; indigenous or local institutions, such as indigenous governance structures, rural occupational groups, and local communities, and formal institutions such as schools, clinics, agriculture, health, and social development, would be able to interact among each other at the local (horizontal) and global (vertical) levels. Similarly, students, teachers, researchers, and staff of agencies that are concerned about global development but are located in spheres outside the primary impact communities, when guided information channels exist, would be able to dial into a community multimedia system to observe and learn about the activities of their development 'partners' from their offices far removed in reality. This way, they would be able to generate more meaningful models in their intervention programs.

At the governmental and multilateral levels, each nation could describe its new comparative and competitive advantages in the networked economy and then operationalize IT around themes to realize their strategic vision. Each community, nation, and sub-region needs to ponder what the Information Society could mean to its inhabitants. Ghana, for example, which was President Clinton's 'gateway' into Africa, and which has become an area of increasing African-American investment activity, has a historical past as a major player in leading sub-Saharan Africa out of colonial rule, and in creating one of the best modern institutions in Africa immediately following independence. Ghana also had one of the best educational systems in Africa: the Ghanaian educational system produced teachers, who taught in Nigeria, Libya, Botswana, and South Africa, among others, but it could be argued that the type of education was not relevant to local people's needs. The disarticulation between the majority's knowledge for tool making, production, processing, social organization, and governance versus the basis of national institutions has meant poor capacity of both formal and informal systems. Ghana therefore could design a networked economy that is guided by developing new formats in education, governance, human resource development, and institutional capacity building that integrates both the indigenous realities and the modern systems they have purported to design and preside over. If human resource development became Ghana's strategic vision, the new education system could evolve by incorporating indigenous knowledge into curricula and establishing vital links among education, research, industry, governance, management, and commerce, for the prosperity and security of its communities. The products of such interrelationships could become that nation's competitive advantage in its sub-region, and the outcomes could be brokered to other communities and nations in the region.

The viability of global peace, security, and prosperity is influenced by the extent to which global and local leaders comprehend the causes of instability and chaos in their own communities and their impact on the world, or how global issues impact local environments. Often, the challenges of one community might not be readily appreciated by outsiders; invariably the non-industrialized nations do not have the opportunity to make their global development counterparts appreciate issues related to local security and prosperity; these communities are perceived as remote and peripheral to core factors that may impact prosperity in the industrialized cultures, until such insecurities build up into a potential force that is capable of fuelling global instability. The global development community has been unable to provide clear definitions and measurement methods of prosperity and security, whether political, economic, or social, therefore some communities are held up to others as models of stability until a sudden event, even a minor disturbance, reveals the inherent weaknesses that may have been ignored by the architects of the community, as the temporary compromises, alliances, and illusions of stability are confronted by the realities of internal dynamics that may have been suppressed by undemocratic and temporary measures.

Communication for development, being a complex issue, requires partnerships to analyze complex oral and rural structures, hence it has become essential and perhaps trendy for groups to constitute themselves into global knowledge networks toward development. Transforming the donor-recipient philosophy of traditional international development agencies has been the concern of some architects of the emerging global knowledge networks (Roger Dumelie, Canadian International Development Agency, personal communication, July 25, 2001). Global development networks are perceived as enabling each element to contribute to the prosperity and security of the others. This development option demands that the various types of organizations that constitute the global network are empowered to contribute to the best of their potentials regardless of status. These networks also attempt to include self-organized and community-focussed or grassroots organizations in their memberships, but such organizations are often poorly resourced; therefore the ability of the grassroots organizations to execute their roles in the global networks may be a limiting factor in the efficiency of such development models. However these grassroots organizations are usually screened for the relevance of their programs to the values of each network, hence they are capable of acting as units of the emerging global development organization, but without the burden of institutional impediments in rapid decision making at the local level.

Strengthening of the capacity of grassroots organizations and other networks within the local impact areas could showcase the benefits of global partnerships in local capacity building. The local members of global networks could represent the various partnership members, including the international development agencies, donor organizations, and specialized units of bilateral regimes at the grassroots as versions of the new global development organization. Their knowledge about the local environment, combined with access to the knowledge and resources of the global development community, would enable understanding of development and market options that can generate outputs in the local market while feeding their outcomes, or lessons learned, into the global development community. These groups could contribute to the pro-active penetration of the network's values into local groups, including governments and institutions, businesses, communities, and individuals. Since these grassroots members would have sought membership in the global network by themselves, they may be more likely to pursue networking and joint programming more actively and effectively than the traditional approach of selecting institutions in the South. This is, perhaps, the organic nature of networking as non-hierarchical and distributed nodes that can enhance creativity, entrepreneurship, new forms of interactions, and increase productivity locally with outcomes or lessons available to the global community. Currently institutions in the South are pre-selected for membership into some of the emerging global knowledge networks by virtue of their existence and not necessarily their ability to execute their roles in development initiatives.

The grassroots members of global knowledge networks and partnerships could become the focal presence of the development community in their respective communities—a place where institutions, businesses, and individuals could purchase knowledge tools and obtain information on knowledge trends, among other knowledge brokerage services. The information and knowledge brokerages would also provide the perspectives of the community they represent during major deliberations such as the G8 Nations' Digital Opportunity Task Force and the World Summit on the Information Society. The performance of these grassroots would be a reflection of the efficiency with which the top (external) communicates with the roots (local) and also determine the efficiency with which products are relevant to local needs. The information kiosks of these networks in the developing world could be considered as field laboratories, and could be actively sold as a place where external experts can undertake studies in the local area and obtain relevant information; this would be similar to the creation of tropical agricultural research posts in the Caribbean and Central America that served many educational and research needs of U.S. institutions.

It is presumed that each member of the global knowledge network would hold a valued stake or shares in the network, but as new members join the network, the average value could increase or decrease depending on the enrichment factor that the new member contributes. Some groups, such as the major development institutions and their 'partners' in the global private sector, may be well endowed and possess the capacity required to join these networks without the need for a transition period during which their capacity is nurtured, but the poor capacity of grassroots organizations and other small groups may require that they are actively groomed into membership. The current practice of rejecting outright groups that did not meet membership requirements may be detrimental to the concept of empowering various communities to participate in local development through partnerships in global networks. In that case, a process of affiliation of such groups with the nearest network element of geographic or thematic proximity may help to nurture the capacity of the prospective applicant to become a substantive global network member, similar to the model of grooming European nations into meeting the standards of the European Union by the time they are ready to join as full and efficient participants.

While the creativity of the poor and national institutions is admirable, an ingenuity gap may exist between a community's needs and its internal knowledge capacity to meet those needs, considering that some of the local challenges are a result of external influences that they may not fully comprehend. Institutions and personnel in many developing countries are capable of undertaking their mandates but may have been more preoccupied with daily bread-and-butter issues than with institutional responsibility. The ability of the local human resources and institutions could be supplemented with a virtual network of global human resources that includes the progenies of indigenous cultures--some of whom constitute the human resources of national institutions locally and others who serve in elite institutions around the world in order to reach indigenous institutions. The Diaspora population has experienced both worlds, and some are champions of the revolution of IT and knowledge networks. The goals to which such Diaspora intellectuals are currently engaged in the industrialized economies may be different from the situations that are concerned here, but these individuals can readily recall the features of the communities in which they were nurtured (because many are in touch with members therein), and can therefore contemplate the unique deployments of IT to nurture indigenous knowledge communities into enhanced knowledge domains. The Diaspora groups could champion the issues of their indigenous homelands within the institutions they now serve abroad. This way, they could become scouts in the strategic product development and market niche expansion of their employers in a win-win situation for both their indigenous and adopted communities. The locals and the Diaspora groups working together, through connectivity, could guide the interaction of global and specialized knowledge centres located in the advanced economies in their indigenous homelands. Acting as honest interpreters in information and knowledge brokerages, they could map locations of IT points-of-presence that would reach the heart of indigenous and oral knowledge blocs for effective local area networks, characterize the knowledge opportunities, and establish knowledge cells.

As knowledge networks evolve, it may be important to develop a system to measure the ability of the various communities to nurture knowledge activities and their performance as a knowledge economy, similar to the practices of other influential communities such as the Fortune 500. These standards could also address terminologies that are unique to the themes of the network concerned. Knowledge about the local needs, the potential of the local economy, lessons from global knowledge networks, and stipulations of international property rights may be some of the inputs into developing standards for the expected knowledge-driven institutional deliverables. These elements could lend to validating ideas about partnership arrangements and network products in the local economy. These standards are also necessary to drive the imaginations of the actors and to ensure that the expected level of 'development' occurs in the capacities of the local partners, elucidate upon the rules of engagement in knowledge sharing, determine what could be considered as a best practice so far as the local economy is concerned, and determine how to measure the outputs of knowledge solutions due to the network's activities.

The broad membership of the various global knowledge networks also brings with it some limitations: members often represent various geographic regions, economies, sectors, themes, and of various organizational sizes. The interests of the various partners may differ, for example while some members and their products and services are expected to operate under competitive market structures, which requires protection of the institution's knowledge assets and products from competitors, others in the knowledge sharing network may be public institutions that face the scrutiny, accountability, and responsibility of tax payers and electoral districts, and the need to justify that their activities *are* effective in reducing poverty and insuring human security in all regions of the world. But the commonalty among the members is the search for knowledge sharing systems in which all elements within the network excel in their domains; therefore the ability to carve common interests while challenging a successful integration of the diverse membership could engender a unique form of synergy in knowledge for development programming.

Furthermore, the types, capacities, and efficiency of the potential stakeholders in any global network would vary by region and culture, regardless of how homogenous the group may strive to become; the assets and needs of network elements may vary, for example governments and institutions, the private sector, and human resources are more developed in Southeast Asia than in Africa. However, knowledge about such variations can become an asset for the network in building partnerships toward developing the unique themes, products, and processes to accentuate local impact. Therefore, while each network element would be evaluated on its merit, a coordinated programming regarding sub-groups such as geographic regions or thematic aspects could accentuate the targeting of prototypes of the unique partnerships that are required for the various cultural, economic, political, and institutional blocs or geographic regions.

Since the current development philosophy emphasizes holistic approaches, networks should strive to include members of the various significant segments of economies. Many networks currently do not include a significant participation of the private sector in general, and often fund management organizations are missing from their folds although their resources are vital to building viable local venture markets that would capitalize the knowledge activities at the local level.

Many global knowledge networks distance their practices from the traditional ivory tower syndrome in which the body accumulates a lot of knowledge but is unable to disseminate the knowledge to the communities in need. The various regional or thematic sub-groups within the global networks could sift through the large volumes of information accrued by these organizations through their electronic dialogues to create new products such as electronic books, and codify the messages in their archives for friendly retrieval on demand. They could also help to build databases of network members, which would contain information on the major activities and achievements of the network and its elements, which could be actively marketed to donors, foundations, and businesses for capital investments and program partnerships.

Furthermore, there should be room for the idea that those who are representing their institutions in the global networks are also the ones who have an interest in the theme of knowledge for development, therefore the notion of emeritus membership should be considered. This way, when such individuals change their occupational titles, they do not have to lose their interaction with the network. This could make each institutional contact play a more active role in representing the values of the network within his/her institution.

A network may be strategically positioned to play a leading role in the subject area initially, however, with an increasing number of similar networks and as technology and culture are changing rapidly, the group may need to continuously monitor the global arena and exhibit flexibility to maintain, rejuvenate, and increase its influence in this important aspect of society and economy.

The current development philosophy of trans-community knowledge networks, partnerships, and global investments in innovation for the prosperity of deprived communities and the rest of the world may be the opportunity for each partner in the development community and impact groups to admit their own lapses and commit to redeeming themselves by thinking more about the people they intend to serve. Assuring equity in livelihood opportunities among the world's communities has reached an action-oriented phase, and the implementation processes will reveal how genuine and ingenious global development policies herald equity among present disadvantaged societies. Each individual, community, or economy should be viewed as possessing the inherent attributes that are required for continuous prosperity and security of the rest, and genuine efforts are required to invest in these entities to realize their full potentials.

About the Author

JOHN SENYO C. AFELE

Dr. Afele is an African-Canadian originally from Ghana. His research interests relate to conceptualising the mining of knowledge from indigenous cultures, optimizing global knowledge flows, and the translation of such reasoning into functional outputs through knowledge partnerships to nurture modern knowledge societies in developing nations. He has served as a member of the executive committee of the Global Knowledge Partnership, the Diaspora Focus Group of the United Nations Economic Commission for Africa's African Development Forum, the Ghana Computer Literacy and Distance Education project, among others; the Voice of America Radio's Voices of Africa program recognized him as one of the voices of Africa in 1999.

Some of his major outputs include the impact of ten major telecommunications and knowledge for development initiatives on Africa, and a landscape of the competitions and collaborations of global knowledge networks, conducted for the Multilateral Initiative to Bridge the Digital Divide of the Swiss Agency for Development and Cooperation; and, identification of some of the governance mechanisms that could enhance knowledge flows and nurture knowledge communities, for the Directorate of International Non-Governmental Organizations at the Canadian International Development Agency. He also contributed to the hypothetical framework of the African Component of the Global University System, and assisted some of the local knowledge networks in Africa in their incubation periods. In 1998, Dr. Afele conceptualized a mobile information van for the Ghana Computer Literacy and Distance Education project to travel 'the last mile' and herald digital opportunities for rural schools and communities.

Dr. Afele has contributed to defining the knowledge needs of communities and institutions in Africa and how telecommunications and knowledge networks can accelerate the intellectualization of their indigenous practices and make science and technology policy relevant to their needs and opportunities. He has been a speaker at several global roundtables and workshops. His thoughts are contained in workshop proceedings, electronic conferences and lists, and publications, such as, African Sociological Review, the Global Knowledge for Development List, Bamako 2000, Helvetas' knowledge for development workshop, the International Food Policy Research Institute, Earthwatch Institute, the 2nd Conference of the European Federation for Information Technology in Agriculture, the 5th Annual Teaching in the Community Colleges online conference's Writing Team on International/Multicultural Issues and New Technologies for Learning, the 1999 Emerging Global Electronic Distance Learning conference, Technet think tank for Identifying Critical Technologies for Developing Countries, the 1999 Ronald H. Brown African Affairs Series during the U.S. Congressional Black Caucus Legislative Forum, the Foundation for Democracy in Africa's U.S.-Africa Trade, Investment & Cultural Arts conferences in Florida, The Internet and National Cultures symposium at the Center for African Studies of Ohio State University, among others. He was also an alternate Canadian delegate to the First Consultation on Agricultural Information Management held at the United Nations Food and Agriculture Organization in Rome.

Dr. Afele's understanding of knowledge and development stems from his cross-cultural experiences: His education and research career have taken him across four continents – Africa, Europe, Asia, and North America. He was born in the village of *Woadze* in the Volta Region of Ghana and obtained his undergraduate degree in agriculture at the University of Ghana, his Master of Science at the Katholieke Universiteit Leuven in Belgium, and doctorate at the University of Guelph in Canada, specializing in crop improvement and biotechnology; he has also been a fellow of the Science and Technology Agency of Japan, stationed at the National Institute of Agrobiological Resources in Tsukuba. His observations about the various societies and technologies associated contributed to his thoughts on building technology platforms that are relevant to the knowledge domains of rural communities in Africa.

His themes on African knowledge and ideas (AKI) are operationalized in his initiative - *International Program for Africa.* This initiative was incubated at the University of Guelph in Canada, where he was the director. International Program for Africa is now a private think tank. His goal is to anchor this initiative in Africa as *Village Telecom* in Ghana, which would serve as an integrated global knowledge hub that could synthesize and customize functional knowledge for various organizational types and communities.

Dr. Afele can be reached at *johnafele@hotmail.com.*

Index

Symbols

2000 presidential elections 174

A

Acacia Initiative 21
Accenture 21
Achebe, Chinua 8
Acquired Immune Deficiency Syndrome
    26
activism 169
advanced economies 7
African Information Society Initiative
    (AISI) 20
African National Congress (ANC) 175
African Virtual University 10
African-American culture 66
Akerlof, George 47
Alzheimer's disease 66
America Online (AOL) 41
American Peace Corp 181
Anan, Kofi 47
Appleby, Sir Richard 140
Arabic Internet Names Consortium
    (AINC) 193
artificial blood 113
artificial intelligence 44
Ashanti Empire 147
Ashanti Golden Stool 67
Asia-Pacific Economic Cooperation
    (APEC) 109
Asian financial crisis 47

Association of South East
    Asian Nations (ASEAN) 20, 109
Atlantis 113
Attac 169

B

Benin Bronze 67
Bell, Alexander Graham 88
Bertini, Catherine 85
Biotechnology research 37
Black Forest 145
Blair, Tony 1
BMW Williams team 118
Bovine Spongiform Encephalopathy
    (BSE) 27
Boxing Hall 92
brain drain 104
brain enrichment 104
brainpower 27
Bread For The World 111
British comedy 140
British empire 174
British secretary 2
Bryant, Kobe 48

C

Canadian Association of University
    Teachers 116
cash crop production 25
Centers for Disease Control (CDC) 60
Chicago Bulls 48
civil society 2

Clashes of cultures 190
Cold War 3
Commonwealth Ministerial Action Group
    174
communicable diseases 8
competitive advantage 95
computer applications 34
confidentiality of communications 91
connectivity 9
connectivity nodes 94
Constituency for Africa (CFA) 110
contraceptives 76
convergent communications 6
Council for Economic Empowerment of
    Women of Africa 93
cultural blocs 109
cybersquatters 132

D

Dar es Salaam 71
debt relief 2
deconstruction 165
democracy 5
developing countries 6
Development Gateway 11
Development Gateway Foundation
    (DGF) 20
Diaspora 106
digital bridges 7, 57
Digital Diaspora 103
digital divide 6
digital opportunities 12
Digital Opportunity Task Force (DOT
    Force) 21
Dioscorea species 75
Diosgenin 76
Distance Learning Centres (DLCs) 21
distributed learning 70
Dow Jones Industrial Average 163

E

e-ASEAN Initiative 20
e-Commerce 61
economic opportunities 2
Education Development Center, Inc.
    164
Elaeis guineensis 75

emerging economies 6
environmental security 6
European Union (EU) 109
executive Forum 97
expert systems 44

F

farming systems 25
Farsi 194
fibre optics systems 88
financial planners 22
food crops 8
Formula One Racing 117
Foundation for Democracy in Africa 111
Free Trade Area of the Americas 103
free-market doctrines 4
Freedom Of Mobile multimedia Access
    (FOMA) 87

G

G8 Nations 2
Geographic Information Systems (GISs)
    24
Ghana Investment Promotion Centre
    132
global community 1
Global Development Learning Network
    (GDLN) 21
Global Development Network (GDN) 10,
    21
global diplomacy 1
Global Gazetteer 45
global institutions 4
global knowledge 5
Global Knowledge Partnership (GKP)
    20
global peace 5
Global Positioning Systems 63
global security 1
Global University System (GUS) 123
globalization 2
GNA Bulletin 58
Gold Coast 192
gong-gong 88
governance 5
grassroots organizations 111

H

Hagel, Chuck 111
Haka 195
Harlem 48
Hawthorne, Sir Nigel 140
Heavily Indebted Poor Country Initiative
    (HIPC) 15
Hemispheric trade bloc 168
HIV/AIDS 2, 139
HIV/AIDS care 37
hoe technology 25
horizontal knowledge channels 57
households 19
human development index 25
Human immunodeficiency virus 26
human intelligence 113

I

impact communities 4
Inca Empire 63
Indian Institute of Science (IIS) 97
indigenous hunters 68
Indigenous knowledge channel systems
    7
Industrial Age 113
industrialized communities 2
industrialized economies 12
informal institutions 6
Information and Communication
        Technologies (ICT) 5
Information Technologies (IT) 5
information brokerages 104
information flow 44
Information for Development (infoDev)
    20
Information linkages 57
Information Society 12
Ingenuity gap 41
Intellectual atrophy 11
Intellectualization of local knowledge
    systems 25
intellectualized indigenous knowledge
    23
International Amateur Athletic
        Federation (IAAF)   92
international development 2

International Monetary Fund (IMF) 9
International Organization for Migration
    103
International Telecommunication Union
    86
International Trade Centre 132
International Women's Tribune Centre
    (IWTC) 93
Internet Café 91
Internet language 191
Internet Service Providers (ISP) 10
Internet traffic 9
investment capital 2

J

Jackson, Phil 47
Jordan, Michael 48
Jospin, Lionel 169

K

Kaunda, Kenneth 142
kente 66
Kentucky Fried Chicken 62
Kilpatrick, Carolyn 110
knowledge brokerages 93
knowledge channels 39
knowledge facilitators 41
knowledge gap 61
knowledge halls 92
knowledge management 32
knowledge networks 10, 23
knowledge outputs 38
knowledge processors 22
knowledge quotient 9, 44
knowledge sharing 4
knowledge vacuum 26
Kwame Nkrumah University of Science
        and Technology 122
Kyoto Protocol on the environment 145
Kyushu-Okinawa Summit 21

L

land of princesses 96
lateral thinking 165
Leach, Jim 111
leadership 1

Leahy, Patrick 111
leapfrogging 12
learner-centred 114
Lego 195
Leland Initiative 21
local area networks (LANs) 93
local environment 5
local groups 5
local prosperity 6
Los Angeles Lakers 47

M

Maasais 66
MacCarthy, Sir Charles 147
mad cow disease 27
Malaysia's Multimedia SuperCorridor
    19
Mandela, Nelson 108
Maori groups 195
Maori language and images 195
Marconi 89
marginal enhancement 114
Markle Foundation 21
Massachusetts Institute of Technology
    108
Médecins Sans Frontières (MSF) 37
micro-knowledge 164
Microsoft 193
Microsoft Windows XP 88
mobile phones 24
modern communications 7
motorized-hoes 61
mouth nations 188

N

nanotechnologies 5
Nastaleeq script 193
nation-building 59
National Basketball Association (NBA)
    47
National Information and Communica-
    tions Infrastructure 20
Network Computer Systems (NCSs)
    107
networked economy 5
new Commonwealth of African and
    Asian countries 175

New Partnership for African Develop-
    ment (NEPAD) 4
New York Stock Exchange 162
Nobel Peace Prize 47
Nobel Prize for Economics 47
Non-Governmental Organizations
    (NGOs) 11
North American Free Trade Agreement
    (NAFTA) 38
NTT DoCoMo 87
nurturing knowledge communities 32

O

oil palm 75
old white Commonwealth 174
Olympic Games 187
O'Neal, Shaquille 48
open universities 114
Organization for Economic Cooperation
    and Development 49, 101
Organization of African Unity 121
Orwell, George 6
outsourcing 131
Oxfam 37

P

patent laws 37
Payne, Donald 111
peacekeeping efforts 68
Pentagon, 162
personal computers (PCs) 10
Philadelphia 76ers 47
Plato 33
Polymerase Chain Reaction (PCR) 14
Port of Dakar 112
Port of Miami 111
Powell, Colin 2
precision farming 63
Prempeh I 192
problem solving 5
professor-centred 114

Q

Quantitative Trait Loci (QTL) 77

R

Ralph Bunche School 48
reality television shows 7
religion 181
Renaissance 113
research and development programs 38
Robinson, Mary 171

S

safe motherhood 139
safe motherhood campaign 24
satellite audio services 90
satellite radio technologies 90
Schumacher brothers 117
Scuderia Ferrari Marlboro team 117
Seychelles 192
Short, Clare 2
Sierra Leone 68
smart communities 19, 23
Smithosonian 192
soccer's World Cup 187
sophisticated technology 92
South African government 37
South African security forces 175
Spence, Michael 47
Sphinx's Beard 67
status quo 114
Stiglitz, Joseph 47
Stone Age 63
strategic partnerships 41
Summer Olympics 92
Summit of the Americas 168

T

talent grooming 33
Tanzam Railway 71
telecentres 90
teledensity 87
telehealth 60
telesaturation 87
telescreens 6
Test of English as a Foreign Language (TOEFL) 70
The Gods Must Be Crazy 185
thinking machineries 113

third-generation wireless telecommuni-cations (3G) 87
Third World governments 4
Time Warner 41
Tobin tax 169
tractorization 63
traditional birth attendants (TBAs) 60
Trans-Atlantic Slave Trade 175
Trans-National Corporation (TNC) 115
translation of knowledge 4
translation of policy 2
Truth and Reconciliation Commission 170

U

U.N. Special Session 2
U.S. Congressional Black Caucus 110
U.S. Federal Reserve 162
U.S. Senate Foreign Relations Committee 111
United Nations Children's Fund (UNICEF) 121
United Nations Development Programme (UNDP) 21
United Nations Economic Commission for Africa (UNECA) 20
United Nations High Commission for Human Rights 170
United Nations Television Forum 190
United Nations University System 118
Urdu 194

V

vertical knowledge 93
videoconferencing 92
virtual education programs 70
Virtual Extension Officer 129
virtual university 10
voice-over-Internet protocols (VoIP) 133
Volta Region of Ghana 45

W

West African Diaspora 77
Wide-Area-Networks (WANs) 93
Wireless Application Protocol (WAP) 87
Woadze 45

Wolfensohn, James 122
World Bank 2, 20
World Conference Against Racism,
    Racial Discrimination 170
World Development Report 101
World Health Organization (WHO) 60
World Links for Development (WorLD)
    10, 21
World Trade Organization (WTO) 51

Y

Yaa Asantewaa 147
yams 75
Yes, (Prime) Minister 140

New Releases on
Global Information Technology

Cases on Global IT Applications and Management:
Successes and Pitfalls

Felix Tan, Ph.D.
University of Auckland, New Zealand

As organizations are competing globally in this new millennium, the effective deployment and exploitation of IT will create the difference between those that are successful and those that are not. What lessons are there to be learned from organizations that run global IT operations and deploy IT in support of their global business operations? *Cases on Global IT Applications and Management: Success and Pitfalls* brings together original cases that report on these aspects of global IT applications and management and benefits educators, researchers and practitioners alike.
ISBN: 1-930708-16-5; eISBN: 1-59140-000-7; c 2002; 322 pp (h/c); US $74.95

Global Perspective of IT Management

Felix B. Tan, Ph.D.
University of Auckland, New Zealand

Managing information technology (IT) on a global scale presents a number of opportunities and challenges. *Global Perspective of Information Technology Management* provides a collection of research works that address relevant IT management issues from a global perspective. As the world economy becomes more interdependent and competition for business continues to be more globally oriented, it has, likewise, become necessary to address the issues of IT management from a broader global focus.
ISBN: 1-931777-11-X; eISBN: 1-931777-32-2; c 2002; 325 pp (s/c); US $59.95

Information Technology Management
in Developing Countries

Mohammad Dadashzadeh, Ph.D.
Wichita State University, USA

The IT revolution has affected the entire world by producing a new, Internet-based, digital economy. The challenges faced by developing countries in harnessing the full potential of IT are not really very different from those that confronted the U.S. in its journey toward the Internet economy. *Information Technology Management in Developing Countries* discusses the possible pitfalls and triumphs involved when implementing this entity into the structure of a developing country.
ISBN: 1-931777-03-9; eISBN: 1-931777-23-3; c 2002; 310 pp (s/c); US $59.95

It's Easy to Order! Order online at
www.idea-group.com
or call our toll-free hotline at 1-800-345-4332!
Mon-Fri 8:30 am-5:00 pm (est) or fax 24 hours a day 717/533-8661

Idea Group Inc.
Hershey • London • Melbourne • Singapore • Beijing

Excellent additions to your library–Please recommend to your librarian.